AF906280

**Financial and Monetary Policy Studies**

Volume 53

The book series 'Financial and Monetary Policy Studies' features the latest research in financial and monetary economics. Books published in this series are primarily monographs and edited volumes that present new research results, both theoretical and empirical, on a clearly defined topic. All books are published in print and digital formats and disseminated globally.

Raluca Iacob

# Blind Spots in the Spotlight

## National Bank of Romania's Answers to the Financial Crisis Aftershocks from the Perspective of Central Bankers, the Public and the Media

Springer

Raluca Iacob
National School of Political Studies
and Public Administration
Bucharest, Romania

ISSN 0921-8580 ISSN 2197-1889 (electronic)
Financial and Monetary Policy Studies
ISBN 978-3-031-04066-5 ISBN 978-3-031-04067-2 (eBook)
https://doi.org/10.1007/978-3-031-04067-2

© The Editor(s) (if applicable) and The Author(s), under exclusive license to Springer Nature Switzerland AG 2022, corrected publication 2022
This work is subject to copyright. All rights are solely and exclusively licensed by the Publisher, whether the whole or part of the material is concerned, specifically the rights of translation, reprinting, reuse of illustrations, recitation, broadcasting, reproduction on microfilms or in any other physical way, and transmission or information storage and retrieval, electronic adaptation, computer software, or by similar or dissimilar methodology now known or hereafter developed.
The use of general descriptive names, registered names, trademarks, service marks, etc. in this publication does not imply, even in the absence of a specific statement, that such names are exempt from the relevant protective laws and regulations and therefore free for general use.
The publisher, the authors and the editors are safe to assume that the advice and information in this book are believed to be true and accurate at the date of publication. Neither the publisher nor the authors or the editors give a warranty, expressed or implied, with respect to the material contained herein or for any errors or omissions that may have been made. The publisher remains neutral with regard to jurisdictional claims in published maps and institutional affiliations.

This Springer imprint is published by the registered company Springer Nature Switzerland AG
The registered company address is: Gewerbestrasse 11, 6330 Cham, Switzerland

*To my grandparents, my roots*

# Acknowledgments

It takes an entire village to raise a child (proverb)

I thank all those who inspired me, motivated me, and helped me in this adventure of knowledge.

I am grateful to my mentor, Dr. Paul Dobrescu, Professor at the National University of Political Studies and Public Administration, Bucharest, for the openness and confidence shown ever since I started looking for a research topic. The feedback from all these years was accompanied by the strongest disclaimer: "For your becoming. This is the road and not another!" At the same time, I thank Dr. Nicoleta Corbu, Professor NUPSPA, who always took the time to gracefully explain to me all the little details of research methods and to answer all my questions.

In addition, I would like to thank all the professors I met at NUPSPA, starting back in 2016. I learned from each and single one of them, the professors in my first year of doctorate and the professors I worked with in my early days at the department or in other projects. Thank you Dr. Alina Bârgăoanu, dean of the faculty of communication and public relations of the NUPSPA, Dr. Daniel Dăianu, Dr. Dumitru Iacob, Dr. Diana Cismaru, Dr. Mălina Ciocea, Associate Professor, Dr. Valeriu Frunzaru, associate professor, Dr. George Tudorie, Lecturer, Dr. Bianca Cheregi, Lecturer, and Dr. Mirela Pirvan, Lecturer.

Thanks also to my colleagues from the Doctoral School. The fact that I always had a "support group" took me out of many moments of hesitation and procrastination, and here my thanks go especially to Georgiana Cristea.

Two other informal and informed mentors have always been by my side: Amalia Fugaru and Liudmila Cernat helped me to formulate and reformulate many questions, not to lose sight of the "red thread," to keep the right measure of the details that count. Graphic designer Florina Paraschiv humanized the research design and all the other schemes, starting from a few drawings in bold and pencil. And on the way to publication, I was joined by a new critical spirit of great help in the critical reading of the entire text—Adina Anghelache.

Among the international experiences that helped me and enriched not only my bibliography, but also my perspectives on my own topic, ECREA Doctoral Summer

School 2019 (Tartu, Estonia) remains the most valuable. I pay special tribute to Risto Kunelius, Professor of Media and Communication Studies (University of Helsinki), Dr. Andra Siibak, Professor of Media Studies, Institute of Social Studies (University of Tartu), Dr. Alenka Jelen-Sanchez, Senior Lecturer, Communications, Media and Culture (University of Stirling), and Pille Pruulmann-Vengerfeldt, Professor of Media and Communication (University of Malmö). The presentations from the international conferences opened a new world to me, one that I am honored to be part of and to grow in—ECPR's General Conference 2019 (Wrocław, Poland), the FSPAC 2019 PhD student conference (Cluj-Napoca), and STRATEGICA International Academic Conference 2017 (Bucharest). I am grateful that, through the vote of confidence received from Springer Publishing—and as a result of which this book has become a reality—I can now bring, to the public, the results of a journey started in 2016.

Certainly, I learned a lot about writing in a scientific style and from the editors of articles published in the journals *Management Dynamics in the Knowledge Economy*, *Romanian Journal of Communication and Public Relations*, and *Mediální studia/ Media studies*.

For the documentation, I would like to thank all the representatives of the National Bank of Romania who were willing to be interviewed for the qualitative research, and I thus allow me access to extremely valuable opinions. At the same time, even if they are unknown to me, I am grateful to all the respondents for answering my questionnaires, which were sometimes quite cumbersome.

Undoubtedly, all these years I have relied heavily on the unconditional understanding, support, patience, and love received from family and friends.

Thank you all, now, at the end of this journey which encompasses many future possibilities, in no small part thanks to you!

# Disclaimer

This research presents the findings of several studies conducted between 2016 and 2020 by Raluca Iacob, author of a PhD thesis in Communications Sciences and researcher at the National University of Political Studies and Public Administration (NUPSPA) (Bucharest). The work focuses on the communication of the National Bank of Romania (NBR) after the 2008 financial crisis. The views expressed are those of the author and do not necessarily reflect the official position of the National Bank of Romania or the European Central Bank.

# Contents

# About the Author

**Raluca Iacob** is a researcher in communications sciences, with over 10 years of working experience in the communication industry, gained as a communications specialist in PR agencies (Smartpoint) and central banks (National Bank of Romania, European Central Bank), and as temporary assistant professor of organizational communication and public relations during her PhD studies at the National University of Political Studies and Public Administration (NUPSPA) (Bucharest). Raluca defended her PhD thesis with an Excellent grade in 2020, with the research focused on the National Banks of Romania's communication after the 2008 financial crisis. Her research activity includes participations in international conferences and doctoral studies: ECREA European Media and Communication Doctoral Summer School 2019 (Tartu, Estonia); ECPR's General Conference 2019 (Wrocław, Poland); FSPAC 2019 PhD students conference (Cluj-Napoca, Romania); the Migration Conference 2018 (Lisbon, Portugal), STRATEGICA International Academic Conference 2017 (Bucharest, Romania); and "Spiru Haret" fellowship within NUPSPA, for research on Romanian Diaspora (2017–2018).

Before entering the field of communication, she worked between 2004 and 2011 as an economic journalist for several media outlets in Romania (Forbes Romania, Adevărul, Curentul, Bursa). She also holds a master's degree in theories of literature from the

University of Bucharest (2004). As a researcher, her main goal is to use both her professional and academic experience in studies with practical application.

# List of Acronyms

| | |
|---|---|
| AFBAR | Association of Financial and Banking Analysts of Romania (Romanian: Asociația Analiştilor Financiar Bancari din România) |
| ALDE | The Alliance of Liberals and Democrats Party (Romanian: Partidul Alianța Liberalilor şi Democraților) |
| ARI | Automated readability index |
| ARUFS | Association of Romanian Users of Financial Services (Romanian: Asociația Utilizatorilor Români de Servicii Financiare) |
| BM | Board meetings |
| BoE | Bank of England |
| BoJ | Bank of Japan |
| CBER | The Council of Banking Employers in Romania (Romanian: Consiliul Patronatelor Bancare din România) |
| CCR | Constitutional Court of Romania |
| CESEE | Central, Eastern and Southeastern Europe |
| EBRD | European Bank for Reconstruction and Development |
| EC | European Commission |
| ECB | European Central Bank |
| ESCB | European System of Central Banks |
| EU | European Union |
| Fed | The Federal Reserve System, the central bank of the USA |
| FOMC | Federal Open Market Committee |
| FSA | The Financial Supervisory Authority (Romanian: Autoritatea de Supraveghere Financiară) |
| GCCC | Group of clients with CHF loans (Romanian: Grupul Clienților cu credite în CHF) |
| GDP | Gross domestic product |
| G20 | The Group of Twenty Finance Ministers and Central Bank Governors |
| IFA | International Financial Architecture |
| IMF | International Monetary Fund |
| MoJ | Ministry of Justice |
| MP | Monetary policy |

| | |
|---|---|
| MRR | Minimum reserve requirements |
| NATO | The North Atlantic Treaty Organization |
| NBFI | Non-bank financial institution |
| NBR | National Bank of Romania |
| NCMO | National Committee for Macroprudential Oversight (Romanian: Comitetul Naţional pentru Supravegherea Macroprudenţială) |
| NGO | Non-governmental organization |
| NPL | Non-performing loans |
| PNL | The National Liberal Party (Romanian: Partidul Naţional Liberal) |
| PSD | Social Democratic Party (Romanian: Partidul Social Democrat) |
| RAB | Romanian Association of Banks (Romanian: Asociaţia Română a Băncilor) |
| RBNZ | The Reserve Bank of New Zealand |
| ROBOR | Romanian Interbank Offer Rate |
| SCM | Superior Council of Magistracy (Romanian: Consiliul Superior al Magistraturii) |
| SMOG | Simple Measure of Gobbledygook index |
| SNB | Swiss National Bank |
| UDMR | Democratic Alliance of Hungarians in Romania (Romanian: Uniunea Democrată Maghiară din România) |
| UK | United Kingdom |
| VAT | Value-added tax |
| WB | World Bank |
| WTO | World Trade Organization |

# List of Figures

# List of Tables

# Chapter 1
# Introduction

*Central banks, like all public institutions, were created by the public to serve the public. Despite a communications revolution, public understanding of central banks remains low and public trust in central banks has fallen. Improving both calls for a second revolution, focused on educating and learning from the general public. The Age of Innocence may be over, but the Era of Engagement has only just begun. (Haldane, 2018, p. 24) (Folk Wisdom)*

This book examines the changes in the communication of the National Bank of Romania (NBR) during the 2008 crisis. To x-ray these changes, we looked at the perspective of the representatives of the central bank, of the specialized public, of the general public, and of the media on how the NBR communicated publicly during the Great Recession.

In this approach, we followed two main directions: strategic communication, on monetary and non-monetary topics, and communication as an instrument of monetary policy. To date, the NBR's public communication has not been addressed in the literature, and the transparency and credibility of the NBR's monetary policy have been marginally researched and often times as subthemes (Dumiter, 2014; Toader & Rus, 2008; Égert, 2006).

Therefore, through this approach we open the way for studies dedicated to the communication of the National Bank of Romania—one of the oldest 20 central banks in the world (Capie et al., 2019)—subsumed exclusively to communication sciences. At the same time, we believe that the analyzed data represents a solid basis for a guide of good practices in central bank communication, useful for both the financial banking industry and the specialized communicators or journalists.

The topic of the book is related to a recent concern of researchers and specialists in central bank communication: how can these institutions enter a real dialogue with the general public, how can they regain, through communication, the confidence lost after 2008, what are the changes in communication expected by the public, and what changes are central bankers willing to take on in order to bring ordinary people closer? In other words—what do you have to do to get started in the second communication revolution?

---

The original version of this chapter was revised: The missing footnotes 1 and 2 have been included now. The corrections to this chapter can be found at
https://doi.org/10.1007/978-3-031-04067-2_9

© The Author(s), under exclusive license to Springer Nature Switzerland AG 2022, corrected publication 2022

R. Iacob, *Blind Spots in the Spotlight*, Financial and Monetary Policy Studies 53,
https://doi.org/10.1007/978-3-031-04067-2_1

Central banks are currently facing a low level of public understanding and trust, even though the transparency of these institutions is on an upward trend. After coming down from the "ivory tower" in terms of monetary policy, most of the world's central banks have stepped up their communication efforts. When specialists emphasize the first revolution in the communication of these institutions, they invoke as a reference system the mantra of Montagu Norman, former governor of the Bank of England (1921–1944), "Never explain, never excuse" or the programmatic hermeticism, designated by Alan Greenspan, former governor of the Federal Reserve System (1987–2006), through expressions such as "Fedspeak" and "mumble with great incoherence."

The turning point in the major shift from hermeticism to transparency is the inflation targeting strategy adopted by central banks in New Zealand, Canada, and the USA 30 years ago, and currently used by central banks around the world. The strategy of setting an inflation target requires regular announcements to the public, such as press releases, conferences, the publication of minutes of monetary policy meetings, and other regular reports.

All this was just the beginning. Nowadays, central bankers make public announcements and statements, give interviews to journalists, organize live broadcasts, participate in communication campaigns, enter controversies with hostile stakeholders, and write blog posts. Furthermore, communication includes the use of new media, production of podcasts and videos, tweets, and posts on social networks Facebook, LinkedIn, YouTube, and Instagram. However, the need to simplify the language and bring it closer to the general public has become increasingly evident. Andy Haldane, former chief economist at the Bank of England (1989–2021), has been a constant voice in this direction, and his speech, "The Great Divide" (Haldane, 2016), is the trigger for the present research. In 2016, Haldane pointed out that, in the context of the economic and financial crisis of 2008, the gap between the financial-banking industry (experts), on the one hand, and the general public (non-experts), on the other—"the great divide"—deepened.

Practically, from the "radical transparency" era,[1] the financial institutions entered, after 2008, the "radical uncertainty"[2] stage and the pre-crisis level of confidence in central banks could not be restored. The erosion of confidence in the financial system, including in these institutions, has several causes. During the 2008 crisis, central banks, which assumed responsibilities that went beyond their traditional mandates and thus became scapegoats for the crisis—"the only game in town" (El-Erian, 2016), were demonized—"villains" (King, 2016). They lost sight of the industry they regulated and supervised because of "blind spots" (Riles, 2018) and "silo thinking" (Tett, 2015) and made controversial decisions.

[1] Against the background of financial globalization, governments have created a number of institutional and cooperation mechanisms, known as International Financial Architecture (IFA). According to Bourne (2016), IFA opened the era of "radical transparency" in which the central bank also has an important word to say, "a state's most influential storyteller" (Bourne, 2016, p. 35).

[2] "Radical uncertainty refers to uncertainty so profound that it is impossible to represent the future in terms of a knowable and exhaustive list of outcomes to which we can attach probabilities" (King, 2016, p. 9).

During the Great Recession, two main directions of action by central banks manifested: reaffirming the flexibility of monetary policy and assigning greater responsibility to these institutions in terms of attention to the financial industry (Ciocca, 2016). Prior to 2008, operationally independent central banks, whose role was to ensure price stability and thus, as a main objective, to target inflation, primarily increased or decreased monetary policy interest rates to achieve this target. The ensuing macroeconomic and financial instability highlighted the limitations of the fundamental objective of these institutions and called into question the extension of their role in the direction of financial stability[3] and, implicitly, of prudential regulation (Nier, 2009).

They were constantly in the spotlight, came to the attention of the media, and were forced to participate in debates on several non-monetary issues such as consumer protection, taxation, changes in the legal framework applicable to the banking system, the level of income of their employees, immunity, and management of international reserves. They lost their general public due to poor communication before the crisis, perpetuated during the Great Recession, but also because the general public had (and still has) a low level of knowledge about the role and objectives of these institutions. Finally, they have lost the public amid a general crisis of global confidence in the authority of governments, institutions, and NGOs—experts in general.

In these circumstances, the first revolution in the communication of these institutions, which consisted in giving up their halo of discretion and mystery by transforming communication into one of the instruments of monetary policy, needs to have a continuation today, specifically, a second revolution in central bank communication, this time based on openness to the general public, whose trust must be regained (Haldane, 2018; Riles, 2018). We believe that central banks need to regain the trust of the general public for two main reasons: to ensure that operational independence meets the terms of the social contract and because trust helps to manage inflationary expectations. Communication from central banks is essential to ensure transparency and is part of their accountability and good governance obligations, as institutions of monetary and supervisory authority independent of the political factor. At the same time, the effectiveness of monetary policy depends on financial markets and the inflationary expectations of private economic agents and consumers. And inflationary expectations are anchored by communication; they are formed in a "communicative culture" (Holmes, 2014), which influences the decisions of economic agents. In short, the communication of central banks contributes both to ensuring operational independence and to the effectiveness of monetary policy.

Most of the literature on central bank communication focuses on the relationship with financial market participants, on informing the specialized public about the objectives, plans, and projections of these institutions, and on communication as a

[3] "Financial stability can be defined as a condition in which the financial system—which comprises financial intermediaries, markets, and market infrastructures—is capable of withstanding shocks and the unravelling of financial imbalances. This mitigates the prospect of disruptions in the financial intermediation process that are severe enough to adversely impact real economic activity" (European Central Bank, 2020).

monetary policy tool, which, however, must not be confused with a public relations function (Holmes, 2014). While the communication of these institutions with the specialized public is a territory explored by several researchers, the general public came to the attention of central banks especially in the post-crisis period. In addition, despite the increased relevance of the general public and the intensification of central banks' communication activities, how the information transmitted reaches the general public and how the media can influence the public's perception of the actions and decisions of these institutions remain less studied topics in academia. At the same time, we want to bring a consistent testimony from a country that is a member of the European Union, but which is not yet in the euro area.

This research thus aims to contribute to filling a gap in the literature and to provide new data on the communication of central banks with various categories of public, as well as the way in which their messages are publicized.

The book focuses on the communication of the National Bank of Romania in the post-crisis period, with emphasis on 2014–2016. By applying several methods and models of qualitative analysis (semi-structured in-depth interviews) and quantitative analysis (questionnaire-based sociological survey and content analysis), we aim to present, from several perspectives, how the NBR communication has changed during the Great Recession. For this purpose, we analyzed the opinion of the institution's representatives, the perception of the general public and of the specialized public, and the frames used by the Romanian online press in the media coverage of one of the most visible non-monetary topics of debate for the NBR—the giving in payment law. The assesment, from the perspective of several stakeholders, of how the NBR's public communication has changed is built around the potential contribution of each category of audience to changing the communication of the central bank: the specialized public (including commercial banks), the general public, the media, and the Parliament. The research model adapts the operation of the frames according to the "cascading network activation" model built by Entman (2003, pp. 419–420), following the flow from the messages sent by the main actors—in this case, the National Bank of Romania, but also the Parliament, the messages taken over by the elites, then by the journalists, the framing of the news until it reaches the general public, and then the reverse flow, in the defined post-crisis context.

The structure of the book follows two main parts. In the first part, we build the theoretical framework relevant to the research conducted, on two main pillars: public communication of central banks and the framing theory; we define the research questions that formed the basis of the approach, research design, and applied methods. The second part of the book—the empirical one—is structured around the three research methods applied between 2017 and 2019: the interview method, the questionnaire-based sociological survey method, and the content analysis method.

Chapter 2 presents the theoretical perspectives on central bank public communication. As the strategic communication of central banks is organically linked to the transparency and trust, the theoretical framework is developed around these two key concepts defined by central bank specialists and researchers.

Transparency is the absence of an information asymmetry between monetary policy makers and other economic agents. We review the two broad categories of studies on transparency, including forward guidance. One side shows that monetary policy has the best effects if it is predictable. However, there is also research showing that increased transparency does not necessarily have a positive effect on the effectiveness of monetary policy or the financial system.

In terms of trust, as money depends on public trust in issuing institutions, we can say that this is the core of the monetary banking system, which makes the "alchemy" defined by King (2016) work. Greenspan (2007, p. 391) argues that "monetary policy should make even a fiat money economy behave 'as though anchored by gold.'" In turn, Qvigstad (2009) considers that, if in the past, the value of money was actually defended with weapons, now it is defended by the trust whose roots lie in the openness and transparency of central banks. Therefore, the strategic communication of central banks must be aimed at gaining and maintaining public confidence. This is even more important in times of financial crisis, which demonstrates that "while a state's financial reputation does not begin with its central banking leadership, it almost certainly ends there" (Bourne, 2016, p. 45).

In the same chapter, we present the results of the main studies on strategic communication of central banks, focusing on the language used (evaluated even by some central bankers as still "impenetrable to the general public"), on defining different categories of stakeholders and the relationship with each of them, on the diversification of communication channels, and on the communication tactics identified mainly in monetary communication.

In Chap. 3, we present the framing theory, which provides us with the analytical framework necessary to analyze how media framed the NBR messages in the post-crisis period. The research uses framing theory and refers to the media as a stakeholder of the central bank, as well as possibly influencing the way the audience selects and interprets different communication situations. In the first part, we present the definitions and results of the main framing theorists, and we look at the literature on how media framing influences public opinion, focusing on the process-based framing interpretation scheme and cascading network activation (Entman, 2003). The important role of journalists in building news, in the process of appreciation and capitalization of certain narrative elements to the detriment of others, is highlighted, and we review the main news values. The theory of framing can also be studied in relation to public relations: the media is dependent on the official statements of representatives of organizations, especially for reporting crisis situations, and thus public relations have the opportunity to shape the tone and content of news.

We also consider relevant to this research the studies on competing frames and elite rhetoric, because, especially in times of crisis, elites compete with each other and launch, strategically, contradictory frames. Chapter 3 concludes with a presentation of the main researches that applied the theory of framing in the analysis of the media coverage of the 2008 financial and economic crisis, both in the international media and in the Romanian press.

Chapter 4 details the general context, the research objectives, and the research questions, as well as the tools used in applying the research methods. Even if through monetary and prudential measures taken in advance by the NBR, Romania avoided a banking crisis, the central bank could not compensate for the macroeconomic imbalances, missed, due to external shocks, the inflation target, and was forced to meet high expectations on the protection of consumers of financial services, which exerted additional pressure.

We define the roles of the main actors that contributed to the change of NBR's communication in the post-crisis period (central bank, Parliament, media, general public, specialized public), and we present the analyzed communication situations. In the same chapter, we explain the motivation of the integrative perspective of the analytical approach, as the empirical data were obtained by applying several methods and models of analysis. On the one hand, we consider that the evaluation of the perception of different categories of actors required the use of different research methods adapted to their profile. On the other hand, the possibility of triangulating the results was sought, to confirm the results by several methods.

We detail the research model of change in bank communication, located at the intersection of several disciplines such as communication sciences, economics, psychology, sociology, and anthropology. We also represent graphically the research design—the second revolution in NBR communication, built on the adaptation of the cascading network activation model (Entman, 2003).

The research proposes to evaluate the messages sent by the NBR and the Parliament as the strongest, the two organizations being the primary source of information. At the same time, between the two (inter)dependent organizations (Riles, 2018), there is a regular, regulated inter-institutional communication, one that also depends on other situations involving the central bank. Being the directly elected power, with the specific role of adopting laws for the country's governance, we appreciate that the Parliament has a proactive role and is the organization that contributes to the context of change in the NBR communication, during the analyzed period. NBR messages firstly reach the elite/specialized public. At the same time, one of the institution's stakeholders is the media, which frames both the messages received directly from the central bank and the messages that the elites formulate and disseminate, based on primary sources. Frames generated by elites (in this case, commercial banks, economic analysts, political analysts, lawyers, academia, communicators, other specialized audiences) may coincide, support, or contradict those transmitted by public authorities and institutions. Through the framing process, the media influences public opinion and the general public's perception of the central bank. In this research, we notice that a part of the specialized public (lawyers, influencers) addressed directly to the general public and took over the role of organizing them in associations and representing them publicly.

Following the reverse flow of the transmission of frames, the messages of the general public are framed primarily by the media, but also by the specialized public that represents them and that transmits their frames in the media and to organizations. The media is the main channel through which the messages of the general public can reach the central bank and can exert an influence on the messages of the elites, ultimately generating changes in the public communication of the NBR that we analyze in the research.

Chapter 5 opens the series of research results, following the analysis of 20 semi-structured in-depth interviews with central bank officials. The interpretation of the data refers to the way in which the NBR managed the communication on non-monetary issues between 2014 and 2016, the main messages transmitted or the labels assigned during the Greek capital bank crisis, the Swiss franc credit crisis, and the legislative changes affecting the banking system, such as the giving in payment law. There are issues related to the frequency of public appearances of NBR representatives after 2008, institutional transparency, the peculiarities of the language used in addressing the general public, including jargon, eroding public confidence in the central bank, the efficiency of the communication channels used, and the role of the media in presenting non-monetary topics during the researched period (2014–2016). The interviews also focused on the NBR's changes in monetary communication. The chapter ends with a series of communication lessons learned after 2008 by the interviewees.

In Chap. 6, the specialized audience ($N = 186$) and the general public ($N = 391$) have the floor. The general objective is to analyze the perception of the two categories of NBR stakeholders in relation to the changes toward greater transparency of public communication, monetary and non-monetary, in the post-crisis period. The questions in the two online questionnaires focused on transparency (frequency of public appearances, assessment of the language used by the institution's representatives or in the official reports of the central bank). At the same time, we assessed the level of public trust in the central bank, the relationship between trust and knowledge of the object of activity of the NBR, and the expectations regarding the changes in the NBR communication, following the same research questions that guided the qualitative analysis of this research.

Chapter 7 presents the content analysis of the articles in the Romanian economic and general media regarding the giving in payment law, using a grid that quantifies five frames: economic consequences, responsibility, conflict, ethics/moral interest, and human interest, based on the criteria developed by Semetko and Valkenburg (2000). The sample to be researched ($N = 420$) was selected from two online portals of the two relevant financial newspapers on the Romanian publishing market: Bursa—bursa.ro ($N = 133$ articles) and Ziarul Financiar—zf.ro ($N = 139$ of articles), the online portal of the quality newspaper *Adevărul*—adevarul.ro ($N = 59$ articles), and the generalist portal hotnews.ro ($N = 89$ articles). The content analysis captures the main trends in the media coverage of the "giving in payment law," the differences between the frames of both the economic media and of the general media, the differences in visibility of supporters and opponents of the giving in payment law during the analyzed period, and the main positions of the media (editorials, comments, opinions, etc.) regarding the NBR's communication strategy in the context of the analyzed legislative change.

This book aims to contribute to the understanding of the way in which the public communication of the National Bank of Romania changed in the post-crisis period. Each assessed audience revealed new meanings of the changes, but also of the implications of the expected changes, of the lessons learned in the post-crisis period, and of the pressure exerted by the public on the central bank in the post-crisis context, but also on the background of technological advancement. We now consider that it is no longer possible for central banks to communicate without taking into account the perception and opinion of different categories of stakeholders. Chapter 8 thus drafts the main conclusions and the limitations of this research, but also the perspectives that this study can open up.

The originality of this book lies first in the construction of a universal central bank communication research design and a useful and easy-to-adapt analysis tool. The research design can be reconfigured according to the realities and specifics of each country or region to analyze how central banks communicate with different audiences. The grid defining the roles of the main actors involved in the second revolution in NBR communication, the interview grid, the structure of the two surveys applied, and the online news analysis grid are useful tools for further research in communication sciences dedicated to monetary and non-monetary communication of central banks.

Second, the analytical preoccupation opens new avenues, as the public communication of the NBR has not been researched. Although it is focusing on a specific case study, the relevance of this research for the communications field is undeniable, as it covers an underexplored topic especially within the non-euro area countries, and one can easily extend the conclusions regarding the mechanisms and the policies studied to other similar markets. Third, the book brings to light new data on the communication of central banks with the general public, a recent topic of interest to central bankers and researchers alike, but little explored compared to the number of studies on monetary communication. Last but not least, the possibility of triangulating the results due to the evaluation of several categories of central bank stakeholders gives complexity and validity to the results obtained.

The timelessness and significance of this research are noticeable as the central banks are already going through a new era of communication challenges triggered by the COVID-19 pandemic. Lessons learned can contribute to what researchers name the second revolution in communication, focusing on opening the central banks to the public and regaining or keeping trust.

## References

Bourne, C. (2016). *Trust, power and public relations in financial markets*. Taylor & Francis.

Capie, F., Fischer, S., Goodhart, C., & Schnadt, N. (2019). *Viitorul băncilor centrale. SIMPOZIONUL TRICENTENARULUI BĂNCII ANGLIEI*. Curtea Veche.

Ciocca, P. (2016). *Stabilising capitalism. A greater role for central banks*. Palgrave Macmillan.

Dumiter, F. C. (2014). Central Bank independence, transparency and accountability indexes: A survey. *Timisoara Journal of Economics and Business, 7*(1), 35–54. Retrieved from https://ideas.repec.org/a/wun/timjeb/tjebv07y2014i01a02.html

Égert, B. (2006). *Central bank interventions, communication and interest rate policy in emerging European economies*. CESifo Working Paper, No. 1869. Center for Economic Studies and ifo Institute (CESifo). Retrieved from https://www.econstor.eu/bitstream/10419/25914/1/528735578.PDF

El-Erian, M. A. (2016). *The only game in town: Central banks, instability, and avoiding the next collapse*. Random House.

Entman, R. M. (2003). Cascading activation: Contesting the White House's frame after 9/11. *Political Communication, 20(4)*, 415–432. https://doi.org/10.1080/10584600390244176

European Central Bank. (2020). *What is the quiet period?* Retrieved from https://www.ecb.europa.eu/ecb/educational/explainers/tell-me/html/what-is-the_quiet_period.en.html

Greenspan, A. (2007). *The age of turbulence: Adventures in a new world.* Penguin Press.

Haldane, A. (2016). *The great divide.* Speech at the New City Agenda Annual dinner. Retrieved from https://www.bankofengland.co.uk/speech/2016/the-great-divide

Haldane, A. (2018). *Folk Wisdom.* Speech at the100th Anniversary of the Bank of Estonia. Retrieved from https://www.bankofengland.co.uk/-/media/boe/files/speech/2018/folk-wisdom-speech-by-andy-haldane.pdf?la=enşihash=DA3CC381EAC763701787B79E68013BE7BB2D2C52

Holmes, D. R. (2014). *Economy of words: Communicative imperatives in central banks.* University of Chicago Press.

King, M. (2016). *The end of alchemy: Money, banking, and the future of the global economy.* Little, Brown.

Nier, E. W. (2009). *Financial stability frameworks and the role of central banks: Lessons from the crisis.* International Monetary Fund. Retrieved from https://www.elibrary.imf.org/view/IMF001/10024-9781451872170/10024-9781451872170/10024-9781451872170_A001.xml?language=enşiredirect=true

Qvigstad, J. F. (2009). *On transparency.* Speech at the Norwegian Academy of Science and Letters on 10 November 2009. Retrieved from https://norges-bank.brage.unit.no/norges-bank-xmlui/bitstream/handle/11250/2567296/On%20transparency.pdf?sequence=1

Riles, A. (2018). *Financial citizenship: Experts, publics, and the politics of central banking.* Cornell University Press.

Semetko, H. A., & Valkenburg, P. M. (2000). Framing European politics: A content analysis of press and television news. *Journal of Communication, 52*(2), 93–109.

Tett, G. (2015). *The silo effect: The peril of expertise and the promise of breaking down barriers.* Simon and Schuster.

Toader, V., & Rus, V. R. (2008). Evaluation of National Bank of Romania monetary policy credibility. *Annals of the University of Oradea, Economic Science Series, 17*(2), 501–506. Retrieved from https://econpapers.repec.org/article/orajournl/v_3a2_3ay_3a2008_3ai_3a1_3ap_3a497-502.htm

# Chapter 2
# Public Communication of Central Banks: Theoretical Perspectives

> *Success should be measured, not by the ability to reach everyone, but rather to influence beyond the small minority of technical specialists and information intermediaries who currently form the core of central banks' audiences.*
> *(Haldane & McMahon, 2018, p. 582)*

Nowadays, researchers and specialists are calling for a second revolution in central bank communication. But what exactly is the first revolution? This chapter touches upon transparency, trust, and fundamental changes in communication before and after the 2008 crisis.

In recent decades, most central banks have intensified their communication efforts, having descended from their monetary policy ivory tower. Central bank communication has changed significantly from the mantra "Never explain, never excuse" formulated by Montagu Norman, governor of the Bank of England (1921–1944), to public announcements, statements, and interviews with journalists, live broadcasts, and participation in communication campaigns, and even blog articles, tweets, posts on Facebook, LinkedIn, and Instagram (Haldane, 2017; Shin, 2017; Bjelobaba et al., 2017; Vardy, 2015).

More than a decade after the onset of the Great Recession, central banks have become more transparent. However, they still face a low level of public understanding and trust. The simultaneous abandonment of their halo of discretion and mystery, about 30 years ago, and the transformation of communication into a monetary policy tool, now require a follow-up. Specifically, researchers (Riles, 2018; Haldane, 2018; Haldane & McMahon, 2018) believe that a second revolution in communication is needed, this time based on openness to the general public. The main argument is that although central banks may seem too disconnected from the experience of the general public, ordinary people—consumers, citizens—are, in fact, the final audience of these institutions and the final test point of action (Riles, 2018; Holmes, 2014).

Moreover, there is a gap in the literature on central banks' communication. While the communication of these institutions with the specialized public is a territory explored by several researchers such as Ehrmann and Talmi (2017), Feroli et al.

© The Author(s), under exclusive license to Springer Nature Switzerland AG 2022 
R. Iacob, *Blind Spots in the Spotlight*, Financial and Monetary Policy Studies 53,
https://doi.org/10.1007/978-3-031-04067-2_2

(2017), Coenen et al. (2017), Belke (2017), Hansen and McMahon (2016), Velthuis (2015), Blinder et al. (2008), Kohn and Sack (2003), and Smart (1999), communication with the general public on nonmonetary issues remains a less addressed topic.

As the strategic communication of central banks is organically linked to their transparency and credibility, we will now examine the links between communication and transparency, accountability, and public trust. Thus, we will follow two main directions: communication as a monetary policy tool and strategic communication on both monetary and nonmonetary topics.

## 2.1 Communication: A Monetary Policy Tool

Communication as an instrument of monetary policy has a recent history of about 30 years. Since the establishment of the world's first central banks in 1668, Riksbank in Sweden—the first central bank to carry out typical clearing operations (e.g., holding accounts for banks that had receivables from each other), and in 1694, the Bank of England—the first central bank which has a monopoly on the issuance of currency—and until the 1990s, when some central banks began to publish monetary policy decisions, these institutions were shrouded in mystery.

Their hermeticism can have at least three explanations: first, obtaining a monopoly on the issuance of money was a competitive undertaking, as even commercial banks could try this activity, and therefore it had to be carried out discreetly; secondly, the central banks' monopoly on the issuance of money started on a geographical basis, it did not influence, from the beginning, the entire population (in the nineteenth century, the Bank of England's sphere of influence was in and around London, according to Bagehot (1901); third, the central banks also carried out commercial operations, the secrecy of which should also be kept safe.

In the twentieth century, according to Bernanke (2007), the fame of hermeticism was mainly because many central bankers, contemporary with Governor Montagu Norman believed that "(. . .) a certain mystique attached to their activities and that allowing the public to glimpse of the inner workings would only usurp the prerogatives of insiders and reduce, if not grievously damage, the effectiveness of policy."

The turning point of the major shift from hermeticism to transparency is in the inflation targeting strategy adopted by central banks in New Zealand, Canada, and the United States 30 years ago (Vega & Winkelried, 2005), and currently used by central banks around the world. The strategy of setting an inflation target requires regular announcements to the public, such as press releases, press conferences, the publication of minutes of monetary policy meetings, and other periodic reports (Table 2.1).

Bernanke (2015, p. 75) describes the Fed's communication from the pre-inflation targeting stage as an act of pantomime: "Without inflation targeting or a coherent communication framework, the Fed had what I called a Marcel Marceau communications strategy. The idea was to watch what I do, not what I say." Moreover, the

**Table 2.1** Communication tools used by central banks to announce monetary policy decisions

| Tools | Central banks: National Bank of Romania (NBR) | European Central Bank (ECB) | Bank of England (BoE) | US Federal Reserve Bank (Fed) | Japan Bank (BoJ) | Reserve Bank of New Zealand (RBNZ) |
|---|---|---|---|---|---|---|
| *Press releases* after board meetings (BMs) on monetary policy issues (MP) | 8 times/year—Decisions are explained | 8 times/year—Decisions are explained | 8 times/year—Decisions are explained | 8 times/year—Decisions are explained | 8 times/year—Decisions are explained | 8 times/year—Decisions are explained |
| *Press conferences* following BMs on MP | 8 times/year briefings | 8 times/year | 4 times/year | 4 times/year | 8 times/year | 8 times/year |
| | No live broadcast of the Governor's speech | Live broadcast of the Governor's speech | Live broadcast of the Governor's speech | Live broadcast of the Governor's speech | Live broadcast of the Governor's speech | Live broadcast of the Governor's speech |
| | Q&A session | Q&A session | Q&A session | Q&A session | Q&A session | Q&A session |
| *Publication of minutes* and/or votes cast during BMs on MP | Yes | Yes | Yes | Yes | Yes | No |
| | With votes cast (non-nominal) | No votes cast | With votes cast (nominal) | With votes cast (nominal) | With votes cast (nominal) | |
| | A week after BMs on MP | 4 weeks after BMs on MP | Simultaneously with the MP decision | 3 weeks after BMs on MP | 4–6 weeks after BMs on MP | |
| *Periodic reports* with background information | Economic bulletin (12/year) (4/year) | Economic bulletin (12/year, 2 weeks after BMs MP) | Inflation report (4/year) | Beige book (summary of comments on the economic situation) (8/year) | Perspective on economic activity and price developments (4/year) | Official cash rate (OCR) announcement (8/year) |
| | Inflation report | Reports on the bond purchase program (12/year) | Financial stability report (2/year) | Fed balance sheet report (4/year) | | Financial stability report (2/year) |

(continued)

**Table 2.1** (continued)

| Tools | Central banks | | | | | |
|---|---|---|---|---|---|---|
| | National Bank of Romania (NBR) | European Central Bank (ECB) | Bank of England (BoE) | US Federal Reserve Bank (Fed) | Japan Bank (BoJ) | Reserve Bank of New Zealand (RBNZ) |
| | Financial stability report (2/year) | Macroeconomic projections for the euro area (4/year) | | Monetary policy report (2/year) | | Monetary policy report (4/year) |
| *Forward guidance* on the evolution of interest rates | No | Yes | Yes | Yes | Yes | Yes |
| | | Starting July 2013 | Starting August 2013 | Starting August 2003 | Since April 1999 | Since June 1997 |

Source: Information from central bank websites, collected in 2019; Data from the research of Moessner et al. (2017)

lack of transparency of the entire financial system was over at the end of the Asian financial crisis (1997–1998), when, amid financial globalization, governments created several institutional and cooperation mechanisms, known as the international financial architecture (IFA) (Elson, 2011). Bourne (2016) points out that the IFA, which includes organizations such as the IMF, WB, G20, NATO, and WTO, has opened the era of "radical transparency" in which the central bank has an important say, "a state's most influential storyteller" (Bourne, 2016, p. 35).

The National Bank of Romania adopted inflation targeting as a monetary policy strategy in 2005. Communication has thus become an important feature of monetary policy whose instruments include, in the case of the NBR, money market operations,[1] permanent facilities granted to credit institutions[2] and minimum reserve requirements[3] (MRRs) (National Bank of Romania, 2020).

In the case of the NBR, the transparency of monetary policy decisions was ensured by publishing the calendar of meetings on monetary policy of the Board, publishing press releases, and having the Chairman of the Board and Governor present these press releases during press briefings after each meeting, presenting inflation reports at quarterly conferences, and publishing the public policy framework. Thus, the NBR fell in line with a broader trend in the evolution of central banks: "(. . .) the NBR Board looked at how the relationship between institutional independence and the transparency of the decision-making process has changed over the past few years at the level of the members of the European System of Central Banks. This analysis has shown that in many central banks in the ESCB the transparency and public disclosure process strengthened and diversified, especially concerning monetary policy decisions and executive management wages. As a result, the NBR Board decided to make public the minutes of the Board's monetary policy meetings and the incomes of the Board member" (National Bank of Romania, 2016).

On the transparency of the decision-making process, King (2016, p. 179) points out that "Transparency is, however, not an end in itself. Any requirement for transparency in a central bank's deliberations should have the aim of improving the quality of its decisions."

Other central banks have followed a similar trend including the monetary policy of the Bank of England, the world's oldest central bank with a monopoly on the issuance of money, saw an increase in the transparency of monetary policy in the early 1990s, with the publication of the inflation target (1992) and inflation reports (1993), and the publication of the minutes of the meetings between the Governor and

---

[1] Open market operations are the most important monetary policy instrument of the NBR. These are carried out at the initiative of the central bank, having the following functions: guiding interest rates, managing the liquidity conditions on the monetary market and signaling the monetary policy orientation (National Bank of Romania, 2020).

[2] Credit institutions can access on their own initiative the two permanent facilities offered by the NBR: the credit facility and the deposit facility (National Bank of Romania, 2020).

[3] The minimum reserve requirements (MRRs) are leu and foreign currency-denominated holdings of credit institutions on accounts opened with the NBR (National Bank of Romania, 2020).

the Chancellor of the Exchequer (1994). Operational independence (1997) has also led to increased transparency.

For researchers it is important to understand the separation, over time, of the role of central banks from government authority (Capie et al., 2012; Bordo, 2007; Bagehot, 1901). In his speech at the PR Manager of the Year Award ceremony, Mario Draghi (2014), former Governor of the ECB (2011–2019), highlighted the role that communication—as one of the monetary policy instruments—due to its major impact, has gained over financial markets and therefore on state economies. At the same time, Draghi points out that due to their increased independence, central banks need to be accountable to the public, which increases the importance of communication. Communication is essential for transparency, accountability, and credibility, and these, in turn, are essential for public support and the independence of central banks.

Studies on central bank transparency, including the forward guidance, can be structured into two broad categories. On the one hand, there are studies that show that monetary policy generates the best effects if it is predictable (Holmes, 2014; Dincer & Eichengreen, 2013; Jeanneau, 2009; Cournède & Minegishi, 2009; Blinder et al., 2008; Bernanke & Woodford, 2007; Woodford, 2005; Bernanke et al., 2001; Faust & Svensson, 2001). On the other hand, there is research showing that increased transparency does not necessarily have a positive influence on the effectiveness of monetary policy or the financial system (Kool & Thornton, 2015; Ehrmann et al., 2012; van der Cruijsen et al., 2010; Cukierman, 2009; Gosselin et al., 2006; Mishkin, 2004; Morris & Shin, 2002).

From the first category, Bernanke et al. (2001) argue that public expectations about the future, including those regarding future monetary policy decisions, are important because they influence current economic behavior. Transparency is related to the ease with which the public anticipates central bank intentions based on observable data (Faust & Svensson, 2001). Jeanneau (2009) shows that better communication regarding the decisions taken by central banks and their actions reduces the uncertainty faced by economic agents.

Based on research conducted between 2008 and 2010 on the monetary regimes of central banks in Wellington, Frankfurt, Stockholm, and London, the anthropologist Holmes (2014, pp. xi–xii) concludes that they all had the same characteristic: "the monetary regime (...) was about language, about communication, and (...) the ultimate aim of these communications was to recruit the public, broadly conceived, to collaborate with central bankers in achieving the ends of monetary policy" (Holmes, 2014, pp. xi–xii). Holmes (2014, p. 64) also shows that "confidence is always and everywhere mediated by culture, a communicative culture" in which expectations regarding the evolution of prices are formed, and these expectations "became manifest in real plans for budgets, for investment, for stocking inventories, for expanding or contracting employment, and, above all, for negotiating wages, for setting prices, for computing various commercial interest rates."

Woodford (2005) considers it important for the public to understand the actions of the central bank not only for reasons of democratic legitimacy, but also for monetary policy to become more effective. Blinder et al. (2008) point out that greater transparency makes monetary policy decisions more predictable and reduces financial market volatility. According to Blinder et al. (2008), central banks communicate about four different aspects of monetary policy: monetary policy objectives and strategy, the reasons behind monetary policy decisions, the economic outlook, and future monetary policy decisions. Crowe and Meade (2008) conclude that the level of transparency of the Bank of England is positively correlated, among others, with the degree of independence of the central bank.

In turn, Cournède and Minegishi (2009) argue that greater transparency is associated with better anchored inflation expectations and thus with more stable inflation. The same aspect is highlighted by researchers Dincer and Eichengreen (2013) who demonstrate, based on a transparency index, using data available for 100 countries by 2006, that greater transparency reduces inflation variations. According to the two researchers, transparency is part of a wider current, which responds to popular pressure to make governing institutions more open to the public, and which is an essential element of accountability in an era of central bank independence. According to the transparency index built by Dincer and Eichengreen (2013), the NBR was valued in 2010 at 7.5 points (indices range from 0 to 15). The most transparent central banks in 2010 were Riksbank in Sweden, Central Bank of Hungary, National Bank of the Czech Republic, Bank of England, Bank of Israel, and the Central Reserve Bank of New Zealand (RBNZ) (Dincer & Eichengreen, 2013).

Following Dincer and Eichengreen's (2013) model, researchers Horvath and Vaško (2016) constructed an index reflecting the financial stability of central banks in 110 countries between 2000 and 2011. The United Kingdom, the Czech Republic, and Hungary occupy the highest positions on the Financial Stability Transparency Index (2011 index values), while Romania is in the ninth place. According to the results of Horvath and Vaško (2016), the transparency of financial stability is higher in more developed countries, especially those with a legal system built on the Nordic and German models; at the same time, increased transparency is valuable in normal financial periods, but in times of financial crisis it can turn into a cause of greater financial stress.

Some researchers define transparency of central banks by the absence of an information asymmetry between monetary policy makers and other economic agents (Geraats, 2002). In order to highlight the economic consequences of transparency, the researcher appeals to two of its effects—uncertainty, generated by asymmetric information, and stimulation, generated by access to confidential information. Geraats (2002) distinguishes five aspects of transparency: political, economic, procedural, policy, and operational transparency. Political transparency refers to monetary policy objectives and decision makers' plans and may include inflation targets or central bank independence; economic transparency focuses on economic information used in monetary policy; procedural transparency describes how monetary policy decisions are made; tactical transparency refers to prompt announcement, explanations of decisions, and projections; operational transparency concerns all actions needed in implementing monetary policy (Fig. 2.1).

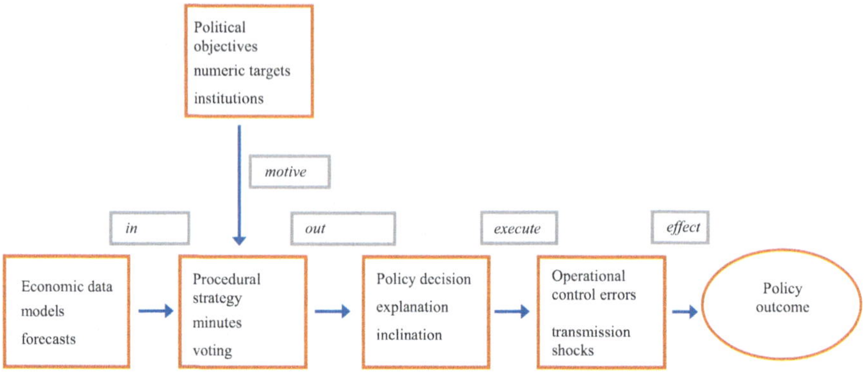


**Fig. 2.1** Conceptual framework for central bank transparency (Geraats, 2002, p. 541)

Also, the response of capital markets to the transparency of central banks is the subject of several studies (Papadamou et al., 2014; Jarocinski & Karadi, 2017).

On the other side of the conceptual framework, are the works that explore the limits and even the adverse effects of increased transparency of central banks. For example, researchers van der Cruijsen et al. (2010) use two theoretical arguments invoked in the debates on transparency—uncertainty and confusion/information overload—to substantiate the best intermediate level of central bank transparency, a level at which the quality of the perception on the estimated inflation is optimized. The conclusion of the study by van der Cruijsen et al. (2010) states that while a certain level of transparency could be useful because it improves the quality of private sector forecasts of inflation, too much transparency can be detrimental.

Ehrmann et al. (2012) to identify the limits of central bank transparency based on an analysis of how 12 central banks in developed economies communicate data on inflation, targets, and forecasts. They emphasize that increased economic transparency can generate strong monetary policy results, even in the case of reduced transparency on the part of central banks. Given the influence that central bank communication has on the ability of financial markets to anticipate monetary policy decisions and their effects, Kool et al. (2011) conclude that central banks should take into account the possible adverse effects of transparency and of the signal that market participants give when they make the decision to inform themselves less. Many other researchers argue that increased transparency does not necessarily increase the effectiveness of monetary policy (Morris & Shin, 2002; Mishkin, 2004; Gosselin et al., 2006; Kool & Thornton, 2015).

Regarding the communication of central banks, Bourne (2016) points out that central bankers were aware that the emphasis placed after the 1990s on the communication of monetary policy to the detriment of financial stability was also marked by mistakes. After 2008, when governments were left without room for fiscal maneuver, central banks became "activists" for economic recovery (Shafik, 2013). According to Bourne (2016), public relations departments supported the organization of training sessions on communication techniques and communication on post-crisis topics, communicators made several TV statements, central banks entered direct dialogue with the public including on social media, and both the number of press conferences and of analysis reports increased.

## 2.2 Confidence in Central Banks

Since money depends on public trust in issuing institutions, trust is the core of the monetary-banking system, which makes the "alchemy" defined by King (2016) work. Therefore, the strategic communication of central banks must be aimed at gaining and maintaining public confidence, which is crucial, including for gaining its support and institutional independence from the political factor.

Some of the causes of the erosion of trust in central banks are the post-crisis general erosion of trust in financial institutions, experts, and elites, the low level of knowledge of central banks by the general public, the assumption of responsibilities by central banks that have exceeded their traditional mandates and their defective communication during the 2008 crisis (Bergbauer et al., 2020; Bourne, 2011, 2016; Haldane, 2016; Tett, 2015; Ehrmann et al., 2013; Owens, 2012; Wälti, 2012; Stevenson & Wolfers, 2011; Fischer & Hahn, 2008).

After 2008, the communication activity of central banks intensified, but the reputation of these institutions began to falter in the context of a global crisis of confidence (Edelman Trust Barometer, 2017). The results of the Edelman Trust Barometer (2017), based on data collected in 2016, reflect the largest decline in trust in government institutions, business, media, and nonprofit organizations to date. More than half of the respondents of the Edelman Trust Barometer (2017) do not agree that financial market reforms have increased economic stability. Along with ministries of finance and regulators, central banks are at the top of the pyramid of trust for financial markets, as adapted by Bourne (2011). The researcher adapted the Pyramid of Confidence built by Costas Lapavitsas to the context of financial institutions for the general public (commercial banks, pension funds, insurance companies) (Fig. 2.2).

Owens (2012) examines how Americans' trust in financial institutions, banks, the stock market, and their perception of the ethical and moral principles of the leaders and representatives of these institutions have evolved over the past 40 years. According to Owens (2012), the largest variations in confidence and the most aggressive public riots are recorded in periods of economic contraction that also correspond to large-scale scandals in the financial sector. Riles (2018) analyzes the relationship between central banks and the general public and draws attention to the general loss of public confidence in the authority of experts. She also highlights the possible causes of this cultural change, such as Hollywood movies about corrupt, incompetent, and dangerous experts and the changes in the media structure in the internet age that make the public have an increasingly important say and control over the flow of news.

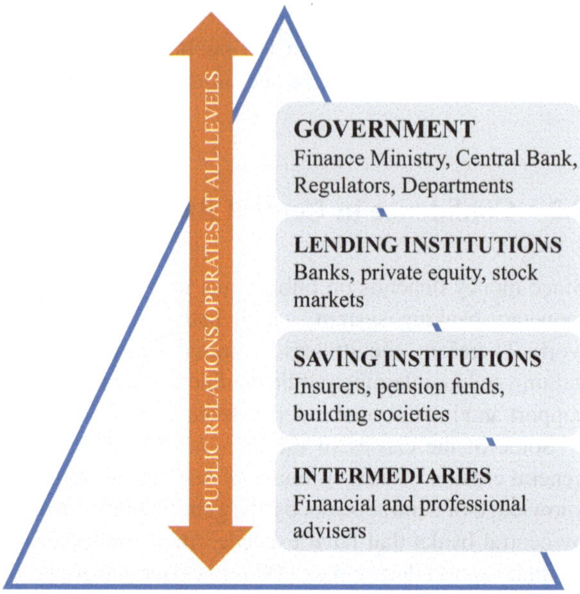


**Fig. 2.2** The pyramid of confidence for retail financial markets (Bourne, 2011)

At the same time, Riles (2018) underlines the danger of prejudice, of blind spots as a result of isolation in one's own knowledge, in fragmentation, in what Gillian Tett defines by "silo thinking" (Tett, 2015). Tett (2015, p. ix) shows that "(...) it seemed that tunnel vision and tribalism had contributed to the disaster. People were trapped inside their little specialist departments, social groups, teams, or pockets of knowledge. Or, it might be said, inside their silos." The general public is not much more connected to the work of central banks, not even a decade after the Great Recession.

For example, according to the YouGov poll (2019), out of a sample of 4843 respondents in the United Kingdom, 33% said the role of the Bank of England was not very clear to them, 11%—that it was not at all clear to them, and 6% do not know. Only 8% appreciated that the role of the BA is very clear. In terms of familiarity with economic jargon, YouGov (2020) shows that 47% of the more than 1500 respondents believe that they know exactly what monetary policy interest rates are, 42%—that they understand to some extent, and only 6% said they had heard the term, but did not know what it meant.

The decline in public confidence in the representative institutions of the financial industry in the post-crisis period, has had an impact on central banks, governments, and politicians alike (Haldane, 2016). This effect of the crisis has been the subject of several studies in recent years (Fischer & Hahn, 2008; Stevenson & Wolfers, 2011; Wälti, 2012; Ehrmann et al., 2013). For example, the latest study published by ECB experts (Bergbauer et al., 2020) shows that confidence in the European Central Bank and population support for the euro have evolved differently since 2008, even though the euro and the ECB are closely linked at the institutional level. Thus, from 2016 to 2019, support for the Euro followed an upward trend, then in the autumn of 2019, more than three quarters of eurozone citizens supported the Euro and only 42% of the eurozone population expressed confidence in the ECB with 44% saying that they did not trust the ECB. "Net trust in the ECB remains in negative territory, while net support for the euro has been increasing steadily since 2013 and reached a record high in autumn 2019" (Bergbauer et al., 2020).

The level of confidence in the ECB is correlated with the level of knowledge of the ECB's mandate and influences the formation of inflationary expectations. The analysis of Bergbauer et al. (2020) shows that confidence in the ECB can be enhanced through enhanced communication on its main aims and objectives and by pursuing its mandate of maintaining price stability.

In turn, researchers Ehrmann et al. (2013) analyze the trust factors in the European Central Bank as measured by the European Commission's Eurobarometer and explain the decline in public confidence in the ECB based on three hypotheses: Economy Hypothesis—erosion in the context of economic evolution, Europe Hypothesis—confidence in the ECB as a European institution was influenced as a result of the global financial crisis exposing the shortcomings of decision makers to prevent and solve global problems, and the Banks Hypothesis—erosion in confidence in the ECB on account of ECB's association with the banking sector which was unjustly supported.

Previously, researchers Fischer and Hahn (2008) showed that general public confidence in the ECB is affected differently by the macroeconomic conditions of an economy, depending on the level of public knowledge about the European Union and the EU institutions (Fischer & Hahn, 2008). In their efforts to establish the main causes of declining public confidence in central banks, researchers Ehrmann et al. (2013) focused on pre-crisis factors and analyzed the idea that a better knowledge of the activity of the central bank—in their analysis the European Central Bank—generates more confidence in normal periods and increases it in times of financial crisis. In the same vein, studies show that a lack of knowledge regarding the ECB does not help the institution to attract public support (Kaltenthaler et al., 2010).

Referring to the ECB's challenge to build trust among the 335 million people in the euro area, Draghi (2014) points out: "We are communicating in 18 countries using 15 different languages (...) We deal with this plurality by making use of the inherent advantage of having a Eurosystem of 18 national central banks—that is, having communications departments in each country that make our messages heard and understood in the local context. But this remains a continuous challenge."

Moreover, poor communication during the crisis eroded public confidence in the main institutions involved in rescuing financial companies. For example, Blinder (2013) considers that, during the crisis, the financial-banking system in the United States lost its audience due to its own, sometimes, "disastrous" discourse.

Regarding central banks, El-Erian (2016) notes that the difference between perception and reality is very large and cannot be justified by the lack of importance of the issues in question or the lack of information. Assuming responsibilities over the mandate, central banks have become "the only game in town" (El-Erian, 2016). King (2016) considers that central banks could maintain their credibility if they recognized their limitations and did not claim to have more information than they have. The transformation from heroes to villains is explained by former BoE governor Mervyn King:

> Central banks were seen as heroes for delivering the decade of the Great Stability and for preventing a relapse into a second Great Depression after 2008. They were seen as villains for having failed to rein in the excesses of the banking system in the first place and then for creating money on a massive scale. Compared with the late 1990s and early 2000s when their reputation peaked, central banks are now on the back foot, defending their hard-won independence from the ambitions of politicians of all colors. (King, 2016, p. 162)

The erosion of trust in central banks calls into question the fact that the banking system works because of the trust in what King (2016) refers to as "alchemy":

> The truth is that money, in all forms, depends on trust in its issuer. Confidence in paper money rests on the ability and willingness of governments not to abuse their power to print money. Bank deposits are backed by long-term risky loans that cannot quickly be converted into money. For centuries, alchemy has been the basis of our system of money and banking. (King, 2016, p. 8)

In the same vein, Greenspan (2007, p. 391) argues that "monetary policy should make even a fiat money economy behave 'as though anchored by gold.'" Qvigstad (2009) argues that while in the past the value of money was defended with weapons, it is currently defended by trust, which in turn, lies in the openness and transparency of central banks. Central banks' public confidence and their enormous power over the economy, gives the citizen "a right to expect—no, to demand—that the bank's actions match its words. To me, that is the hallmark of credibility: matching deeds to words" (Blinder, 1998, p. 64).

Periods of financial crisis demonstrate that "while a state's financial reputation does not begin with its central banking leadership, it almost certainly ends there" (Bourne, 2016, p. 45). From "radical transparency," financial institutions entered, after 2008, the "radical uncertainty"[4] stage, which they tried to overcome, including through communication.

## 2.3 Strategic Communication of Central Banks

The main studies on the strategic communication characteristics of central banks aim to identify the optimal communication strategy to ensure the effectiveness of monetary policy. More specifically, strategic communication defined as the use of communication by an organization to fulfill its mission and to strengthen its strategic positioning translates, when analyzing central banks, into the assessment of how central banks' communication increases the predictability of their decisions, anchors inflationary expectations of economic agents, and reduces volatility in financial

[4] "Radical uncertainty refers to uncertainty so profound that it is impossible to represent the future in terms of a knowable and exhaustive list of outcomes to which we can attach probabilities" (King, 2016, p. 9).

markets (Hallahan et al., 2007; van Riel & Fombrun, 2007; Argenti et al., 2005; Grunig et al., 2002). At the same time, research on the strategic communication of central banks focuses on the contribution of communication to central banks' reputation in the eyes of different categories of public and on gaining and maintaining public confidence, a goal that guarantees the functioning of the entire monetary-banking system.

### 2.3.1 Language

A team of researchers from Stanford University showed that financial-banking institutions are more and more unclear in the language they use. Moretti and Pestre (2015) applied a computerized analysis of language of 65 years' worth of World Bank speeches years (1946–2012), generically called bankspeak. They identified a sharp decline in factual accuracy, which has been replaced by what sociologists call "Management discourse" (Boltanski & Chiapello, 2007). Researchers at Stanford University show that structural change is profound: verbs have been replaced by nouns (for example, people and countries no longer "cooperate," there is only "cooperation"), the number of temporal adverbs ("now," "recently," or "later") decreased by more than 50% between 1946 and 2008, and the number of acronyms used increased rapidly. Boltanski and Chiapello (2007, p. 14) consider that management discourse, "which aims to be formal and historical, general and local, which mixes general precepts with paradigmatic examples, today constitutes the form par excellence in which the spirit of capitalism is incorporated and received."

The degree of accessibility of transmitted messages is becoming the subject of research for central bankers concerned with reducing uncertainty through communication. For example, Coenen et al. (2017) show that the length of sentences and the difficulty of the language used in the opening statements of the ECB's press conferences, which explain monetary policy decisions, as well as in the Fed's monetary policy statements, have evolved over time and now require the audience to have13–15 years of formal education for a correct understanding of the content. Haldane (2016, p. 19) analyzes the linguistic complexity of the materials published between 2012 and 2014 by the Bank of England and admits that even his own speeches are "impenetrable to most." Researchers measured fragments of speeches, reports and news about BoE using several indices and indicators. The most commonly used were Coleman—Liau and ARI indices, which are calculated based on the length of sentences and words; SMOG, calculated based on the number of multisyllabic words in a sentence; the Gunning fog index, calculated on the basis of the number of multisyllabic words and the length of sentences; the Flesh—Kinkaid level, which reflects the length of words and the average number of syllables per word; the Coleman indicator, which reflects the length of sentences and the number of monosyllabic words.

The results of the measurements show that materials published by BoE and commercial banks generally use long words, phrases, and paragraphs, as opposed to general or tabloid newspapers and as opposed to political speeches, which are much more accessible to audiences. At the same time, considering the degree of literacy, Haldane and McMahon (2018) estimate that BoE materials are inaccessible to about 90% of the general public. Bulíř et al. (2013) analyze the accessibility of inflation reports and press statements made in the last 10 years by seven central banks in advanced and emerging economies: Central Bank of Chile, BoE, Bank of Thailand, National Bank of the Czech Republic, ECB, National Bank of Poland, and Riksbank (Sweden). Applying the Flesh-Kincaid index and content analysis, the researchers show that central bank materials in the United Kingdom and Sweden require, on average, 12 years of schooling to be understood by the public, those in Czech Republic—14 years, while the documents issued by the other banks are addressed to an audience with at least 16 years of schooling.

Haldane (2016) considers that, building upon the openness to the public, reflected in recent years in the increasingly detailed and extensive materials published by BoE, there is currently a need for greater concern about the nature of communication and a simplification of communication. Haldane et al. (2020, p. 36) add: "Communication may need to be simple, relevant and story-based to become convincing and credible to a wider audience. Traditional central bank communications tend to fail on all three fronts."

One of Haldane's (2016) suggestions is for banks to publish different versions of the reports, adapted to the audience categories (customers, investors). To reach the general public, Bank of England's chief economist aims to use "a language that is hopefully non-elitist, in a format that means I am listening as much or more as I am speaking" (Haldane, 2016, p. 16). Furthermore, Isărescu (2016) observes that "despite the abundant information provided by a wide spectrum of communication vehicles, our messages reach only a small section of the general public. That is why we must strive to give up professional jargon so that we can explain to the public in the most accessible language the reasons behind monetary policy decisions."

Regarding forward guidance, an unconventional monetary policy instrument used by central banks such as the Fed, the ECB, the Bank of England, the Bank of Japan, is the clear communication of intentions concerning subsequent monetary policy decisions. The clear communication of intentions effectively informs credit institutions, financial market participants, companies, and the general public on how credit costs could evolve. Researchers Campbell (2013) and Campbell et al. (2012) distinguish between Odyssean and Delphic guidance.

More specifically, banks are either consistent with the announcements made, keep past verbal commitments, and take announced measures even in contexts that would favor different measures, just as Odysseus resisted the alluring songs of the Sirens, or make predictions, but not promises, through messages like the obscure answers given by the Delphi oracle. After 2008, the most common types of prospective guidance were data based, followed by the qualitative guidance (which refers to neither a time horizon nor economic conditions) and the calendar-based guidance (Blinder et al., 2017). The Fed's prospective calendar-based guidance has been criticized (Blinder, 2013; El-Erian, 2019). El-Erian (2019) considers that the Fed should give up prospective guidance, a strategy that has proven, over time, vulnerable to misinterpretations. Coenen et al. (2017) demonstrate that forward-looking guidance, launched by the ECB in response to the 2008 crisis, is more effective and credible in that it reduces economic uncertainty, especially when it is based on indicators, and clarity can be achieved through the emphasis on detailing them and when the institution refers to an asset acquisition program.

Researchers such as Tobback et al. (2017) and Apel and Grimaldi (2012) grouped and analyzed central banks' communication on the following monetary policy decisions, referring to two different languages used: hawkish, which conveys a possible increase in interest rates, and dovish, based on which an interest rate cut can be anticipated. For example, using quantitative content analysis of the minutes of the monetary policy meetings of the Bank of Sweden, Apel and Grimaldi (2012) identified dovish or hawkish adjectives in phrases and their frequency, and constructed an index (Net Index) with which to interpret the dovish or hawkish character of each minute.

### 2.3.2 Publics

Strategic organizational communication focuses on communication with different categories of stakeholders, as defined by researchers such as Bryson (2004) as a person or group who is affected by an organization or can affect it; by Grunig and Repper (1992) as different categories of audiences, active or passive, who have links with the organization, such as employees or investors; or by Freeman (1984, p. vi): "a stakeholder is any group or individual who can affect, or is affected by, the achievement of a corporation's purpose. Stakeholders include employees, customers, suppliers, stockholders, banks, environmentalists, government and other groups who can help or hurt the corporation." Taxonomies of organizations' audiences distinguish between internal and external stakeholders (Newsom et al., 2010); between primary stakeholders—who have contractual or formal relationships with the organization and secondary stakeholders (Clarkson, 1995); define the priority audience, which is given special attention (Newsom et al., 2010); opponent stakeholders who stand out in times of crisis, sometimes even among the public considered allies (Fusalba, 2012) etc. According to Coombs (2014, p. 19), "A crisis is the perception of an unpredictable event that threatens important expectations of stakeholders related to health, safety, environmental, and economic issues, and can seriously impact an organization's performance and generate negative outcomes."

Central banks, together with analysts, investment banks, and commercial banks, are part of the financial community (Freeman, 1984, p. 56) and thus build their reputation and autonomy by meeting the expectations of different categories of publics. For example, Riksbank (Bank of Sweden), the most transparent central bank according to Dincer and Eichengreen (2013), details, in the general framework of its communication policy the main target groups: members of the Riksdag (Swedish parliament), financial agents, authorities public, researchers, business sector, social partners, media and central bank employees (Riksbank, 2020). One of the stated objectives is to "Contribute to good knowledge and thereby to a high level of confidence in the Riksbank's activities, analysis and policy decisions."

Most of the literature dedicated to central bank communication focuses primarily on the relationship with financial market participants (monetary, foreign exchange), on informing the specialized public about the objectives, plans and projections of these institutions, on communication as a monetary policy tool, which, however, should not be misinterpreted as a public relations function (Holmes, 2014). Central banks are "the pivot of the monetary system," "the bankers' bank" (Tucker, 2018, p. 396), and their status as politically independent institutions should transform them, along with other independent organizations, in "legitimacy seekers" (Tucker, 2018, p. 15). The specialized public, consisting of bankers, analysts, investors, representatives of academia, becomes the first public to which central banks address to in the field of strategic communication, through public speeches, academic conferences, seminars, and other special events.

Riles (2018) notes that the social relations between central bankers and financial market elites, two sources of information and means of implementing monetary policy, are an important source of legitimacy of central banks. Other specialized publics are the competent national and international institutions, organizations, and forums with which the central banks establish cooperation relations.

Researchers show that the general public came to the attention of central banks especially in the post-crisis period (Haldane et al., 2020; Haldane & McMahon, 2018; Riles, 2018; Binder, 2017; Haldane, 2016).

Binder (2017) emphasizes that it is important to anchor the inflationary expectations of not only financial market participants, but also of consumers. In addition, "If effective communication with households is essential to good governance, its absence—limited or ineffectively transmitted communication—could result in public dissatisfaction, possibly leading to calls to reduce the bank's power and independence" (Binder, 2017, p. 240). For their part, Haldane et al. (2020) believe that central banks need to gain the trust of the general public for two main reasons: to ensure that operational independence meets the terms of the social contract for society as a whole and that trust helps to manage inflationary expectations.

Currently, financial sector audiences include, according to Haldane (2016), not only decision makers, banks, and investors, but also politicians, civil society, businesses, representatives of various industries, religious groups, and the media. Haldane (2018) calls for a second revolution in central bank communication, this time focused on educating the general public, but also on learning from the general public.

After over 20 years of studying the culture of central banks and the social relations formed between financial regulators and other financial market participants, the anthropologist Annelise Riles (2018) is also looking at the general public. Riles (2018) identifies the need for a new way of understanding the role, purpose, and challenges of central banks and financial governance in a highly charged post-crisis context, characterized, inter alia, by government bailout plans, negative interest rates, populist and nationalist movements pointing the finger at central bankers when referring to the source of evil in the economy. According to Riles (2018), experts are not the only customers of the global financial system and the exclusion of the general public's perspective on the economy has serious consequences for the entire economy, especially against the background of the latest financial crisis.

For the general public, the media is the primary source of information about central banks (Berger et al., 2006) the general public is indirectly reached by the bank primarily through the media (Böhm et al., 2012). In a study of the ECB's relationship with the media, Velthuis (2015) identifies three ways in which central banks can use the media to influence how the public perceives their actions: as a neutral tool for disseminating information, as an amplification tool for reaching audiences, and as a propaganda tool for reaching audiences. Haldane and McMahon (2018) explain that to connect with the general public, central banks must experiment with new methods and media. Researchers emphasize the need for central banks to learn to work "with a more diverse swath of media than the usual mainstream financial press, and with far greater sophistication, if they wish to get ahead of the falsehoods and conspiracies that proliferate with lack of understanding" (Riles, 2018, p. 64).

However, despite the increased relevance of the general public and the intensification of central banks' communication, how disseminated information reaches the general public and how the media can influence public perception of the actions of these institutions remain less studied.

Politically independent central banks include the political class among the main audiences to which they are addressed. The members of central banks Board are appointed by the Parliament, and central banks periodically submit reports to the Government and the Parliament regarding their activity and participate in public hearings. At the same time, it is necessary for the central bank "to coordinate its policies (monetary policy and financial stability policy) with governmental policies (budgetary and public debt management). It is also important for the central bank to publicly express its position on government policies" (Cerna, 2019). Researchers draw attention to the interdependence between the economic and political spheres (Riles, 2018). Moreover, Cerna (2016) shows that "behind the legal independence of the central bank can be hidden a political complicity or an exchange of political-bureaucratic privileges. Therefore, an important current direction of research is the decoding of hidden communication channels between the central bank and the political sphere." An example of accepting the politicization of a central bank is, according to Riles (2018), the Bank of Japan, which in 2012 was forced to implement the measures proposed by Prime Minister Shinzo Abe to overcome economic stagnation, a project known as "Abenomics." On the other hand, Riles (2018) highlights the Fed's reactions, namely ignoring the situation and denying any possible political interference in the central bank's decision-making process, which in recent years, under Donald Trump's administration, have been under constant attacks and criticism regarding the Fed's independence and its monetary policy decisions.

In recent years, central banks have shown a constant concern to listen and interact directly with different audiences. For example, in 2019, the Fed launched a series of events brought together under the slogan Fed Listens open to the general public,

**Table 2.2** Central banking followers on social networks

| Social network | Community (followers, friends, subscribers) |
|---|---|
| Twitter | 1,036,117 |
| LinkedIn | 886,125 |
| Facebook | 188,306 |
| YouTube | 81,315 |
| Instagram | 29,356 |
| Total | 2,221,219 |

Source: Official accounts managed on social networks by EU central banks (including the Bank of England), January 2020

business, and academia to assess monetary policy strategy, tools and its communication practices during the 2008 crisis (Federal Reserve, 2019). The Bank of England has developed a network of 12 regional agencies and maintains direct links with around 10,000 companies. The same agencies regularly organize round tables with groups of 20–24 people representative of the local population, who explain to BoE representatives the main problems they face (Haldane et al., 2020). In 2012, the European Central Bank launched the "€uro Generation" competition for high school students in the euro area, in which it also organizes online events, in which ECB decision makers answer questions (European Central Bank, 2019).

### *2.3.3 Communication Channels*

The most important communication channels for the central bank public are the websites on which all public speeches, analyses, periodic reports, minutes of monetary policy meetings, and other materials are published. Central bank communication researchers analyze the adoption of new media channels, such as Twitter, Facebook, YouTube, Instagram, LinkedIn (Haldane et al., 2020; Binder, 2017; Haldane, 2017; Shin, 2017; Bjelobaba et al., 2017; Vardy, 2015), and preliminary results show that the audience reached through these new media channels remains quite small. For example, Haldane et al. (2020) show that none of the central banks analyzed has a community of more than 0.5% of the country's population, and give the example of the Fed, with a community of 0.5 million followers, while the current president of the United States, Donald Trump, has a community of over 61 million followers, or almost 20% of the US population.

Statistics on the online presence of EU central banks in early 2020 (Table 2.2) show a growing community. In January 2020, a total of more than 2.2 million followers, subscribers and friends followed EU central banks on their official social media accounts. The trend is increasing compared to 2019, when the online community was 1.5 million, according to public data centralized for this research and reflects the fact that central banks are increasingly using these new media in organizational communication.

The largest online community of all the central bank is on Twitter, with over one million followers for 24 accounts, followed by LinkedIn with over 880,000 community members and Facebook with a total of 188,000 friends. The European Central Bank (ECB) has the largest Twitter community (over 520,000 followers in January 2020), followed by the Bank of England (over 290,000 followers), the Banque de France (over 31,000 followers), De Nederlandsche Bank NV, the Narodowy Bank Polski and the Czech National Bank. As for LinkedIn, there are 25 official accounts managed by EU central banks, with the ECB (over 180,000 followers), BoE and the Banque de France in the top 3, followed by the Banco de Portugal, the Bank of Italy, the Bank of Greece, the Banco de España and the Bank of Ireland. Of the 18 official Facebook accounts of European central banks, the Hungarian National Bank (over 58,000 friends) ranks first, followed by the Narodowy Bank Polski (over 31,000 friends) and BoE (over 24,000 friends).

Often, research focuses on social networks as communication channels of different organizations: governments, corporations, small businesses, academia, financial institutions, nonprofit organizations, etc. Researchers analyze "the ways in which individuals internalize the convergence of public and private, operate in the social, and absorb technological convergence as audiences, publics, and citizens" (Papacharissi, 2010, p. 50), "the interplay between communication and power relationships in the technological context that characterizes the network society" (Castells, 2007, p. 238), the political power of social media (Shirky, 2011), social media democracy (Loader & Mercea, 2011), or analyze social media communication structures as reflections of Habermasian concept of public sphere constructs (Bruns & Highfield, 2015).

The way in which organizations use social media in strategic communication and public relations has become the subject of research for numerous studies. Researchers analyze the impact of social networks on organizations (Balagué & Fayon, 2016; Treem & Leonardi, 2013) or focus on good practices for professionals who intend to use them (Charest et al., 2013). Other studies have been built around the confidentiality and intimacy of Facebook communication (Stutzman et al., 2013; Tufekci, 2012; van Manen, 2010; Boyd, 2008). Researchers Macnamara & Zerfass (2012, p. 7) analyze the challenges of finding an optimal dosage that balances openness and sincerity, strategy, and management of organizations in different countries that use social media. Researchers Macnamara and Zerfass (2012, p. 7) emphasize its main features: "openness for participation and interactivity involving dialogue, conversation, collaboration and co-creativity harnessing collective intelligence. Explicit in definitions and descriptions of this environment is relinquishing control that characterizes one-way, top-down information distribution models, as well as a requirement for authenticity instead of pre-packaged content."

Referring to the interactivity between audiences and organizations, Carr and Hayes (2015, p. 7) show that "publics will increasingly expect a personal face to represent organizations and corporations on social media, fostering interaction at all times of the day." The analysis uses the concept of engagement in social media, described by researchers who emphasize the role of facilitator of interactions, creator of new ways to reach different stakeholders and involve them in various activities.

For example, Cornelissen (2014, p. 393) considers that "the challenge for organizations increasingly is to have a 'discreet' presence on Facebook in the personal context of users which is not about 'selling' but about creating a personal image for the company and its brands, and in such a way that it presents interesting contents for users that strengthens or reaffirms the company's image and reputation." According to Taylor and Kent (2014), "engagement is part of dialogue and through engagement, organizations and publics can make decisions that create social capital."

Researchers of central bank culture also call for dialogue between financial experts and the public and posit that central bank should adapt to new media (Riles, 2018). Regardless of communication channels, audiences, tactics, or language, central bankers believe that "But the revolution in central bank communication is not driven by technological advances. Rather, it is the product of advances in our understanding of how to make monetary policy most effective" (Yellen, 2012).

### *2.3.4 Tactics*

The literature on central bank strategic communication presents the impact of several tactics on achieving stated goals and building reputation (Blinder et al., 2017; Tutino, 2016; Ehrmann & Fratzscher, 2009; Cukierman, 2009; Ehrmann & Fratzscher, 2005; Jansen & de Haan, 2006; Issing, 2005, etc.).

The first steps taken by central bankers towards communication were marked by a calculated hermeticism, in the deliberate practice of ambiguity as an opportunity for the organization to create meaning. In Weick's definition (1995, pp. 91–92): "Ambiguity refers to an ongoing stream that supports several different interpretations at the same time." For example, Alan Greenspan, former governor of the Fed for almost 20 years (1987–2006), who opened the institution to the public in 1994 by deciding to publish real-time interest rate decisions, refers to the deliberate use of central banking jargon as "Fedspeak": "I took care, naturally, to couch any discussion of possible future moves in Fedspeak to keep from roiling the markets"/. (Greenspan, 2007, p. 150); "I carefully hedged what I had to say in my usual Fedspeak" (Greenspan, 2007, p. 176); "For the record, even as I learned "Fedspeak," I would joke to the staff, "Whatever happened to the English language?"" (Greenspan, 2007, p. 102).

Some theorists who analyze total silence as a response strategy of an organization, especially in the context of crisis communication, show that it can be perceived as an offense, can amplify media pressure, and in many situations "silence can be interpreted as the object of a crisis itself" (Libaert, 2009, p. 75). Organizations resort to silence when they want to avoid feeding a spiral of public controversy, when the crisis situation is outclassed, on the public agenda, by other more important topics or when they assess that the crisis situation may remain secret (Libaert, 2008). Smith (2005, p. 113) considers that strategic silence can shorten the duration of a crisis and that "Strategic silence can work when publics accept that an organization is remaining silent not out of guilt or embarrassment but rather because it is motivated by higher intentions such as compassion for victims, respect for privacy or other noble considerations, or simply because it is working on the problem and refuses to be side-tracked into talking much about it."

Even if silence is defined as "the most radical form of indirect communication," Dimitrov (2015, p. 648) argues that "Most communication takes place trough silence and invisibility. Meaning arises and is conveyed with and without language. Silence and invisibility remain the widely untapped reservoir of communication wisdom."

In the case of central banks, strategic silence takes two forms: on the one hand, there are tactics by which representatives are forbidden to communicate in public within a time frame set by each institution, by its own regulations, in relation to the date of publication of the main decisions, and, on the other hand, crisis response strategy. Ehrmann and Fratzscher (2009) examine the Fed's self-imposed strategy to remain silent around monetary policy decisions (which they metaphorically call purdah[5])—for 7 days before and 3 days after the Federal Open Markets Committee (FOMC) meeting. Researchers put forward evidence about the importance of the timing of communication for financial markets: "markets tend to be more sensitive around policy decisions, and that statements in such a period may induce excessive market volatility" (Ehrmann & Fratzscher, 2009, p. 15). Blinder et al. (2008) compare the communication strategy of monetary policy decisions of the Fed, ECB and BoE and show that one of the objectives of communication, including through the synchronization of messages, is to prepare markets for the next measures to come.

Maor et al. (2013) believe that banking system regulators choose between silence and communication based on the possible impact of opinions outside the organization on their reputation. Specifically, the three researchers who analyzed the response strategy of the Israeli Department of Banking Supervision to various allegations covered by the media concluded that a regulator can generally remain silent when faced with criticism in the areas of in which it enjoys a very good reputation (prudential regulation), as such criticisms do not pose a threat to the autonomy and authority of the institution.

Silence can also be adopted when the received criticism does not directly affect reputation (the authors did not record the requests sent by journalists to the authority but assumed that the proactive request for an official reaction is part of journalism ethics). Maor et al. (2013) show that such an institution will choose to communicate about activities in which the reputation is not yet strengthened (regulations on lending conditions to individual customers), as well as in the case of extensive media coverage.

[5] *Purdah* = a state of seclusion or concealment, according to Merriam–Webster, as of March 2020: https://www.merriam-webster.com/dictionary/purdah Until 2014 the ECB called the quiet period "purdah," but changed the name due to its outdated gender connotations (European Central Bank, 2020).

At the opposite pole of strategic silence is the transmission of the same information by several representatives of the same central bank, on several communication channels simultaneously. Bernanke (2004) acknowledges the pressure that the diversity of Fed representatives' views exerts on the effectiveness of communication, and even if diversity sometimes generates cacophony, "Although at times it feels cacophonous, the willingness of FOMC members to present their individual perspectives in speeches and other public forums provides the public with useful information about the diversity of views and the balance of opinion on the Committee."

Blinder et al. (2008) define cacophony as the situation in which monetary policy decisions taken by the central bank are explained by a committee, and not by a single representative of the institution, by a single voice. More disparate voices could confuse rather than clarify the public, especially when the messages are contradictory. Researchers believe that to solve the problem, clarity and not silence is the best solution. In the same direction, Tutino (2016, p. 4) states that "Moreover, a more effective communication strategy for the central bank (author's note: Fed) could be to speak less often and make each speech count by delivering a more focused, cohesive and concise message." However, there is no consensus on the best communication strategy. While the Fed adopts an individualistic approach, Ehrmann and Fratzscher (2005) show that the ECB and the BoE use a collegiate approach, in that they prioritize the opinion of committees and consensus among members; at the same time, the consensus of the opinions expressed does not always overlap with a consensus in decision-making. Researchers demonstrate the effectiveness of both strategies and believe that the best way to design a communication strategy cannot be established. At the same time, Marcussen (2009) argues that it is not necessary for central banks with a good track record in making decisions to talk as much as central banks that have a low level of credibility.

## 2.4 Changes Triggered by the Great Recession

After the 2008 financial crisis, central banks faced new challenges, such as the risk of deflation,[6] low interest rates[7] and uncertainties about the economic outlook (Cournède & Minegishi, 2009). "The mythical 'Central Banker era' is over," proclaimed Bourne (2016, p. 45), referring to criticism received by central banks after 2008. Institutions have been accused of poor governance, inadequate inflation targeting, inadequately taken monetary measures, but also of ignoring the experts

[6]Continuous and widespread decline in prices in the economy, which do not account for improvements in the production process, is not favorable, as it can lead to a spiral of falling prices (European Central Bank, 2017).

[7]The nominal interest rate is the agreed and paid rate. For example, homeowners pay the nominal interest rate for their mortgage loan and depositors receive it for their deposits. Debtors pay the nominal rate, and depositors receive it (European Central Bank, 2016).

who predicted the crisis. According to Bourne (2016), all these events and their consequences took the communication teams by surprise.

Researchers agree that central banks communicated more once they entered the rugged terrain. For example, more than 90% of academics and more than 80% of central bank governors who responded to a questionnaire launched in 2016 by Blinder et al. (2017) argued that, compared to the pre-crisis period, central bank communication has intensified. Researchers consider that the most important change in central bank communication is the wider use of perspective communication, especially when interest rates are at historically low levels (Filardo & Hofmann, 2014; Blinder et al., 2017).

Regarding the evaluation of the criticisms received during the crisis, again, the perception of those inside the industry is different from that of the outside public. As Blinder et al. (2017) show, while 40% of academics consider that their country's central bank has received "a lot of criticism," only about 10% of central bankers consider that they have received "a lot of criticism." When assessing the criticisms that central banks received in their efforts to combat the crisis, 30% of central bankers reported that their institution was not criticized at all. They are also less concerned about the government's threats to central bank independence, with almost 70% of central bankers not reporting any threats to independence or just small attempts—as opposed to almost 40% of academics who see moderate threats, or even substantial ones (Blinder et al., 2017). Borio (2011) highlights three main challenges for central banks in the post-crisis period: economic, intellectual, and institutional, referring to the hostile economic environment, the failure of paradigms and macroeconomic models used before 2008 and the threats to their independence. The researcher shows that price stability managed through successive changes applied to monetary policy interest rates has not provided any guarantee against financial and macroeconomic instability (Borio, 2011).

Coenen et al. (2017) points out that in times of crisis, when banks use unconventional measures, communication about central bank policy becomes even more important in public discourse, for two main reasons: on the one hand—some of the measures are quasi-fiscal and involve a risk for the taxpayer, and on the other hand—some unconventional instruments have more palpable distribution effects (Coenen et al., 2017). Winkler (2000) argues that good communication must meet three criteria: be clear, be effective, and be honest. King (2016, p. 179) also focuses on sincerity when he emphasizes that "It is also important for central banks to be honest about what they don't know." The former governor of the Bank of England believes that now, trust in central banks needs to be gained much more transparently.

Although the usefulness of the unconventional measures applied is not yet fully proven, researchers Blinder et al. (2017) anticipate that some of these—such as communication of perspectives—are irreversible and that central banks will continue to intensify their communication activity.

The crisis of confidence that affected central banks after 2008 brought to light a vulnerability of the entire financial sector: a real gap between the perception of those inside the financial industry and those outside, between the discourses of elites and the opinions of the general public (Haldane, 2016). Under these conditions, Haldane

(2016) assigns to communication the responsibility of recovering, in the post-crisis period, the confidence deficit generated during the crisis between the financial-banking system on the one hand and markets and the general public on the other. Among the solutions proposed by the chief economist of the Bank of England is for financial institutions to become more accessible to the general public. Haldane (2018) builds upon this idea and shows that, despite the communication revolution that central banks generated when they transformed communication into a monetary policy instrument, the level of public understanding of central banks remains low, and just as low is the level of public trust.

Researchers and central bankers alike have identified central bank communication vulnerabilities amid the Great Recession and are now calling for a second revolution in the communication of these institutions, this time based on openness to the general public. After 2008, central bankers had more public appearances compared to the pre-crisis period as "'activists' for economic recovery" (Shafik, 2013). They assumed responsibilities that often exceeded their mandates, in an economy from which however, the big projects were missing. At the same time, they intensified their communication activity to regain the lost trust of the public. At the heart of the monetary-banking system, trust is what makes the "alchemy" defined by King (2016) work. Therefore, the strategic communication of central banks must be aimed at gaining and maintaining confidence, which is also crucial for gaining public support and institutional independence.

Where are the central banks in relation to this desideratum? Have they capitalized on the 2008 crisis or wasted it on communication? Given that the central bankers themselves admit that their own discourses are "impenetrable to most" (Haldane, 2016), we appreciate that all communication efforts must have as a starting point a revolution of the language used. Bridges to the public should be built, using non-elitist language, the abandonment of professional jargon and a simplification of communication, in a format that can be read and listened to. Central banks are not only obliged to fulfil their mandate, but, as Issing (2005, p. 74) observes even before 2008, they must give society compelling reasons for the measures they take. And the success or failure of monetary policies, as well as the preservation of historical authority, is also based on the ability of central bankers to communicate clearly, openly, sincerely, with all categories of public about their actions.

The slow recovery of economic growth after 2008 has discouraged the recovery of confidence in central banks more than all communication mistakes could have done (Bourne, 2016). However, we believe that the communication activity of central banks, no matter how professional, cannot overcome the crisis of confidence on its own and cannot reduce the real gap between the perception of those inside the financial industry and those outside. Central banks still face a low level of public understanding and trust more than a decade after the onset of the Great Recession. Public confidence invested in central banks and their significant influence over the economy give the citizen the right to demand that the actions of these institutions duplicate words. Therefore, it is necessary that the central transformation, which is reflected in the communication, take place primarily at the level of their activity itself. Central banks should surpass their framing as "scapegoats" of the crisis. After all, their main role in the financial crises—that of preventing the collapse of the banking sector—has been fulfilled, with central banks preventing the onset of a second Great Depression after 2008.

## References


Apel, M., & Grimaldi, M. (2012). *The information content of central bank minutes*. Riksbank Research Paper Series (92). Retrieved from https://www.econstor.eu/bitstream/10419/81866/1/715517821.pdf

Argenti, P. A., Howell, R. A., & Beck, K. A. (2005). The strategic communication imperative. *MIT Sloan Management Review, 46*(3), 83.

Bagehot, W. (1901). *Lombard street, a description of the money market*. Kegan Paul, Trench, Trubner.

Balagué, C., & Fayon, D. (2016). *Facebook, Twitter et les autres...: quels réseaux sociaux pour votre entreprise?* Pearson.

Belke, A. (2017). *Central bank communication: Managing expectations through the monetary dialogue*. Ruhr Economic Papers (No. 692). https://doi.org/10.4419/86788802

Bergbauer, S., Hernborg, N., Jamet, J. F., Persson, E., & Schölermann, H. (2020). *Citizens' attitudes towards the ECB*. The Euro and Economic and Monetary Union. ECB Economic Bulletin, Issue 4/2020. Retrieved from https://www.ecb.europa.eu/pub/economic-bulletin/articles/2020/html/ecb.ebart202004_01~9e43ff2fb2.en.html#toc8

Berger, H., Ehrmann, M., & Fratzscher, M. (2006). *Monetary policy in the media*. ECB working paper no. 679. https://doi.org/10.2139/ssrn.931350

Bernanke, B. S. (2004). *Fedspeak*. Speech at the meetings of the American Economic Association, San Diego, CA. Retrieved from https://www.federalreserve.gov/boarddocs/speeches/2004/200401032/default.htm

Bernanke, B. S. (2007). *Federal reserve communications*. Speech at Cato institute (25th Annual Monetary Conference), Washington, DC. Retrieved from https://www.federalreserve.gov/newsevents/speech/bernanke20071114a.htm

Bernanke, B. S. (2015). *The courage to act: A memoir of a crisis and its aftermath*. W. W. Norton.

Bernanke, B. S., & Woodford, M. (Eds.). (2007). *The inflation-targeting debate* (Vol. 32). University of Chicago Press.

Bernanke, B., Laubach, T., Mishkin, F. S., & Posen, A. S. (2001). *Inflation targeting: Lessons from the international experience*. Princeton University Press.

Binder, C. (2017). Fed speak on main street: Central bank communication and household expectations. *Journal of Macroeconomics, 52*, 238–251. https://doi.org/10.1016/j.jmacro.2017.05.003

Bjelobaba, G., Savic, A., & Stefanovic, H. (2017). *Analysis of central banks platforms on social networks*. UBT International Conference, pp. 16–21. Retrieved from https://knowledgecenter.ubt-uni.net/cgi/viewcontent.cgi?article=1223&context=conference

Blinder, A. S. (1998). *Central banking in theory and practice*. MIT Press.

Blinder, A. S. (2013). *After the music stopped: The financial crisis, the response, and the work ahead*. Penguin.

Blinder, A. S., Ehrmann, M., Fratzscher, M., de Haan, J., & Jansen, D. J. (2008). Central bank communication and monetary policy: A survey of theory and evidence. *Journal of Economic Literature, 46*(4), 910–945. Retrieved from https://pubs.aeaweb.org/doi/pdfplus/10.1257/jel.46.4.910

Blinder, A., Ehrmann, M., De Haan, J., & Jansen, D. J. (2017). Necessity as the mother of invention: Monetary policy after the crisis. *Economic Policy, 32*(92), 707–755. https://doi.org/10.1093/epolic/eix013

Böhm, J., Král, P., & Saxa, B. (2012). The Czech National Bank's monetary policy in the media. *European Journal of Political Economy, 28*(3), 341–357. https://doi.org/10.1016/j.ejpoleco.2012.01.004

Boltanski, L., & Chiapello, E. (2007). *The new spirit of capitalism*. Verso.

Bordo, M. (2007). *A brief history of central banks*. Economic Commentary. Retrieved from https://www.clevelandfed.org/newsroom-and-events/publications/economic-commentary/economic-commentary-archives/2007-economic-commentaries/ec-20071201-a-brief-history-of-central-banks

Borio, C. E. (2011). Central banking post-crisis: What compass for uncharted waters? In C. Goodhart, D. Gabor, J. Vestergaard, & I. Ertürk (Eds.), *Central banking at a crossroads—Europe and beyond* (pp. 191–2016). Anthem Press.

Bourne, C. (2011). *Public relations' role as trust strategist: A specialist niche evolves from turbulence*. EUPRERA Annual Conference 2011. Retrieved from http://orca.cf.ac.uk/29796/1/BourneTrust%20Strategist.pdf

Bourne, C. (2016). *Trust, power and public relations in financial markets*. Taylor & Francis.

Boyd, D. (2008). Facebook's privacy trainwreck: Exposure, invasion, and social convergence. *Convergence, 14*(1), 13–20. https://doi.org/10.1177/1354856507084416

Bruns, A., & Highfield, T. (2015). Is Habermas on twitter? Social media and the public sphere. In A. Bruns, G. Enli, E. Skogerbo, A. Larsson, & C. Christensen (Eds.), *The Routledge companion to social media and politics* (pp. 56–72). Routledge.

Bryson, J. M. (2004). What to do when stakeholders matter: Stakeholder identification and analysis techniques. *Public Management Review, 6*(1), 21–53.

Bulíř, A., Čihák, M., & Jansen, D. J. (2013). What drives clarity of central bank communication about inflation? *Open Economies Review, 24*(1), 125–145. https://doi.org/10.5089/9781463931148.001

Campbell, J. (2013). Odyssean forward guidance in monetary policy: A primer. In*Forward guidance: Perspectives from central bankers, scholars and market participants* (pp. 130–152). Vox eBook. Retrieved from https://fraser.stlouisfed.org/files/docs/historical/frbchi/economicperspectives/frbchi_econper_2013q4.pdf

Campbell, J. R., Evans, C. L., Fisher, J. D., Justiniano, A., Calomiris, C. W., & Woodford, M. (2012). *Macroeconomic effects of federal reserve forward guidance* [with comments and discussion]. Brookings Papers on Economic Activity, pp. 1–80.

Capie, F., Fischer, S., Goodhart, C., & Schnadt, N. (2012). *The future of central banking: The tercentenary symposium of the Bank of England*. Cambridge University Press.

Carr, C. T., & Hayes, R. A. (2015). Social media: Defining, developing, and divining. *Atlantic Journal of Communication, 23*(1), 46–65. https://doi.org/10.1080/15456870.2015.972282

Castells, M. (2007). Communication, power and counter-power in the network society. *International Journal of Communication, 1(1), 29*, 238–266. Retrieved from https://ijoc.org/index.php/ijoc/article/viewFile/46/35

Cerna, S. (2016, November 6). Banca centrala prin prisma teoriei birocratiei. Cum sa decodificam canalele ascunse de comunicare între banca centrală şi lumea politică. *Ziarul Financiar*. https://www.zf.ro/opinii/banca-centrala-prin-prisma-teoriei-birocratiei-cum-sa-decodificam-canalele-ascunse-de-comunicare-intre-banca-centrala-si-lumea-politica-15919510

Cerna, S. (2019, December 20). Independența băncii centrale, politica bugetară și gestionarea datoriei publice. *Hotnews.ro*. https://www.hotnews.ro/stiri-opinii-23561276-independenta-bancii-centrale-politica-bugetara-gestionarea-datoriei-publice.htm

Charest, F., Gauthier, A. M., & Grenon, F. (2013). Appropriation et stratégies d'intégration des médias sociaux par les professionnels de la communication. *Communication et organisation, 43*, 269–280. https://doi.org/10.4000/communicationorganisation.4259

Clarkson, M. E. (1995). A stakeholder framework for analyzing and evaluating corporate social performance. *Academy of Management Review, 20*(1), 92–117.

Coenen, G., Ehrmann, M., Gaballo, G., Hoffmann, P., Nakov, A., Nardelli, S., Persson, E., & Strasser, G. (2017). *Communication of monetary policy in unconventional times*. ECB Working Paper, No. 2080. https://doi.org/10.2866/72507

Coombs, W. T. (2014). *Ongoing crisis communication: Planning, managing, and responding*. Sage.
Cornelissen, J. (2014). *Corporate communication: A guide to theory and practice* (4th ed.). Sage.
Cournède, B., & Minegishi, M. (2009). *The role of transparency in the conduct of monetary policy*. OECD Economics Department Working Papers, No. 724. OECD. https://doi.org/10.1787/221128317344
Crowe, C., & Meade, E. E. (2008). Central bank independence and transparency: Evolution and effectiveness. *European Journal of Political Economy, 24*(4), 763–777. Retrieved from https://www.elibrary.imf.org/doc/IMF001/09223-9781451869798/09223-9781451869798/Other_formats/Source_PDF/09223-9781451914337.pdf
Cukierman, A. (2009). The limits of transparency. *Economic Notes, 38*(1–2), 1–37. Retrieved from https://www.tau.ac.il/~alexcuk/pdf/limits-of-transparency-12-07-revision.pdf
Dimitrov, R. (2015). Silence and invisibility in public relations. *Public Relations Review, 41*(5), 636–651. https://doi.org/10.1016/j.pubrev.2014.02.019
Dincer, N., & Eichengreen, B. (2013). Central bank transparency and independence: Updates and new measures. *International Journal of Central Banking, 10*(1), 189–253. https://doi.org/10.2139/ssrn.2579544
Draghi, M. (2014). *Central bank communication*. Speech at PR Manager of the Year Award. Retrieved from https://www.ecb.europa.eu/press/inter/date/2014/html/sp140804.en.html
Edelman Trust Barometer. (2017). *Trust in crisis*. Retrieved from https://www.edelman.com/research/2017-edelman-trust-barometer
Ehrmann, M., & Fratzscher, M. (2005). Communication by central bank committee members: Different strategies, same effectiveness? *Journal of Money Credit and Banking, 39*(2–3), 509–541. Retrieved from https://www.econstor.eu/bitstream/10419/152922/1/ecbwp0488.pdf
Ehrmann, M., & Fratzscher, M. (2009). Purdah—On the rationale for central bank silence around policy meetings. *Journal of Money, Credit and Banking, 41*(2–3), 517–528.
Ehrmann, M., & Talmi, J. (2017). Starting from a blank page? Semantic similarity in central bank communication and market volatility. *Journal of Monetary Economics, 111*, 48–62.
Ehrmann, M., Eijffinger, S., & Fratzscher, M. (2012). The role of central bank transparency for guiding private sector forecasts. *The Scandinavian Journal of Economics, 114*(3), 1018–1052.
Ehrmann, M., Soudan, M., & Stracca, L. (2013). Explaining European Union citizens' trust in the European Central Bank in normal and crisis times. *The Scandinavian Journal of Economics, 115*(3), 781–807.
El-Erian, M. A. (2016). *The only game in town: Central banks, instability, and avoiding the next collapse*. Random House.
El-Erian, M. A. (2019). A simple idea to improve fed communication. Opinion published by *Bloomberg*. Retrieved from https://www.bloomberg.com/opinion/articles/2019-02-18/fed-to-avoid-market-miscommunication-abolish-the-dot-plot
Elson, A. (2011). *Governing global finance: The evolution and reform of the international financial architecture*. Palgrave Macmillan.
European Central Bank. (2016). *What are interest rates and what is the difference between nominal and real interest rates?* Retrieved from https://www.ecb.europa.eu/ecb/educational/explainers/tell-me/html/nominal_and_real_interest_rates.en.html
European Central Bank. (2017). *Why are stable prices important?* Retrieved from https://www.ecb.europa.eu/ecb/educational/explainers/tell-me-more/html/stableprices.en.html
European Central Bank. (2019). *ECB youth dialogue initiative*. Retrieved from https://www.ecb.europa.eu/ecb/educational/youth-initiatives/ecb-youth-dialogue/html/index.en.html
European Central Bank. (2020). *What is the quiet period?* Retrieved from https://www.ecb.europa.eu/ecb/educational/explainers/tell-me/html/what-is-the_quiet_period.en.html
Faust, J., & Svensson, L. E. (2001). Transparency and credibility: Monetary policy with unobservable goals. *International Economic Review, 42*(2), 369–397. Retrieved from https://www.nber.org/papers/w6452.pdf

Federal Reserve. (2019). *Fed listens events*. Retrieved from https://www.federalreserve.gov/monetarypolicy/review-of-monetary-policy-strategy-tools-and-communications-fed-listens-events.htm
Feroli, M., Greenlaw, D., Hooper, P., Mishkin, F. S., & Sufi, A. (2017). Language after liftoff: Fed communication away from the zero lower bound. *Research in Economics, 71*(3), 452–490.
Filardo, A. J., & Hofmann, B. (2014, March). Forward guidance at the zero lower bound. *BIS Quarterly Review*. Retrieved from https://www.bis.org/publ/qtrpdf/r_qt1403f.pdf
Fischer, J. A., & Hahn, V. (2008). *Determinants of trust in the European Central Bank*. SSE/EFI Working Paper Series in Economics and Finance. Retrieved from https://www.econstor.eu/bitstream/10419/56308/1/56082744X.pdf
Freeman, R. E. (1984). *Strategic management: A stakeholder approach*. Pitman.
Fusalba, T. (2012). *Managementul crizei*. Editura C.H.Beck.
Geraats, P. M. (2002). Central bank transparency. *The Economic Journal, 112*(483), F532–F565. Retrieved from http://www.wm.tu-berlin.de/fileadmin/fg124/geldtheorie/literatur/geraats.pdf
Gosselin, P., Lotz, A., & Wyplosz, C. (2006). *How much informat ion should interest rate-setting central banks reveal?* Centre for Economic Policy Research. Retrieved from https://www.researchgate.net/profile/Charles_Wyplosz/publication/4759038_How_Much_Information_Should_Interest_Rate-Setting_Central_Banks_Reveal/links/00b7d51c3679da1eb1000000/How-Much-Information-Should-Interest-Rate-Setting-Central-Banks-Reveal.pdf
Greenspan, A. (2007). *The age of turbulence: Adventures in a new world*. Penguin Press.
Grunig, J. E., & Repper, F. C. (1992). Strategic management, publics, and issues. *Excellence in Public Relations and Communication Management, 73*(1), 117–157.
Grunig, L. A., Grunig, J. E., & Dozier, D. M. (2002). *Excellent public relations and effective organizations. A study of communication management in three countries*. Lawrence Erlbaum Associates.
Haldane, A. (2016). *The great divide*. Speech at the New City agenda annual dinner. Retrieved from https://www.bankofengland.co.uk/speech/2016/the-great-divide
Haldane, A. (2017). *A little more conversation. A little less action*. Speech at the Federal Reserve Bank of San Francisco. Retrieved from https://www.bis.org/review/r170403e.pdf
Haldane, A. (2018). *Folk wisdom*. Speech at the100th anniversary of the Bank of Estonia. Retrieved from https://www.bankofengland.co.uk/-/media/boe/files/speech/2018/folk-wisdom-speech-by-andy-haldane.pdf?la=enşihash=DA3CC381EAC763701787B79E68013BE7BB2D2C52
Haldane, A., & McMahon, M. (2018). Central bank communications and the general public. *AEA Papers and Proceedings, 108*, pp. 578–583. https://doi.org/10.1257/pandp.20181082.
Haldane, A., Macaulay, A., & McMahon, M. (2020). *The 3 E's of central bank communication with the public*. Bank of England, Staff Working Paper No. 847. Retrieved from https://www.bankofengland.co.uk/-/media/boe/files/working-paper/2020/the-3-es-of-central-bank-communication-with-the-public.pdf?la=enşihash=B3D34A003BB6F2B7D5653B265966DF11C8F75154
Hallahan, K., Holtzhausen, D., Van Ruler, B., Verčič, D., & Sriramesh, K. (2007). Defining strategic communication. *International Journal of Strategic Communication, 1*(1), 3–35.
Hansen, S., & McMahon, M. (2016). Shocking language: Understanding the macroeconomic effects of central bank communication. *Journal of International Economics, 99*, S114–S133.
Holmes, D. R. (2014). *Economy of words: Communicative imperatives in central banks*. University of Chicago Press.
Horvath, R., & Vaško, D. (2016). Central bank transparency and financial stability. *Journal of Financial Stability, 22*, 45–56.
Isărescu, M. C. (2016, June 7). *Trebuie să renunţăm la jargonul profesional şi să explicăm publicului deciziile de politică monetară în limbaj accesibil*. Article published by Agerpres, based on the presentation given at the IMF-World Bank Annual Constituency Meeting. Retrieved from http://www.agerpres.ro/economie/2016/06/07/isarescu-trebuie-sa-renuntam-la-jargonul-profesional-si-sa-explicam-publicului-deciziile-de-politica-monetara-in-limbaj-accesibil-11-47-05

Issing, O. (2005). Communication, transparency, accountability: Monetary policy in the twenty-first century. *Federal Reserve Bank of St. Louis Review, 87 (March/April 2005)*. Retrieved from http://homepage.ntu.edu.tw/~nankuang/Money%20and%20Banking%20Supplement/12/Communication,%20Transparency,%20Accountability.pdf

Jansen, D. J., & de Haan, J. (2006). Look who's talking: ECB communication during the first years of EMU. *International Journal of Finance și Economics, 11*(3), 219–228.

Jarocinski, M., & Karadi, P. (2017). *Central bank information shocks*. Presented at the 2017 Meeting Papers, Society for Economic Dynamics. Retrieved from https://www.econstor.eu/bitstream/10419/179348/1/ecb-wp2133.en.pdf

Jeanneau, S. (2009). *Communication of monetary policy decisions by central banks: What is revealed and why*. BIS Papers. Retrieved from https://www.bis.org/publ/bppdf/bispap47.pdf

Kaltenthaler, K., Anderson, C. J., & Miller, W. J. (2010). Accountability and independent central banks: Europeans and distrust of the European Central Bank. *JCMS: Journal of Common Market Studies, 48*(5), 1261–1281.

King, M. (2016). *The end of alchemy: Money, banking, and the future of the global economy*. Little, Brown.

Kohn, D. L., & Sack, B. (2003). *Central bank talk: Does it matter and why?* Divisions of Research & Statistics and Monetary Affairs, Federal Reserve Board. Retrieved from https://www.federalreserve.gov/PubS/feds/2003/200355/200355pap.pdf

Kool, C., & Thornton, D. L. (2015). *How effective is central bank forward guidance?* Utrecht School of Economics. Tjalling C. Koopmans Research Institute. Discussion Paper Series 12-05.

Kool, C., Middeldorp, M., & Rosenkranz, S. (2011). Central bank transparency and the crowding out of private information in financial markets. *Journal of Money, Credit and Banking, 43*(4), 765–774.

Libaert, T. (2008). *Comunicarea de criză*. Editura C.H.Beck.

Libaert, T. (2009). *Planul de comunicare. Cum să-ți definești și să-ți organizezi strategia de comunicare*. Editura Polirom.

Loader, B. D., & Mercea, D. (2011). Networking democracy? Social media innovations and participatory politics. *Information, Communication and Society, 14*(6), 757–769. https://doi.org/10.1080/1369118X.2011.592648

Macnamara, J., & Zerfass, A. (2012). Social media communication in organizations: The challenges of balancing openness, strategy, and management. *International Journal of Strategic Communication, 6*(4), 287–308.

Maor, M., Gilad, S., & Bloom, P. B. N. (2013). Organizational reputation, regulatory talk, and strategic silence. *Journal of Public Administration Research and Theory, 23*(3), 581–608. https://doi.org/10.1093/jopart/mus047

Marcussen, M. (2009). Scientization of central banking: The politics of a-politicization. In K. Dyson & M. Marcussen (Eds.), *Central banks in the age of the Euro: Europeanization, convergence, and power* (pp. 373–390). Oxford University Press.

Mishkin, F. S. (2004). *Can central bank transparency go too far?* National Bureau of Economic Research. Retrieved from https://www.nber.org/papers/w10829.pdf

Moessner, R., Jansen, D. J., & de Haan, J. (2017). Communication about future policy rates in theory and practice: A survey. *Journal of Economic Surveys, 31*(3), 678–711. https://doi.org/10.1111/joes.12169

Moretti, F., & Pestre, D. (2015). Bankspeak: The language of World Bank reports. *New Left Review, 92*(2), 75–99.

Morris, S., & Shin, H. S. (2002). Social value of public information. *American Economic Review, 92*(5), 1521–1534.

National Bank of Romania. (2016). *Press release on increasing the transparency of information on NBR activity*. Retrieved from https://www.bnr.ro/page.aspx?prid=11979

National Bank of Romania. (2020). *Monetary policy instruments*. Retrieved from https://www.bnr.ro/Monetary-Policy-Instruments-3647.aspx

Newsom, D., Turk, J., & Kruckeberg, D. (2010). *Totul despre relațiile publice*. Editura Polirom.

Owens, L. A. (2012). The polls—Trends: Confidence in banks, financial institutions, and wall street, 1971–2011. *Public Opinion Quarterly, 76*(1), 142–162.

Papacharissi, Z. (2010). *A private sphere: Democracy in a digital age*. Polity Press.

Papadamou, S., Sidiropoulos, M., & Spyromitros, E. (2014). Does central bank transparency affect stock market volatility? *Journal of International Financial Markets, Institutions and Money, 31*, 362–377. https://doi.org/10.1016/j.intfin.2014.05.002

Qvigstad, J. F. (2009). *On transparency*. Speech at the Norwegian Academy of Science and Letters on 10 November 2009. Retrieved from https://norges-bank.brage.unit.no/norges-bank-xmlui/bitstream/handle/11250/2567296/On%20transparency.pdf?sequence=1

Riksbank. (2020). *The Riksbank's communication policy*. Retrieved from https://www.riksbank.se/globalassets/media/riksbanken/lagar-regler%2D%2Dpolicy/communication-policy.pdf

Riles, A. (2018). *Financial citizenship: Experts, publics, and the politics of central banking*. Cornell University Press.

Shafik, N. (2013, March 7). *Communication, engagement and effective economic reform: The IMF experience*. Retrieved from https://www.imf.org/en/News/Articles/2015/09/28/04/53/sp030713

Shin, H. S. (2017). *Can central banks talk too much?* Speech at the ECB conference on "Communications challenges for policy effectiveness, accountability and reputation". Retrieved from https://www.bis.org/speeches/sp171114.pdf

Shirky, C. (2011). The political power of social media: Technology, the public sphere, and political change. *Foreign affairs, 90*, 28–41.

Smart, G. (1999). Storytelling in a central bank: The role of narrative in the creation and use of specialized economic knowledge. *Journal of Business and Technical Communication, 13*(3), 249–273.

Smith, R. D. (2005). *Strategic planning for public relations*. Lawrence Erbaum Associates.

Stevenson, B., & Wolfers, J. (2011). Trust in public institutions over the business cycle. *The American Economic Review, 101*(3), 281–287.

Stutzman, F. D., Gross, R., & Acquisti, A. (2013). Silent listeners: The evolution of privacy and disclosure on Facebook. *Journal of Privacy and Confidentiality, 4*(2), 7–41.

Taylor, M., & Kent, M. L. (2014). Dialogic engagement: Clarifying foundational concepts. *Journal of Public Relations Research, 26*(5), 384–398.

Tett, G. (2015). *The silo effect: The peril of expertise and the promise of breaking down barriers*. Simon and Schuster.

Tobback, E., Nardelli, S., & Martens, D. (2017). *Between hawks and doves: Measuring central bank communication*. ECB Working Paper, No. 2085. https://doi.org/10.2866/977130

Treem, J. W., & Leonardi, P. M. (2013). Social media use in organizations: Exploring the affordances of visibility, editability, persistence, and association. *Annals of the International Communication Association, 36*(1), 143–189.

Tucker, P. (2018). *Unelected power: The quest for legitimacy in central banking and the regulatory state*. Princeton University Press.

Tufekci, Z. (2012). Facebook, youth and privacy in networked publics. In *Proceedings of the International AAAI Conference on Web and Social Media, 6*(1), 338–345.

Tutino, A. (2016). Central Bank communication must overcome the Public's limited attention span. *Economic Letter, 11*(6), 1–4. Retrieved from http://www.dallasfed.org/assets/documents/research/eclett/2016/el1606.pdf

van der Cruijsen, C. A., Eijffinger, S. C., & Hoogduin, L. H. (2010). Optimal central bank transparency. *Journal of International Money and Finance, 29*(8), 1482–1507.

van Manen, M. (2010). The pedagogy of Momus technologies: Facebook, privacy, and online intimacy. *Qualitative Health Research, 20*(8), 1023–1032. https://doi.org/10.1177/1049732310364990

van Riel, C. B., & Fombrun, C. J. (2007). *Essentials of corporate communication: Implementing practices for effective reputation management*. Routledge.

Vardy, J. (2015). *Reputational risk management in central banks* (No. 2015–16). Staff Discussion Paper, Bank of Canada.

Vega, M., & Winkelried, D. (2005). Inflation targeting and inflation behavior: A successful story? *International Journal of Central Banking, 1*(3), 153–175.

Velthuis, O. (2015). Making monetary markets transparent: The European Central Bank's communication policy and its interactions with the media. *Economy and Society, 44*(2), 316–340. https://doi.org/10.1080/03085147.2015.1013355

Wälti, S. (2012). Trust no more? The impact of the crisis on citizens' trust in central banks. *Journal of International Money and Finance, 31*(3), 593–605.

Weick, K. E. (1995). *Sensemaking in organizations*. Sage.

Winkler, B. (2000). *Which kind of transparency? On the need for clarity in monetary policymaking*. ECB Working Paper, No. 26. European Central Bank (ECB). Retrieved from https://www.econstor.eu/bitstream/10419/152460/1/ecbwp0026.pdf

Woodford, M. (2005). *Central bank communication and policy effectiveness*. National Bureau of Economic Research. Retrieved from https://www.nber.org/papers/w11898.pdf

Yellen, J. L. (2012). *Revolution and evolution in central Bank communications*. Speech at the Haas School of Business, University of California, Berkeley, CA. Retrieved from http://www.federalreserve.gov/newsevents/speech/yellen20121113a.htm

YouGov. (2019). *How clear, if at all, are you about what role the Bank of England carries out?* Retrieved from https://yougov.co.uk/topics/science/survey-results/daily/2019/04/24/12913/3

YouGov. (2020). *Survey on economic jargon*. Retrieved from https://docs.cdn.yougov.com/1nu27z8r6f/YouGov%20Survey%20Results%20-%20Budget%20Day.pdf

# Chapter 3
# Framing Theory

*Like the framing of a house, a news frame creates a structure on which other elements are built*
*(Capella & Jamieson, 1997, p. 38)*

How should news be configured in order to shape the mindset of readers? This chapter provides a theoretical support for the origins of the media framing theory, definitions, typologies, and what were the main features of the financial and economic crisis of 2008.

The 2008 crisis provides a generous framework for observing and analyzing the communication of the various categories of actors involved in managing and overcoming the situation. This research aims to present how the communication of the National Bank of Romania changed in the post-crisis period and to identify and analyze, on the one hand, the frames used by the Romanian online media in its coverage of one of the most visible nonmonetary topics of debate for the NBR during the analyzed period—the giving in payment law, and, on the other hand, the messages sent by bank representatives referring to the monetary and nonmonetary communication of this period. At the same time, we test the perception of the general public and of the specialized public on the changes in the communication of the central bank.

To this end, the research uses the theory of framing and refers to the media as a stakeholder of the central bank, as well as a possible influencer of how the audience selects and interprets different communication situations. In the research, we will use a series of terms and phrases explained in this chapter such as frames, framing theory, agenda setting, priming theory, and gatekeeping.

## 3.1 Framing Paradigm

Framing theorists (Gitlin, 1980; Iyengar & Kinder, 1987; Gamson & Modigliani, 1989; Entman, 1993; Shah et al., 1996; Iyengar, 1991; de Vreese, 2002; Entman, 2003; de Vreese, 2005; Matthes & Kohring, 2008; Scheufele & Iyengar, 2011;

© The Author(s), under exclusive license to Springer Nature Switzerland AG 2022 
R. Iacob, *Blind Spots in the Spotlight*, Financial and Monetary Policy Studies 53,
https://doi.org/10.1007/978-3-031-04067-2_3

McLeod & Shah, 2015, etc.) discuss how media framing can influence and shape public opinion and can impact individual interpretations by emphasizing the importance of certain characteristics of a subject and the way in which audiences perceive reality based on accessibility and interpretive patterns.

Over the last four decades, the concept of "frames" has been defined in different ways, and research on the effects of frames has been based on various theoretical premises, with affiliations in several sciences, such as anthropology, sociology, psychology, political science, and communication sciences. In one of his first definitions, sociologist Erving Goffman explains frames as "interpretive schemes" that turns "what would otherwise be a meaningless aspect of the scene into something that is meaningful" and "allows its user to locate, perceive, identify, and label a seemingly infinite number of concrete occurrences defined in its terms" (Goffman, 1986 [1974], p. 21). Goffman (1986 [1974]) introduces the concept of "framing" in relation to the organization of lived experiences, starting from the conclusions of the anthropologist and psychologist Gregory Bateson about the patterns of play activities of otters. Building on this perspective, researchers have referred to framing as interpretive schemes with origins in culture and society, related to individual consciousness (Entman, 1993; Pan & Kosicki, 1993; Gamson et al., 1992; Benford & Snow, 2000; Reese, 2001; van Gorp, 2007, etc.).

According to Entman (1993), the concept of "framing" is a way of "describing the power of a text that transmits information" (Entman, 1993, p. 51). Entman emphasizes that the selection and prominence, salience of the subjects are the main processes through which the framing is done. "To frame is to select some aspects of a perceived reality and make them more salient in a communicating text, in such a way as to promote a particular problem definition, causal interpretation, moral evaluation, and/or treatment recommendation for the item described" (Entman, 1993, p. 52). Starting from the experiments of Kahneman and Tversky, who showed that the chosen frames guide the audience's attention to certain aspects of reality, Entman (1993) also emphasizes that framing can also distract the attention of receivers from other aspects. Thus, "Most frames are defined by what they omit as well as include" (Entman, 1993, p. 54). Entman (1993) shows that, in the communication process, frames can be identified both in communicators who use them deliberately or not, in the text, by using keywords, phrases, stereotypical images, sources, etc., in receivers that can or cannot reflect the cadres of communicators, and in the culture considered the source of the common frames, recurring in the same social group. In the same vein, Gitlin (1980) views frames as models that organize the world for both journalists and readers: "Media frames are persistent patterns of cognition, interpretation, and presentation, of selection, emphasis, and exclusion, by which symbol-handlers routinely organize discourse, whether verbal or visual" (Gitlin, 1980, p. 7).

Researchers Gamson et al. (1992, p. 374) consider that "a wide variety of media messages can act as teachers of values, ideologies, and beliefs and that they can provide images for interpreting the world whether or not the designers are conscious of this intent." Analyzing news discourse on public policy issues, researchers Pan and Kosicki (1993, p. 57) evaluate the news media frame as "a cognitive device used in information encoding, interpreting, and retrieving; it is communicable; and it is related to journalistic professional routines and conventions."

Capella and Jamieson (1997, p. 38) consider that "Like the framing of a house, a news frame creates a structure on which other elements are built." Reese (2001, p. 9) describes framing "as an exercise in power, particularly as it affects our understanding of the political world." van Gorp (2007, p. 64) refers to the frames used by journalists and takes one step further the expression media package launched by Gamson and Modigliani (1989), when describing the frame package as "a cluster of logical organized devices that function as an identity kit for a frame." The kit proposed by van Gorp (2007) consists of three components: (1) framing devices, which consist of chosen words, metaphors, descriptions, arguments, images, etc.; (2) reasoning devices, such as wording on justifications, causes, and consequences; (3) the cultural phenomenon, which functions as a central theme (archetype, mythical figure, value, story).

In turn, Benford and Snow (2000) clarify the link between framing concepts and processes and other conceptual and theoretical formulations relevant to social movements, such as ideologies. Researchers analyze strategic processes related to the framing of social movements, when collective action frames are used to achieve certain goals (for example, to recruit new followers, to attract the support of spectators) and which can be redefined in a dynamic social context.

Scheufele and Iyengar (2011) structure two main perspectives in substantiating the research of the classification: psychological and sociological. The psychological approach—known as the "equivalence frames"—is grounded in the research of Kahneman and Tversky (1979) and is based on two hypotheses: "framing refers to differential modes of presentation for the exact same piece of information" and "participants interpret the stimulus in line with the context in which it is framed (...) but have no reason to assume that it could also be seen differently if framed in an alternative way" (Scheufele & Iyengar, 2011, p. 5). From a sociological perspective, framing is defined as "information that conveys differing perspectives on some event or issue" and considers that "this tradition can also be labeled 'emphasis' framing, since the observed framing effects represent differences in opinion that cannot be attributed exclusively to differences in presentation" (Scheufele & Iyengar, 2011, pp. 6–7).

Exploring the long history of framing and the different conceptualizations of the framing theory, recent studies call for a "return to the origins" approach. Cacciatore et al. (2016, p. 15) propose "framing research be both terminologically and conceptually refocused around equivalence-based definitions" and "a much narrower conceptual understanding." Also, researchers Cacciatore et al. (2016) drew attention to the challenges of differentiating framing effects from other persuasive media mechanisms while applying emphasis framing.

In practice, there are two approaches to identifying and analyzing frames in news: qualitative, inductive, such as discourse analysis (Pan & Kosicki, 1993; Gamson & Modigliani, 1989); and quantitative, based on deductive content analysis, using predefined frames (Semetko & Valkenburg, 2000; Tankard, 2001; Dimitrova et al., 2005; Matthes & Kohring, 2008; Corbu et al., 2015). According to Capella and Jamieson (1997, p. 47), a framing must meet three criteria: be identifiable on the basis of conceptual and linguistic characteristics; be usually observed in journalistic practice and be differentiable from other frames.

Researchers Matthes and Kohring (2008) describe five methodological approaches to the analysis of media frames, the first four approached are: inductive—hermeneutical (interpretation links frames to the broader cultural framework); linguistic (frames are identified by following the selection, structure, and placement of certain words and phrases in a text), manual holistic (frames are identified by a qualitative analysis of texts and then coded as variables of a whole, in a manual analysis of content), computer-assisted (mapping of frames, based on the identification of certain words used together, using cluster algorithms) and deductive approach (using frames from the literature and encoding them in standard content analysis).

Based on findings by Iyengar (1991), Semetko and Valkenburg (2000), Dahinden (2006), researchers Pühringer et al. (2008, p. 5) describe five categories of general frameworks: the conflict framework which reflects a conflict of interest between different categories of social actors (key values for power relations, capital distribution); the economic framework, an economic perspective that emphasizes efficiency and effectiveness; the progress framework—science has an important role in presenting the subject (values: expertise, truth); the moral framework—the values in question are ethical, moral and legal; and the episodic framing—the subject is presented from an individual perspective, and the values are part of the emotional register (sympathy and antipathy).

Researcher de Vreese (2005, p. 54) proposes a distinction between specific frames, related only to certain topics or events, and generic frames, which go beyond thematic limitations and can be used in connection with different topics, including different cultural contexts or moments, different on the time axis.

Researchers Semetko and Valkenburg (2000, pp. 95–96) operate with five categories of framing: the conflict frame—which focuses on conflicts between individuals, groups, or institutions that attract the audience's attention; the human interest frame—which highlights emotional aspects, journalists are concerned with giving a human face to the subject; the economic consequences frame—which emphasizes the economic consequences of a situation on a country, institutions, organizations, people; the morality frame—which highlights the religious or moral implications of the subject; and the responsibility frame—which identifies those who caused the situation or those who must contribute to overcoming the problem (institutions, politicians, groups, etc.).

Knight (1999, pp. 388–389) classifies frames into: fact-based frames, using official evidence; interest-based, especially in discussing arguments or bills; value-based framing, which emphasizes the contradictions between good and evil, moral and immoral; relational-based framing, focused on the emotional connections between those who enter debates; and crisis framing, framing messages such as trust issues, control, and collaboration history.

Goffman, E. (1986 [1974]) describes the primary organizational frames: natural frames, unguided, physical events; and social frameworks, which involve rules and provide a guiding context.

## 3.2 News Framing and Public Opinion

There is a rich literature on how media framing influences public opinion. For example, according to Nisbet (2010, p. 47), "media frames work by connecting the mental dots for the public. They suggest a connection between two concepts, issues, or things, such that after exposure to the framed message, audiences accept or are at least aware of the connection."

Framing research is often found in the structure of agenda setting. As Cacciatore et al. (2016, p. 11) point out, "framing has been said to overlap with or, in some cases, be subsumed by theories like priming and agenda-setting."

Framing is the third concept to be studied by researchers concerned with the effects of the media. Early theorists (Cohen, 1963; McCombs & Shaw, 1993) focused on the public agenda setting theory and showed how the media can influence public opinion because media pay attention to certain topics. In their 1993 study, McCombs and Shaw (1993, p. 63) describe the evolution of agenda setting theory and show that "Agenda setting is a process that can affect both what to think about and how to think about it" and anticipate the importance and role of media framing. Iyengar and Kinder (1987) analyze the power of television to influence political decisions, due to its priming effect: "By priming certain aspects of national life while ignoring others, television news sets the terms by which political judgments are rendered and political choices made" (Iyengar & Kinder, 1987, p. 4).

Some researchers include all three of these theories—agenda setting, priming, and framing under the same theoretical "umbrella" (e.g., Iyengar & Kinder, 1987; McCombs, 2002):

> The effects of mass communication may be due to the high volume of exposure. The effects at the first level of agenda setting demonstrate this phenomenon. But as both agenda setting and priming show, increased attention to the specific content in the media—including the tone of those messages—provides a detailed understanding of the images in our minds and the attitudes and opinions that flow from these images. (McCombs, 2002)

Other researchers view framing and public agenda setting as distinct theories (e.g., Domke et al., 1998; Price et al., 1997). Priming is seen as a result of setting the calendar, while framing corresponds to the second level of agenda setting. Price et al. (1997, p. 486) use, for example, "applicability effects" when describing framing, "but once activated, ideas and feelings retain some residual activation potential, making them more likely to be activated and used in making subsequent evaluations—these are called accessibility effects."

Scheufele and Iyengar (2011) consider agenda setting and priming as accessibility-based effects—as a logical extension of agenda setting. "An issue can

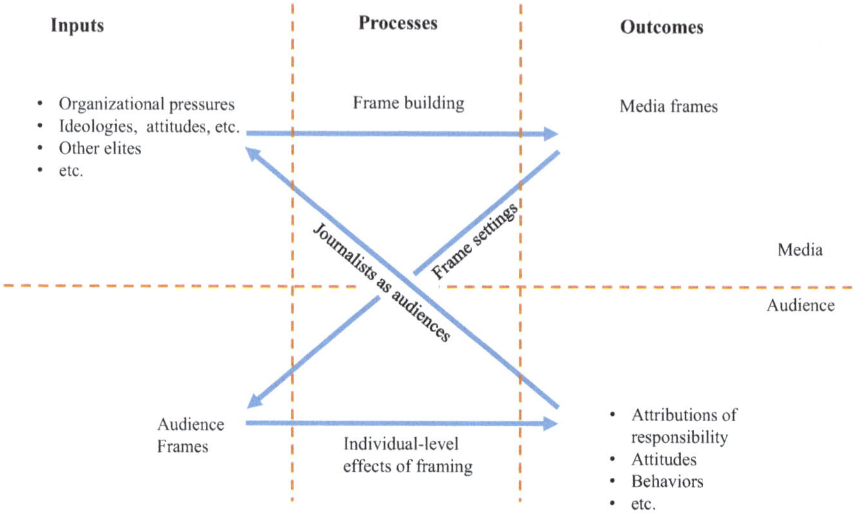


**Fig. 3.1** The interpretation scheme of the process-based model of framing research (Scheufele, 1999, p. 115)

be primed or made salient among mass audiences, even if they have never heard about it before," while "applicability models, in contrast, assume that effects, such as framing, are contingent or at least variant in strength, depending on an audience member's pre-existing schema(s)" (Scheufele & Iyengar, 2011, pp. 13–14).

Regardless of these differences, most researchers dedicated to the effects of media on public opinion indicate that media frames can influence audience's frames (Scheufele, 1999). Dietram Scheufele (1999) develops a process-based model for framing, in which the results of some processes become stimuli for subsequent processes. Researchers identify four processes (Fig. 3.1): frame building—the process of building media framing based on stimuli such as organizational pressures, professional values, elites, and ideological framework; frame setting—the process by which media frames are transmitted to audience frames; the effects of framing at the individual level (attitudes, behaviors, etc.); and the link between individual frames and media frames (predisposition of journalists and elites in the recruitment process).

Entman (2003, p. 420) analyzes the functioning and transmission of frames starting from the state authorities and continuing the chain of other elites, media, news frames and the public, and proposes cascading network activation (Fig. 3.2).

As in the case of real-world waterfalls, each level in the metaphorical waterfall makes its own contribution to the mixing and flow (transmission) (of ideas), but the ability to promote the spread of frames is also highly stratified, both between levels, as well as within each level. As with real waterfalls, moving down a waterfall is relatively easy, but spreading the ideas above, from lower to higher levels, requires extra energy—a pumping mechanism, so to speak.

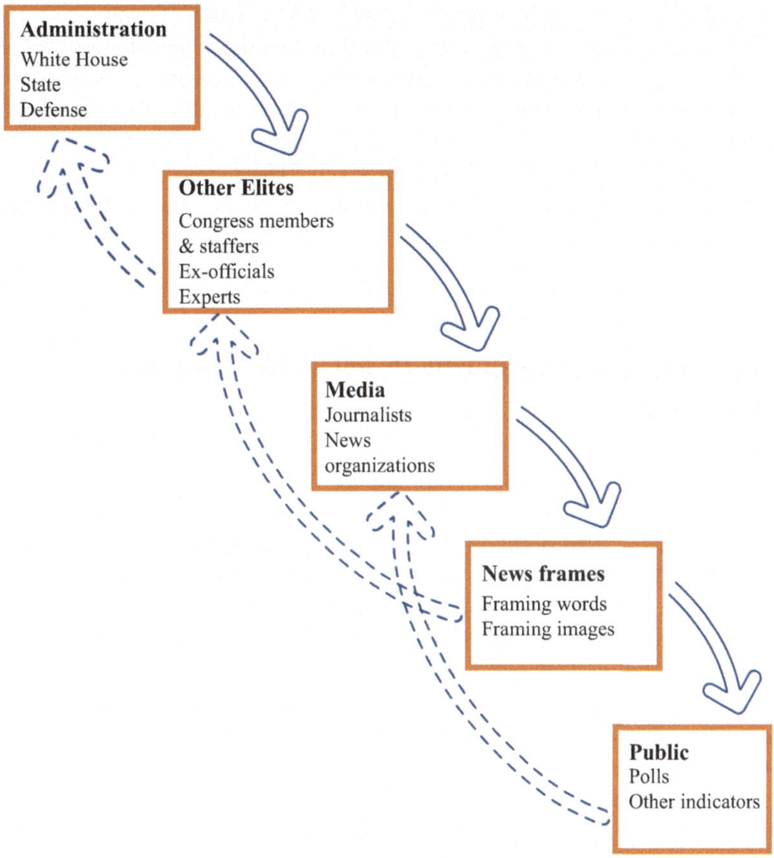


**Fig. 3.2** Cascading network activation scheme (Entman, 2003, p. 419)

Entman (2003) considers that the ideas transmitted from the top level, in the case of the proposed analysis—of the White House administration (president, advisers), are the strongest, then follow those of the elites who are part of the Congress, experts, lobbyists, interest groups, public relations firms, etc. The network of journalists is made up of reporters, editorialists, producers, and newspaper owners, who establish professional and social networks, formal and informal, inside the industry, but also outside and through which the frames of the elites are transmitted. Entman (2003, p. 420) argues that "it is not always easy to determine where the line between 'elite' and 'journalist' should be drawn, or who influences whom. Arguably, a few top editors, correspondents, and editorialists exercise more sway over the spread of ideas than all but the most powerful public officials." According to the model proposed by Entman (2003), the media is the main channel through which the frames of the public can reach the administration and can exert an influence on the frames of the elites. The cascade activation model identifies four variables that, according to Entman (2003) explain the formation and results of competing frameworks: motivations, which generates mental associations for all actors (elite, journalists, audience); power and strategy developed by the administration and other elites, defined as external forces that can stimulate certain mental associations; and cultural congruence, ensured by the essence of the news itself, and which measures the ease with which a frame is transmitted at different levels in the framing process and can generate similar reactions on each level: "The more congruent the frame with schemas that dominate the political culture, the more success it will enjoy" (Entman, 2003, p. 422).

## 3.3 Framing and Journalistic Practice: News Values—Gatekeeping

Journalists play an important role in building the news because, by the nature of the profession, they appreciate and capitalize on certain narrative elements to the detriment of others. Research on journalism has identified several values that contribute to the configuration of news, called news values. For example, in the now-classic study, Galtung and Ruge (1965) identified 12 factors and their dynamic combinations: frequency, threshold (intensity), unambiguity, meaningfulness, consonance (predictability, demand), unexpectedness (unpredictability, rarity), continuity, composition, reference to elites (statesmen), reference to elites (other influential people), reference to persons, and reference to negative subjects.

In turn, Shoemaker and Reese (2014) argue that news values become predictable and influence what recipients find interesting. They formulate six values of the news: prominence and importance, conflict, and controversy, the unusual, the human interest, timeliness, and proximity. The values of modern news, as identified by Harcup and O'Neill (2017) are: exclusivity, bad news, conflict, surprise, audio–visual components, shareability, entertainment, drama, follow-up, the power elite, relevance, magnitude, celebrity, good news, and news organization's agenda.

At the same time, journalists have a key role in selecting the news. Whitney and Becker (1982) show that when it comes to media choices made as a gatekeeper, the proportion of articles can have a greater effect than the values of the news. Heinderyckx and Vos (2016) delve into the history of gatekeeping theory, starting with David Manning White's classic study—The "Gate Keeper": A Case Study in the Selection of News, published in 1950, which defines gatekeeping as a selection process determined by the supposed relevance of certain topics to certain audiences, and discuss the relevance and reform of gatekeeping in the digital age. Researchers appreciate that, in the perspective defined by Shoemaker et al. (2009), gatekeeping is a process of selection and processing of unlimited information into a limited number of messages that reach various audiences daily, "there is no doubt that gatekeeping will remain relevant for as long as news will be processed and disseminated to an audience" (Heinderyckx & Vos, 2016, p. 36).

Researchers debate the purpose, nature, temporality, agencies, and context of this process. According to Heinderyckx and Vos (2016), in terms of purpose, currently gatekeeping also contributes to defining the identity of journalists; the nature of the process—the media looks at an increasing traffic (clickbait) and recommendation (buzz) when selecting content from multiple sources and channels. "Gatekeeping in the digital age has considerably shifted from a logic of relevance (Harcup & O'Neill, 2001) towards one of popularity" (Heinderyckx & Vos, 2016, p. 39). The time required for selection is much shorter, and the selection of news in the digital age also refers to the replacement of news on the main page or the deletion of news from archives, and "The art of taking stories off digital outlets is mysterious, like traditional gatekeeping, but in a different way" (Heinderyckx & Vos, 2016, p. 40). Regarding the role of gatekeeping agents, Heinderyckx and Vos (2016) point out that it has become characteristic not only of journalists, but also of other actors such as civil society organizations, citizen journalists, and interest groups. The context of gatekeeping is changing with the media industry, including with the expansion of technology.

## 3.4 Framing and Public Relations

The framing theory can also be studied relative to public relations. According to researchers Wilcox et al. (2015), the media are dependent on the official statements of representatives of organizations, especially for reporting crisis situations, and thus public relations can shape the tone and content of a news story. Hallahan (1999) considers that framing theory thus becomes a useful paradigm, including for researching the strategic creation of public relations messages and audience responses. Systematizing the theories regarding the framing theory and based on the object to be framed, Hallahan (1999) describes seven framing models applicable to public relations: situations, attributes, choices, actions, problems, responsibilities, and novelties. "If public relations are defined as the process of establishing and maintaining mutually beneficial relations between an organization and publics on whom it depends (Cutlip, Center & Broom, 1995), the establishment of common frames of reference about topics or issues of mutual concern is a necessary condition for effective relations to be established" (Hallahan, 1999, p. 207). When defining the media package, Gamson and Modigliani (1989) refer to a process that includes cultural resonances, sponsor activities, and media practices. Referring to sponsors, the researchers show that they can come from organizations that hire specialists to mediate interviews, statements, etc. with journalists, and most of them are recruited even from the professional category of journalists.

Official statements are used by journalists to build frames. Randall (2016, p. 245) points out that "The great reporters save quotation for when someone says something in an original way, with an authentic voice, or when they want to capture some characteristic of the interviewee, be it authority, cheekiness, pomposity, sharpness, etc." Referring to the post-crisis communication of organizations, Seeger et al.

(2005, p. 79) show that "The ways in which participants, stakeholders and leaders frame and make sense of these events, as reflected in post-crisis discourse, shape both the nature and degree of change."

## 3.5 Competing Frames and Rhetoric of Elites

Researchers (Reese, 2010; 't Hart & Tindall, 2009; Callaghan & Schnell, 2001; Benford & Snow, 2000; Pan & Kosicki, 1993, etc.) show that elites can compete with each other and strategically launch contradicting frames. For example, Callaghan and Schnell (2001) examine on the one hand, the frameworks of politicians and interest groups regarding arms control in the United States, and, on the other hand, the frameworks of media materials that reflected them between 1988 and 1996 and support that, in addition to the agenda setting and priming, the media also have the power to shape public discourse by selecting several frames provided by the elite. The results of a study by Callaghan and Schnell (2001) show that politicians for and against legislation have built frames and "worked hard to put their preferred themes on the agenda" (p. 183). At the same time, the media intervened in the framing process and acted in three directions: they structured the general tone of the debates, built different frames from those of the elites, and focused more on public policy discourse and less on the "culture of violence." Callaghan and Schnell (2001) conclude that "To maximize coverage, successful political players must work within the known set of media-imposed constraints. They need to provide drama and good visuals, simplify arguments, communicate through events, and generally fit conventional news narratives (. . .)" (Callaghan & Schnell, 2001, p. 203). Boin et al. (2008) discuss the challenges that crises pose to political and administrative elites in imposing winning frames:

> The battle over crisis frames unfolds in the arenas in which learning and accountability take place. In a liberal democracy, many actors can join this battle. Those who manage to gain the most support for their definition of the situation and the solutions that accompany it will have the most leverage in determining the fate of political leaders, public policies and public institutions. (Boin et al., 2008, p. 18)

In the analysis of crisis framing, Boin et al. (2008) consider that the nature of crises (difficult to understand—e.g., the September 11, 2001, attacks, the 2004 Asian tsunami, the Katrina hurricane in New Orleans in 2005; mismanaged—characterized by real or invented management failures, agenda setting crises, those that touch nerve and degenerate (students' uprising in Paris, 1968), historical achievements of leaders and contextual factors, such as synchronization. Boin et al. (2008) believe that media represent an additional contextual factor, as they make the public arena available, take over, amplify, and challenge the frames of the crisis launched by leaders. "Their neutrality is often doubted, sometimes justifiably so. Investigative reporting or editorial agendas can easily become a crisis catalyst. When public attention is squarely focused on the crisis story, media reporting can hurt and boost political and bureaucratic reputations, particularly if the various competing media organizations tell the same story and voice the same opinions" (Boin et al., 2008, p. 21).

Based on previous research, Reese (2010) describes several types of elite frames: frames placed, built, and promoted by elites who compete against other elites, in competing social and political circles, in order to achieve certain results. Reese (2010) also identifies the use of competing frames within the same group, for the internal mobilization of groups, so as to compete with other groups in the public arena, frames built to resonate with the life experience of the targeted group or frames built by elites that contradict public opinion.

How a crisis is understood by the public can be influenced by framing contests, "battles between competing definitions of the situation, between the various actors that seek to contain or exploit crisis-induced opportunity space for political posturing and policy change" ('t Hart & Tindall, 2009, p. 23). Researchers point out that framing can have a limited impact on individuals, especially when exposed to "competitive frames of varying quantities and strengths" (Chong & Druckman, 2007, p. 104).

## 3.6 Framing the Financial Crisis

The theory of framing was initially used to understand the role that the media plays in political life. Over time, researchers have expanded the use of framing theory and applied it in the analysis of the media coverage of the 2008 financial and economic crisis (Damstra & Vliegenthart, 2018; Falasca, 2014; Bach et al., 2013; Schifferes & Coulter, 2013; Mylonas, 2012; Radu & Ştefăniţă, 2012; López & Llopis, 2010; Fuchs & Graf, 2010; 't Hart & Tindall, 2009; etc.). As Schifferes and Coulter (2013, p. 19) point out, analyzing online news about the 2008 crisis published by BBC News, "The complex nature of the financial crisis meant that even in the digital age, the role of journalists in framing news coverage and interpreting events to the general public was crucial." "Crises mobilize the mass media, which will put an intense spotlight on the issues and actors involved" ('t Hart & Tindall, 2009, p. 22), and how causes and responsibilities are framed can have a major impact on public support for institutions and main actors. According to the two researchers, in the context of a crisis, framing efforts refer to (1) the nature and severity of a crisis; (2) the causes of the crisis; (3) responsibility for the occurrence or intensification of the crisis; and (4) the consequences of the crisis on public policy (actions taken by the authorities) ('t Hart & Tindall, 2009).

't Hart and Tindall (2009) consider that the major challenges for elites in the 2008 crisis are similar to those of leadership crisis management: finding meaning; correct and rapid diagnosis—very few analysts and decision makers anticipated and predicted the crisis; making strategic decisions under time pressure and social pressure, in uncertain situations—during the crisis, institutions and decision makers were heavily criticized for decisions on interest rates, stimulus packages, saving financial companies from public money; coordination—the need to synchronize politicians and central bankers in messages sent to the public; delimitation—public debates regarding the companies that received or not aid; consolidation—each crisis leaves unemployment and business sectors affected, even as financial markets resume their rise, but such consequences continue to be in crisis and new financial assistance is being sought from policy makers; building meaning—how should decision makers communicate an unprecedented crisis.

Next, we will present the results of the main research regarding the framing of the 2008 crisis in the international media and in the Romanian press.

### 3.6.1 In the International Media

Schifferes and Coulter (2013) analyze the financial crisis news published by the BBC News online portal between September and December 2008. Regarding the main sources and actors of the material, the results of the study show that most were focused on the actions of a relatively small number of individuals and institutions. Among the most prominent figures in crisis management were Gordon Brown (Prime Minister of the United Kingdom during the crisis), George Bush (President of the United States), Alistair Darling (Chancellor of the Central Bank of the United Kingdom), Ben Bernanke (Fed Governor), Barack Obama (next US President), and Mervyn King (Governor of the Bank of England). Gordon Brown, Alistair Darling, and Mervyn King had the most favorable coverage, being portrayed as actively involved in combating the effects of the crisis. Schifferes and Coulter (2013) show that the media coverage of institutions has shifted its focus from individual cases represented by rescued institutions to responses and actions taken by US and UK central banks. The tone of the BBC News coverage was not necessarily alarming, according to the assessments of the two researchers, but there were sudden changes in sentiment between positive and negative topics. Schifferes and Coulter (2013) debate the role of journalists as gatekeepers in the context of the financial crisis and consider that the understanding of this role could be improved, through research on journalists' perceptions, backgrounds, and education, on their understanding of the phenomenon and their interactions with editors. Business journalists, the researchers point out, explained the financial crisis using three mainframes: scandal (blaming bankers); moral panic (blaming the public); and reform (blaming decision makers). In turn, Berry (2016) examines how BBC News dealt with the growing public deficit in the United Kingdom in 2009, its consequences, and possible solutions. The results of the research show how the political and financial elites dominated the media coverage, which generated a limited number of opinions on the implications and possible strategies for reducing the deficit. The recurring and undisputed view presented by journalists was that Britain was in danger of being abandoned by international creditors, and austerity policies were the most promoted solution, which, according to Berry (2016), raises questions on the impartiality of journalism and the watchdog role of public television.

Riaz et al. (2011) analyze the rhetoric of elites, as reflected in the statements selected by The Economist in articles published between 2007 and 2009 and identify the main positions on the crisis (status quo, neutral, and change), as well as the rhetorical procedures used in the communication of positions (call to the authority of experts, finding the culprit, using scenarios, avoiding critical discussions). The results of the study show that the main pressure for changing public policies came from academia, which used past scenarios and blame, but avoided critical discussions through overgeneralization. Banks have focused on changing practices, using future scenarios, identifying culprits outside the industry, and relying on the authority of expertise. The Fed has stood out by maintaining the pre-crisis situation in terms of regulatory issues, using different scenarios and the authority conferred by the expertise. However, Riaz et al. (2011) consider that the predominant neutral position of the elites is the main result of the study, interpreted, on the one hand, as tacit support of some institutions, and, on the other hand, as the result of the publication's efforts to frame the subject by giving certain actors the opportunity to speak about the crisis.

López and Llopis (2010) make a comparative study of the conceptual metaphors used by the English publication *The Economist* and the Spanish newspaper *El Economista* between 2007 and 2008, noting that articles in the British press included a greater number of metaphors used in a negative sense, compared to Spanish articles.

Analyzing how German newspapers have reflected the financial crisis since its inception, Bach et al. (2013) indicate several frames: the frame of complexity risk, of globalization, of solidarity, of greed, of regulation, of self-regulation, of systemic threat, and of moral hazard. Fuchs and Graf (2010) could not identify, following the analysis of speech applied to the German media (Die Zeit, Financial Times Deutschland, TAZ, Bild, Süddeutsche Zeitung), between October and December 2007–2009, a coherent and common definition of the crisis mainly due to the heterogeneous way of presenting the crisis and the political response. Fuchs and Graf (2010) look at how geographic focus changes—in 2007—with a focus on the United States, when the crisis is not a problem for Germany, in 2008—the crisis affects Germany, Europe, and other regions, in 2009—the US context is only mentioned, while Germany is in the spotlight.

Mylonas (2012) applies an analysis of the Bild-Zeitung headlines in relation to the crisis that hit Greece and examines five frames: economic—in relation to austerity policies; eschatological—about the catastrophic effects of the mystified crisis as a phenomenon that works according to natural principles; narcissistic—which presents austerity and loans as "help" and "fight" against the crisis, emphasizes the unity between the German people and the German companies, classified as "victims"; cultural—Greece is mystically portrayed as a "natural miracle," but Greeks are blamed for the local, European, and global expansion of the capitalist crisis; and hostile—in which Bild becomes the representative of German taxpayers, expressing anger at the burden of rescuing others.

Zeri (2014) uses three frames to examine how four Greek political blogs covered the 2009 crisis: the first frame deals with how political and social actors involved in debates perceive democratic political institutions, the second examines the discourse on the loss of national sovereignty, and the third framework analyzes how the public interest is understood and reflected. The study's findings show that both far-right and far-left blogs appeal to "the same rigid ideological raster that excludes an understanding of the principles and grounds of democracy" (Zeri, 2014, p. 1).

Damstra and Vliegenthart (2018) investigate how the print media framed the crisis in the Netherlands between 2007 and 2013. Researchers have identified five major frameworks: business, financial, individual, Eurozone, and moral values. The researchers concluded that the media coverage of the economic crisis was uniform, and even though the audience profile was different, the publications similarly covered the topic.

Falasca's study (2014) aims at framing the financial crisis in Sweden, based on the statements of political actors between September and December 2008. If, initially, the bankruptcy of Lehman Brothers was a sufficient pretext for articles on the general socio-economic future, as the effects of the crisis were being felt on the Swedish banking and labor markets, the coverage of the financial crisis became a political issue, and the research shows how politicians' stances have intensified. Falasca (2014, p. 12) shows "two major governmental frames emerged, the bank crisis frame (...) and the crisis of economic growth frame in the third phase emphasising the financial rather than the political dimension of the crisis." Other used frames were the labor market crisis, the state finance crisis, the business crisis, and the private economy.

### *3.6.2 In the Romanian Press*

The 2008 global crisis it is the effects as felt in Romania, became topics constantly covered by both local media and communication researchers who analyze how they were publicized and the possible effects on audiences of the frames used (Vincze, 2014; Bârgăoanu et al., 2013; Radu & Ştefăniţă, 2012; Abrudan, 2009).

Using the framing theory, Abrudan (2009) conducts one of the first quantitative and qualitative analyses of content based on articles about the crisis, published between 2008 and 2009, in the dailies Jurnalul naţional, Gândul, and Cotidianul, in the financial publications Capital, Săptămâna financiară and Ziarul Financiar, in the tabloids Libertatea and Click! as well as in the Hungarian language publications Krónika and Új Magyar Szó. In the case of dailies, the dominant scenarios were pessimistic, the only positive aspect covered in the analyzed period was the increase in the consumption of products with low and medium prices; the tabloids initially treated the subject in a superficial way and sought the sensational; Hungarian language publications used the word crisis to capture readers' attention, just as dailies, the financial media and the tabloids did. The research observes that the description of the crisis changes from the search for the causes of the crisis, at the beginning of the period, to the crisis as the cause for many other processes and concludes that "Apparently the financial crisis is shown to be responsible for everything that is negative in Romania, therefore not referring only to the Romanian economy" (Abrudan, 2009, p. 78).

Vincze (2014) shows that in the Romanian news, the crisis became a visible topic in the autumn of 2008, peaked in the first half of 2009, then declined until mid-2011, when the media exposed the sovereign credit crisis. Based on the analysis of two generalist dailies—Adevărul and România Libera, and two online news portals—hotnews.ro and ziare.com, Vincze (2014) claims that, in terms of the prominence of the subject, the crisis was more visible in hotnews.ro and in România Libera, which more often included the term "crisis" in titles and in lead articles. At the same time, the two publications paid more attention to economic issues, while Adevărul focused on the social sphere and jobs, and ziare.com, on business and banking. "At the same time, news about social issues and jobs were empathic, the unemployment rate being a central issue in these articles" (Vincze, 2014, p. 10). Vincze's (2014) study also highlights changes in the use of the term "crisis," from defined structures such as "economic crisis," "financial crisis," and "credit crisis" to the generic use of the term "crisis," such as "crisis period," "crisis period," "price crisis," and "wedding crisis" usage that contributed to the creation of a sense of generalized crisis (Vincze, 2014,).

Radu and Ştefăniţă (2012) look at the online environment, as a vehicle for informing the public about the European economic crisis, with a focus on hotnews.ro and ziare.com from 2009 to 2011. The researchers identify an increase in the visibility of the crisis in the analyzed period and points out that media framing emphasizes the framework of responsibility, followed by that of conflict and conspiracy:

> The responsibility frame prevails, suggesting the need for identifying solutions and ideas to manage the crisis. It also implies the tendency of pinning down and punishing at all costs those to blame for the current situation. This approach may prove constructive in the short-term, but destructive in the long run, because it blocks us in a paradigm focused on chasing the guilty ones. (Radu & Ştefăniţă, 2012, p. 44)

Bârgăoanu et al. (2013) studied the role of the media in shaping the expectations of Romanians regarding their economic prospects, the future of Romania, and the future of the EU, based on a national survey and analysis of disseminated content, between March first and March 28th, 2012, by three TV channels (TVR1, PRO TV, and Antena 1) and by four online portals (adevarul.ro, ziare.com, hotnews.ro, gandul.info). The conclusion of the analysis is that "Romanians" government evaluations are not mediated by mass media, as the mass media's tone plays little or no importance in the economic expectations "process formation" (Bârgăoanu et al., 2013, p. 240).

* * *

From the perspective of the framing theory, to define the post-crisis period, this research starts from the definition of crisis proposed by 't Hart (1993), namely—"a crisis can be defined as a breakdown of familiar symbolic frameworks legitimating the pre-existing sociopolitical order" ('t Hart, 1993, p. 88). After 2008, including in Romania, we witnessed an unexpected collapse and destruction of known frames and a reconfiguration, reconstruction, repositioning as the main events unfolded.

Changing the roles of the main actors in the crisis—politicians, public institutions, individuals or the general public, the media, etc., new attributes and responsibilities, decisions and their effects—have all led to changes that can be seen through the application of the framing theory.

We believe that the framing theory provides sufficient arguments to support the hypothesis stating that how the media framed, after 2008, the official statements of central bank representatives on the management of the financial crisis could have had a major impact on public confidence in these institutions. The present research is based on framing as a factor influencing public opinion, uses the perspective of framing emphasis and stays within the quantitative analysis school of thought, which is focused on deductive content analysis, using predefined frames in the evaluation of media articles. At the same time, it follows the process of transferring messages from the elite to different categories of stakeholders, through the media.

## References


Abrudan, M. (2009). Quantitative and qualitative analysis of Romanian newspapers concerning the topic of global economic crisis. *Revista Română de Comunicare și Relații Publice, 11*(2), 67–80. Retrieved from http://integru.org/web/wp-content/uploads/2011/09/RJCPR_16full.pdf#page=67

Bach, T., Weber, M., & Quiring, O. (2013). News frames, inter-media frame transfer and the financial crisis. *Zeszyty Prasoznawcze, 56*(1). https://doi.org/10.4467/2299-6362PZ.13.008.1026

Bârgăoanu, A., Corbu, N., & Radu, L. (2013). The role of government evaluations and EU identity in shaping economic expectations during the crisis. The case of Romania. *European Journal of Science and Theology, 9*(4), 225–241. Retrieved from https://www.researchgate.net/profile/Nicoleta_Corbu/publication/288471450_The_role_of_government_evaluations_and_EU_identity_in_shaping_economic_expectations_during_the_crisis_the_case_of_Romania/links/5a0ea7c1aca27244d2859c69/The-role-of-government-evaluations-and-EU-identity-in-shaping-economic-expectations-during-the-crisis-the-case-of-Romania.pdf

Benford, R. D., & Snow, D. A. (2000). Framing processes and social movements: An overview and assessment. *Annual Review of Sociology, 26*(1), 611–639.

Berry, M. (2016). No alternative to austerity: How BBC broadcast news reported the deficit debate. *Media, Culture and Society, 38*(6), 844–863. https://doi.org/10.1177/0163443715620931

Boin, A., McConnell, A., & Hart, P. T. (2008). *Governing after crisis: The politics of investigation, accountability and learning*. Cambridge University Press.

Cacciatore, M. A., Scheufele, D. A., & Iyengar, S. (2016). The end of framing as we know it. . . and the future of media effects. *Mass Communication and Society, 19*(1), 7–23. https://doi.org/10.1080/15205436.2015.1068811

Callaghan, K., & Schnell, F. (2001). Assessing the democratic debate: How the news media frame elite policy discourse. *Political Communication, 18*(2), 183–213.

Capella, J., & Jamieson, K. (1997). *Spiral of cynism. The press and the public good.* Oxford University Press.

Chong, D., & Druckman, J. N. (2007). A theory of framing and opinion formation in competitive elite environments. *Journal of Communication, 57*(1), 99–118. https://doi.org/10.1111/j.1460-2466.2006.00331.x

Cohen, B. (1963). *The press and foreign policy*. Princeton University Press.

Corbu, N., Ştefăniţă, O., Oprea, D., & Udrea, G. (2015). The European Union–From Agenda Setting and Media Frames to Citizens' Conversations. *Romanian Journal of Communication and Public Relations, 17*(1), 41–57. Retrieved from https://www.journalofcommunication.ro/index.php/journalofcommunication/article/download/114/167

Dahinden, U. (2006). *Framing: eine integrative Theorie der Massenkommunikation*. Konstanz: UVK-Verl

Damstra, A., & Vliegenthart, R. (2018). (Un) covering the economic crisis? Over-time and inter-media differences in salience and framing. *Journalism Studies, 19*(7), 983–1003. https://doi.org/10.1080/1461670X.2016.1246377

de Vreese, C. H. (2002). *Framing Europe: Television news and European integration*. Aksant Academic.

de Vreese, C. H. (2005). News framing: Theory and typology. *Information Design Journal and Document Design, 13*(1) Retrieved from https://asset-pdf.scinapse.io/prod/2089363775/2089363775.pdf

Dimitrova, D. V., Kaid, L. L., Williams, A. P., & Trammell, K. D. (2005). War on the Web: The immediate news framing of Gulf War II. *Harvard International Journal of Press/Politics, 10*(1), 22–44. https://doi.org/10.1177/1081180X05275595

Domke, D., Shah, D. V., & Wackman, D. B. (1998). Media priming effects: Accessibility, association, and activation. *International Journal of Public Opinion Research, 10*(1), 51–74.

Entman, R. M. (1993). Framing: Toward clarification of a fractured paradigm. *Journal of Communication, 43*(4), 51–58.

Entman, R. M. (2003). Cascading activation: Contesting the White House's frame after 9/11. *Political Communication, 20*(4), 415–432. https://doi.org/10.1080/10584600390244176

Falasca, K. (2014). Framing the financial crisis: An unexpected interaction between the government and the press. *Observatorio, 8*(1), 01–21. Retrieved from http://www.scielo.mec.pt/scielo.php?script=sci_arttext&pid=S1646-59542014000100001

Fuchs, D., & Graf, A. (2010). *The financial crisis in discourse: Analyzing the framing of banks, financial markets and political responses*. Universität Münster, FB Erziehungswissenschaft und Sozialwissenschaften, Institut für Politikwissenschaft. Retrieved from https://nbn-resolving.org/urn:nbn:de:0168-ssoar-344922

Galtung, J., & Ruge, M. H. (1965). The structure of foreign news: The presentation of the Congo, Cuba and Cyprus crises in four Norwegian newspapers. *Journal of Peace Research, 2*(1), 64–90.

Gamson, W. A., & Modigliani, A. (1989). Media discourse and public opinion on nuclear power: A constructionist approach. *American Journal of Sociology, 95*(1), 1–37.

Gamson, W. A., Croteau, D., Hoynes, W., & Sasson, T. (1992). Media images and the social construction of reality. *Annual Review of Sociology, 18*(1), 373–393.

Gitlin, T. (1980). *The whole world is watching: Mass media in the making and unmaking of the new left*. University of California.

Goffman, E. (1986). *Frame analysis. An essay on the organization of experience*. Northeastern University Press. (Original work published in 1974).

Hallahan, K. (1999). Seven models of framing: Implications for public relations. *Journal of Public Relations Research, 11*(3), 205–242. Retrieved from http://www.pitt.edu/~mitnick/BPweb/HallahanSevenModelsFramingJPubRelRes.pdf

Harcup, T., & O'Neill, D. (2017). What is news? News values revisited (again). *Journalism Studies, 18*(12), 1470–1488. https://doi.org/10.1080/1461670X.2016.1150193

Heinderyckx, F., & Vos, T. P. (2016). Reformed gatekeeping. *CM: Communication and Media, 11*(36), 29–46. https://doi.org/10.5937/comman11-10306

Iyengar, S. (1991). *Is anyone responsible? How television frames political issues*. University of Chicago Press.

Iyengar, S., & Kinder, D. R. (1987). *News that matters: Agenda-setting and priming in a television age*. University of Chicago Press.

Kahneman, D., & Tversky, A. (2013) [1979]. Prospect theory: An analysis of decision under risk. In *Handbook of the fundamentals of financial decision making: Part I* (pp. 99–127). World Scientific.

Knight, M. G. (1999). Getting past the impasse: Framing as a tool for public relations. *Public Relations Review, 25*(3), 381–398.

López, A. M. R., & Llopis, M. Á. O. (2010). Metaphorical pattern analysis in financial texts: Framing the crisis in positive or negative metaphorical terms. *Journal of Pragmatics, 42*(12), 3300–3313. https://doi.org/10.1016/j.pragma.2010.06.001

Matthes, J., & Kohring, M. (2008). The content analysis of media frames: Toward improving reliability and validity. *Journal of Communication, 58*(2), 258–279. https://doi.org/10.1111/j.1460-2466.2008.00384.x

McCombs, M. (2002). *The agenda-setting role of the mass media in the shaping of public opinion*. In Mass Media Economics 2002 Conference, School of Economics, London. Retrieved from http://sticerd.lse.ac.uk/dps/extra/McCombs.pdf

McCombs, M. E., & Shaw, D. L. (1993). The evolution of agenda-setting research: Twenty-five years in the marketplace of ideas. *Journal of Communication, 43*(2), 58–67.

McLeod, D. M., & Shah, D. V. (2015). *News frames and national security. Covering big brother*. Cambridge University Press.

Mylonas, Y. (2012). Media and the economic crisis of the EU: The 'culturalization' of a systemic crisis and Bild-Zeitung's framing of Greece. *tripleC: Communication, Capitalism & Critique. Open Access Journal for a Global Sustainable Information Society, 10*(2), 646–671.

Nisbet, M. (2010). Knowledge into action: Framing the debates over climate change and poverty. In P. D'Angelo & J. Kuypers (Eds.), *Doing framing analysis: Empirical and theoretical perspectives* (pp. 43–83). Routledge.

Pan, Z., & Kosicki, G. M. (1993). Framing analysis: An approach to news discourse. *Political Communication, 10*(1), 55–75.

Price, V., Tewksbury, D., & Powers, E. (1997). Switching trains of thought: The impact of news frames on readers' cognitive responses. *Communication Research, 24*(5), 481–506. https://doi.org/10.1177/009365097024005002

Pühringer, K., Dahinden, U., Rademacher, P., Gerth, M., & Siegert, G. (2008). *Challenges to political campaigns in the media: Commercialization, framing, and personalization*. National Centre of Competence in Research (NCCR) Challenges to Democracy in the 21st Century Working Paper, 20, p. 75.

Radu, L., & Ştefăniţă, O. (2012). Framing the economic crisis in the Romanian online media. *Romanian Journal of Communication AND Public Relations, 14*(2), 29–46. Retrieved from https://journalofcommunication.ro/oldsite/archive2/026/26/rjcpr_26_full.pdf#page=30

Randall, D. (2016). *The universal journalist*. Pluto Press.

Reese, S. D. (2001). Framing public life. A bridging model for media research. In S. D. Reese, H. G. Oscar, & E. G. August (Eds.), *Framing public life: Perspectives on media and our understanding of the social world* (pp. 7–31). Lawrence Erlbaum Associates.

Reese, D. (2010). Finding frames in a web of culture the case of the war on terror. In P. D'Angelo & J. A. Kuypers (Eds.), *Doing news framing analysis: Empirical and theoretical perspectives* (pp. 17–42). Routledge.

Riaz, S., Buchanan, S., & Bapuji, H. (2011). Institutional work amidst the financial crisis: Emerging positions of elite actors. *Organization, 18*(2), 187–214. https://doi.org/10.1177/1350508410389630

Scheufele, D. A. (1999). Framing as a theory of media effects. *Journal of Communication, 49*(1), 103–122. https://doi.org/10.1111/j.1460-2466.1999.tb02784.x

Scheufele, D. A., & Iyengar, S. (2011). The state of framing research: A call for new directions. In*The Oxford handbook of political communication theories* (pp. 1–26). Oxford University Press. https://doi.org/10.1093/oxfordhb/9780199793471.013.47

Schifferes, S., & Coulter, S. (2013). Downloading disaster: BBC news online coverage of the global financial crisis. *Journalism, 14*(2), 228–252. https://doi.org/10.1177/1464884912460171

Seeger, M. W., Ulmer, R. R., Novak, J. M., & Sellnow, T. (2005). Post-crisis discourse and organizational change, failure and renewal. *Journal of Organizational Change Management, 8*(1), 78–95. https://doi.org/10.1108/09534810510579869

Semetko, H. A., & Valkenburg, P. M. (2000). Framing European politics: A content analysis of press and television news. *Journal of Communication, 52*(2), 93–109.

Shah, D. V., Domke, D., & Wackman, D. B. (1996). "to thine own self be true": Values, framing, and voter decision-making strategies. *Communication Research, 23*(5), 509–560.

Shoemaker, P. J., & Reese, S. D. (2014). *Mediating the message in the 21st century: A media sociology perspective*. Routledge.

Shoemaker, P. J., Vos, T. P., & Reese, S. D. (2009). Journalists as gatekeepers. In K. Wahl-Jorgensen & T. Hanitzsch (Eds.), *The handbook of journalism studies* (pp. 73–87). Routledge.

Tankard, J. W., Jr. (2001). The empirical approach to the study of media framing. In S. D. Reese, O. H. Gandy Jr., & A. E. Grant (Eds.), *Framing public life: Perspectives on media and our understanding of the social world* (pp. 95–106). Routledge.

't Hart, P. (1993). Symbols, rituals and power: The lost dimensions of crisis management. *Journal of Contingencies and Crisis Management, 1*(1), 36–50. https://doi.org/10.1093/parlij/gsg096

't Hart, P., & Tindall, K. (2009). Understanding crisis exploitation: Leadership, rhetoric and framing contests in response to the economic meltdown. In*Framing the global economic downturn. Crisis rhetoric and the politics of recessions.*

Van Gorp, B. (2007). The constructionist approach to framing: Bringing culture back in. *Journal of Communication, 57*(1), 60–78. https://doi.org/10.1111/j.1460-2466.2006.00329.x

Vincze, H. O. (2014). 'The crisis' as a journalistic frame in Romanian news media. *European Journal of Communication, 29*(5), 567–582. https://doi.org/10.1177/0267323114541610

Whitney, D. C., & Becker, L. B. (1982). 'Keeping the gates' for gatekeepers: The effects of wire news. *Journalism Quarterly, 59*(1), 60–65. Retrieved from http://www.aejmc.org/home/wp-content/uploads/2012/09/Journalism-Quarterly-1982-Whitney-60-5.pdf

Wilcox, D. L., Cameron, G. T., & Reber, B. H. (2015). *Public relations: Strategies and tactics*. Pearson Education.

Zeri, P. (2014). Political blogosphere meets off-line public sphere: Framing the public discourse on the Greek crisis. *International Journal of Communication, 8*, 1579–1595. Retrieved from https://ijoc.org/index.php/ijoc/article/viewFile/2012/1152

# Chapter 4
# Research Design and Elements

The research model of changes in central bank communication rests at the intersection of several disciplines such as communication, economics, psychology, sociology, and anthropology. In the following, we will define the roles of the main actors that have a contribution to the change of NBR communication in the post-crisis period and we will detail the integrative perspective of the analytical approach.

The present research is aimed at collecting data that would facilitate an understanding of how the NBR communication changed in the post-crisis period, inscribing the NBR in what central bankers and researchers call the second communication revolution (Haldane, 2018; Haldane & McMahon, 2018). The general objective of this research is to investigate the perception on the change of NBR's communication in the post-crisis period, of the NBR representatives, on the one hand, and, of both the specialized and the general public, on the other hand. At the same time, we analyze the frames used by the Romanian online press in its coverage of the giving in payment law, as this is one of the most visible nonmonetary topics of debate for the NBR in the analyzed period. Our timeframe is 2014–2016, an intense communication period for the NBR, and we focus on NBR communication on nonmonetary communication topics such as the crisis of Greek capital banks, the Swiss franc credit crisis, and the banking sector legislative projects initiated by the Parliament. Also in this timeframe, there is an essential change in the monetary communication of the NBR, which adopts the publication of the minutes of the monetary policy meetings.

Before briefly presenting the three communication situations analyzed, some considerations regarding the spread of the 2008 crisis in the Romanian market are useful.

© The Author(s), under exclusive license to Springer Nature Switzerland AG 2022

R. Iacob, *Blind Spots in the Spotlight*, Financial and Monetary Policy Studies 53,
https://doi.org/10.1007/978-3-031-04067-2_4

## 4.1 Propagation of the 2008 Crisis in Romania

After the 2008 autumn, the Romanian banking system, like other banking systems in Central and Eastern Europe, proved vulnerable to a sudden slowdown in foreign lending (Klingen, 2013). Georgescu (2018) demonstrates that lending had been generally unsustainable right before the crisis (2003–2008). At the population level, credit had expanded rapidly, 13.5 times in just 5 years (from 2 billion euros to 26.9 billion euros), a rise spurred by aggressive promotional campaigns of commercial banks (Georgescu, 2018, p. 372). After 2008, the Romanian banking system was affected by the rise of nonperforming loans, if in September 2009, their percentage was 6.4%, in March 2014 it had exceeded 22% (National Bank of Romania, 2020).

Between 2003 and 2009, monetary measures, which consisted of changes in minimum reserve requirements ratios (MRRs) and money and foreign exchange market operations, as well as prudential measures to limit foreign currency lending had been adopted. These measures increased the resilience of the "banking system, by creating additional reserves of liquidity and capital which helped banks overcome the crisis without needing public funds" (Georgescu, 2018, p. 366).

Prior to 2008, the NBR took prudential measures and increased the MRR on foreign currency liabilities from 20% in early 2002 to 40% in early 2006 to mitigate capital inflows, but Isărescu (2009a, p. 2) shows that they were not very efficient: "Even if confronted with administrative barriers, markets will still identify solutions to meet demand (...). We resorted to administrative barriers, yet their efficiency was subdued and we realised that side effects outweighed benefits. Hence we removed those barriers relatively quickly."

However, after 2008, Romania did not go through a banking crisis, the commercial banks were well capitalized and did not need to be saved with public money (Popovici, 2014; Roman & Şargu, 2013). The main response of the NBR to the 2008 crisis was to sign agreements with the parent banks of the biggest nine credit institutions operating with foreign capital in Romania, which in spring 2009 had a total market share of approximately 70% (National Bank of Romania, 2009a, 2009b; International Monetary Fund, 2009).

Under the agreements known as the "Vienna 1.0 Initiative," the parent banks of Erste Group Bank, Raiffeisen International, Eurobank EFG, National Bank of Greece, Société Générale, Alpha Bank, Volksbank, Piraeus Bank, and UniCredit Group, committed to maintaining the general exposure of the respective banking groups to Romania.

At the same time, they undertook to increase the capital of their subsidiaries in order to maintain a capital adequacy rate of 10% for the entire duration of Romania's Economic Program. In 2012, amid the liquidity crisis in the eurozone, the "Vienna 2.0 Initiative" was launched and Western banks vowed to maintain an adequate credit supply for their economies in the Central, Eastern, and Southeastern Europe (CESEE) countries, Romania included. On account of this policy, during the Greek banking crisis, the Romanian banking system had a solvency rate of over 14% and the Greek banks had a good capitalization on the Romanian market.

Morosan and Scurtu (2019) show that the drastic measures imposed by the NBR had both direct and indirect consequences on commercial banks, whose profits were affected due to spending on provisions. After 2008, the activity of the Romanian banking system gradually subsided. Between 2008 and 2016, 1800 territorial banking units were closed, 17,000 employees were let go (to 55,000 in 2016), and, following mergers and acquisitions, the number of credit institutions was 37 from 43 in 2008 (Georgescu, 2018, vol. 2, p. 369).

The Romanian government's response to the 2008 crisis came 2 years later and its austerity measures and structural reforms were among the most severe in Europe (Stoiciu, 2012; Glassner & Watt, 2010). For example, the salaries of public sector employees were cut by 25%, pensions by 15%, and VAT was increased from 19 to 24%.

However, given that there was no banking crisis in the Romanian market, what exactly was the Romanian crisis of 2008? The main channels through which the international crisis spread were trade, external financing, exchange rates, and trust (Croitoru, 2009). Isărescu (2009b) shows that, on the trade channel, the crisis reduced the growth of exports; on the financial channel—it limited access to external financing; on the exchange rate channel, the depreciation of the national currency reflected the decrease of external financing; and on the trusted channel, the crisis generated a withdrawal of investors, and the period was marked by speculative attacks (October 2008) on the money-foreign exchange market in Romania.

Another effect identified by Isărescu (2009b, p. 4) is, "the diminishing of net assets held by both population and companies, as a result of both the high share of foreign currency loans (correlated with the depreciation of the leu—the national currency of Romania) and the decrease of the prices of movable and immovable assets from speculative, unsustainable, 'bubble' values."

On March 24, 2009, the Romanian Government signed a loan agreement with the IMF, EU, WB, and EBRD worth 19.95 billion euros. In the opinion of researchers Dăianu and Murgescu (2013, p. 13):

> These external interventions (author's note: financial assistance from IMF, EU, WB, and the Vienna Initiative) entailed the front-loading of a major fiscal adjustment. Yet, this programme was fraught with pitfalls. One of its major weaknesses was to neglect the significance of EU funds absorption as a countercyclical weapon in the economy during a period of major fiscal adjustment. It was only in the second half of 2010 that policymakers in Bucharest and experts in Brussels and elsewhere properly understood this significance, albeit to no concrete avail, since the absorption levels continued to stay.

Moreover, Georgescu (2018, vol. 2, p. 357) emphasizes that "intense external capital flows were not a charitable gesture from foreign investors to the Romanian population and companies in need of financing," but were stimulated by the attractive interest rates in Romania compared to those in the eurozone, both before and after the crisis. At the time of signing the loan agreement in May 2009, the economic assessment showed that between 2003 and 2008, Romania registered an economic boom that led to the overheating of the economy and to unsustainable imbalances

(National Bank of Romania, 2009b). Foreign direct investment and capital inflows contributed to a significant increase in consumption and investment, average GDP growth exceeded 6% per year and exports to EU member states increased.

The overheated economy and the rapid capital inflows put pressure on monetary policy, which led, as we have shown, to an average increase in credit of 50% between 2006 and 2007. Despite increases in interest rates and minimum reserve requirements ratios, as well as other measures aimed at slowing credit growth, the NBR did not achieve the proposed inflation target. The opacity of commercial banks, which ignored the signals sent by the monetary authority, is one of the causes of the missed inflation target, as identified by Balaban and Ailenei (2012). Researchers (Georgescu, 2018; Boiciuc, 2015; Dumitru & Stanca, 2010) show that fiscal policy was strongly pro-cyclical, which led to an increase in the budget deficit from below 1% of GDP in 2005 to almost 5% of GDP in 2008, to an overheated economy and to massive economic corrections between 2009 and 2011.

Dăianu and Murgescu (2013) show that, in the years before the Great Recession, Romania registered a fragile economic growth, characterized by very large external deficits, inadequate distribution of resources, and a high degree of external private debt. Additionally, Romania "is also afflicted by structural institutional weaknesses and less effective public policies (. . .) The current financial crisis has caused an economic setback and dented Romania's growth potential" (Dăianu & Murgescu, 2013, p. 29). "The current crisis in Romania is primarily the expression of the failure of governments to establish capitalism" (Croitoru, 2012b, p. 2), and "putting capitalism in its place remains the greatest challenge for Romania, as it has become for the whole world" (Croitoru, 2012b, p. 5).

Dobrescu (2016, pp. 352–353) emphasizes that, in the post-crisis period, when development was crucial, Romania did not even have the building blocks of development (an industrial base, an education system, performing agriculture, etc.), as these had been destroyed after the 1989 revolution. Dobrescu (2016) points to major mistakes following the 1989 revolution: the fact that we did not build "a coherent foreign policy of good neighborliness," the fact that we waste important resources due to internal division: "The main collapse is the collapse of trust, which daily erodes the feeling of belonging and the need for identity, the supreme values of a national community" (Dobrescu, 2016, p. 353).

In conclusion, the crisis of 2008 spread to Romania on account of chronic economic underdevelopment, and the erosion of confidence in political and economic institutions, including the central bank, intensified. Romania avoided a banking crisis thanks to the measures taken by NBR. However, NBR was not able to compensate for the macroeconomic imbalances, missed the inflation target, and had to face high consumer protection expectations, which exerted additional pressure, on an already weak system.

## 4.2 Communication Situations

The NBR's public communication changed, after 2008, mainly due to the intensification of nonmonetary communication, which eclipsed the communication of monetary policy objectives. The NBR was at the forefront of public debates that were not related to monetary policy objectives, but which attracted the attention of large audiences due to the importance of the topics.

For example, NBR officials made official statements regarding amendments to the Fiscal Code (2014); the credit crisis in Swiss francs (2015–2016); the crisis of the Greek capital banks (2015); changes in the lending law (giving in payment law, freezing of the exchange rate Swiss franc—leu) (2015–2017); the role of the NBR in the management of Romania's international reserves, especially the management of the gold reserve (2018–2019); foreign exchange and money market mechanisms (depreciation of the national currency and the rise of the ROBOR reference rate (2017–2019); taxation of the financial system (2018); capping the indebtedness of the population (2018). But the first episode of crisis communication for the central bank can be traced back to October 2008, when "there was a speculative attack on the leu" (Croitoru, 2011, p. 5). Croitoru (2011) believes that the NBR's "reputation of being very sensitive to the magnitude of the depreciation/appreciation of the leu" as well as the guarantee/certainty that NBR will intervene to avoid a massive depreciation of the Romanian currency represented "a favorable premise for triggering the speculative attack" (Croitoru, 2011, p. 36).

All these public debate topics required more active public communication on behalf of the NBR, which was on an upward trend in transparency, but, at the same time, on a downward trend in terms of public confidence. The erosion of trust in the NBR did not take place immediately after the onset of the crisis, but began a few years later. For example, in March 2016, 44% of Romanians, said that their level of trust in the NBR was high or very high, compared to 51.3% in December 2014 (INSCOP Research, 2016), and the level of trust has not been recovered. In 2019, only 35.6% of Romanians said that their level of trust in the central bank was high or very high (INSCOP Research, 2019).

Following are the brief presentations and definitions of the three communication situations analyzed in this chapter.

**The Crisis of the Greek Capital Banks** Amid the spread of the crisis in Europe, in the form of the sovereign debt crisis and the banking crisis, NBR representatives expressed concern about the situation in Greece.

For example, in 2011, NBR Governor, Mugur Isărescu, declared that he strictly monitored the contagion channels of the Greek crisis and stressed that the Romanian banking system had no direct exposure to the sovereign debt crisis in Greece (Isărescu, 2011); at that time, Greek banks controlled 16% of total banking assets in Romania. The peak of the crisis in Greece was reached in mid-2015, when the credit ratings of the four largest banks in Greece were changed to "insolvency" (European Court of Auditors, 2017).

At that time, in Romania only four Greek banks were operating in Romania: Alpha Bank, Bancpost, Piraeus, and Banca Românească, which owned 12% of the total assets of the banking system (National Bank of Romania, 2015c). Among NBR's main official messages (2015c) we mention: "banks with Greek majority capital have a moderate role in the Romanian banking sector," are "Romanian legal entities," "Romanian banks with Greek capital," "all these banks are subject only to the Romania legislation and are directly supervised by the National Bank of Romania," "are not dependent on the financing of the parent banks" (National Bank of Romania, 2015c).

**Swiss Francs Credit Crisis** The indebtedness of the Romanian population doubled from 25% in March 2005 to 53% in December 2007 (Georgescu, 2018, p. 430). According to Georgescu (2018), the rapid rise in lending and the effects of the crisis have led to the accumulation of a large volume of nonperforming loans generated mostly by companies, and in the case of the population—the largest arrears were recorded by consumer loans. Home loans accounted for one-third of the total value of nonperforming household loans.

The Romanian banking system was affected by a credit crisis in Swiss francs triggered on January 15, 2015, when the Swiss National Bank (SNB) announced that it no longer supports a stable euro/franc exchange rate at the level of 1 euro = 1.20 Swiss francs (Swiss National Bank, 2015). The SNB decision generated a rapid and aggressive reaction in the foreign exchange markets and the Swiss franc appreciation against the euro by over 20% in just 1 week was felt hard by the Romanian debtors.

At the time of the onset of the Swiss franc crisis, 11 commercial banks in Romania held loans in Swiss francs in their portfolios: Bancpost (32% of loans), Volksbank (which merged in 2015 with Banca Transilvania) (24%), Piraeus Bank (20%), Raiffeisen Bank (11%), Banca Românească (7%), OTP Bank (2%) (Tempea, 2015), the remaining 4% of customers being debtors of other credit institutions such as Credit Europe Bank, Millennium Bank (which merged in 2015 with OTP Bank), Nextebank, Garanti Bank, and BRD-SocGen.

The loans in Swiss francs granted in Romania, compared to other European countries such as Hungary and Poland, were limited and did not present a systemic risk, according to the main message of the NBR (2015b). Loans in Swiss francs had, at the end of 2015, a low share in GDP (1.4% in the case of Romania, being 5 times, respectively, 7 times lower than in Poland and Hungary) and a low share in total loans in banks' balance sheets (4.7% compared to Poland and Hungary with levels 3 and 5 times higher, respectively) (National Bank of Romania, 2015b).

Of the approximately 475,000 Romanians with loans secured by a property, most had contracted them in foreign currency (over 315,000), and the balance of these loans was 53.89 billion lei (approx. 11.9 billion euros). Debtors with loans in Swiss francs represented 10% of the number of borrowers with foreign currency loans, the balance of these loans being 7.32 billion lei (approx. 1.6 billion euros) (National Bank of Romania, 2015a). Other messages of the central bank on this subject were: "customers must negotiate with commercial banks to find customized solutions," "NBR cannot intervene on the leu—Swiss franc exchange rate."

**Legislative Changes with an Impact on the Banking System** In Romania, lending in Swiss francs began in 2005, first offered by OTP Bank and largely stopped by 2008 when a large part of credit institutions began to abandon offers (BRD stopped offering loans in Swiss francs in February 2007) (Popa, 2008). Researchers such as Alt et al. (2017), David et al. (2015), and Brown et al. (2009) researched the effects of lending in Swiss francs on the Romanian market, both on debtors and on commercial banks. Banks that offered lending in Swiss francs included in their products fixed interest rates for the first months after granting and lower interest rates compared to those charged for loans in other currencies. Researchers point out several issues related to social responsibility in the communication of these banks. For example, Alt et al. (2017) analyze the commercial banks' advertisements published between 2004 and 2007 in Evenimentul Zilei and Ziarul financier newspapers, discussing the clarity of information, from font size, format, page orientation, colors, visibility, and exchange rate information and conclude, based on the results, that regulators should review the advertisements for clarity.

Against the background of the 2008 crisis, the Swiss franc became one of the safe haven[1] assets, which determined the constant appreciation of the currency, including the Romanian national currency. In September 2011, the Swiss National Bank introduced a threshold for the franc precisely because of the overvaluation of the Swiss franc against the euro. For over 3 years (September 2011–January 2015), in practice, the SNB maintained the euro/franc exchange rate at the same parity, and when it gave up this temporary measure, the appreciation of the refugee asset continued even more aggressively.

At the same time, the leu also depreciated against the euro and the US dollar. All these developments in the foreign exchange market overlapped with the decline in debtors' incomes amid the 2008 crisis and paved the way for several legislative proposals initiated by the National Liberal Party (PNL) and the Social Democratic Party (PSD) (two main Romanian political parties—the first is right leaning and the second is left leaning). These proposals applied to legal relations between consumers and credit institutions, nonbanking financial institutions. For example, the draft of the giving in payment law (draft adopted by Law no. 77/2016) was initiated at the end of 2015 by "PNL deputy Daniel Zamfir and to which the lawyer Gheorghe Piperea contributed, being signed by almost 140 other parliamentarians of PNL, PSD, UDMR, ALDE and of minorities' political parties (author's note: Romanian political parties)" (Ghinea, 2015).

In its final form, the Law no. 77/2016 provides that debtors who have borrowed up to 250,000 euros for the purchase, construction, extension, etc. of a dwelling, and who have secured the loan with at least one residential building, have the right to have their debts established by the credit agreements settled by the payment of the mortgaged building in favor of the creditor. Earlier, in 2014, PSD member of

---

[1] Safe heaven assets are investment that keeps its value, especially when other investments are falling or may fall in value (according to Cambridge Dictionary definition: https://dictionary.cambridge.org/dictionary/english/safe-haven)

Parliament Ana Birchall had tabled a bill aimed at converting foreign currency loans to the exchange rate at the time of the loan (the historical exchange rate), but the bill was not adopted.

Even before 2015, debtors in Swiss francs, but also in other currencies, filed individual or class action lawsuits, against banks and the NBR. The debtors were represented by associations and communities, the most visible being the Parakletos Association, founded by clients and the lawyer Gheorghe Piperea (Parakletos Association, 2020), the Association of Romanian Users of Financial Services and the Banking Client Advice Association and Insured persons in Romania, the Contrabănci.com platform that defines itself as "the community of customers abused by the banking system" (Contrabănci.com, 2020). During the analyzed period, the most visible consumer group on Facebook was the Group of Customers with loans in CHF, a group that launched, in 2018, the Association CREDERE (CREDERE, 2020; GCCC, 2020; Olescu, 2018), an association that aims to provide consumers and SMEs with legal and financial guidance.

The main messages of the NBR regarding the legislative changes focused on the assessment of financial losses for credit institutions if the legislative changes would have been passed. For example, in January 2015, for the conversion of Swiss franc loans at the historical exchange rate, the NBR estimated a loss of 3.2 billion lei (approx. 707 million euros) for the banks, representing 0.4% of GDP (National Bank of Romania, 2015d). Some of the other messages were: "banks' losses will be passed on to all customers receiving banking services," "the NBR does not intervene in the legal relations between credit institutions and their customers," "the relationship between the bank and the customer consuming financial services falls under consumer protection," "imposing financial losses through an administrative decision can be challenged in court as an unconstitutional act, based on the violation of article 44 (1-6) which guarantees the right to property" (National Bank of Romania, 2015d).

## 4.3 Defining the Main Actors

The roles of all actors considered during research, those of the NBR and of its audiences, are defined by the Romanian legislature (Annex A). This framework is based on three reference studies (Tucker, 2018; Riles, 2018; Tognato, 2012) on the need to seek new sources of legitimacy for central banks, especially in a difficult post-crisis context.

As institutions that are independent of political influence, central banks should become "legitimacy seekers" (Tucker, 2018, p. 15). Subsequently, Riles (2018) notes that the social relations between central bankers and financial market elites—considered both sources of information and means of implementing monetary policy—are an important source of legitimacy of central banks and proposes the in(ter)dependence perspective. For his part, Tognato (2012), a sociologist of central banks, points out that "we also see money and central banking entering the field of national identity" (p. 5) and that "Wherever monetary affairs exit the realm of economic calculation and turn into a matter of national identity, public preferences about inflation become a proxy of public preferences about national identity" (Tognato, 2012, p. 4).

To evaluate the change response strategy, the present research uses the four basic models proposed by Freeman (1984, p. 23) in the analysis of how organizations respond to external changes, based on the theories of Ackoff (1974) and Post (1978): "Inactivity"—organizations ignore changes and continue the activity as before; "Reactivity"—organizations wait for something to happen and respond to that change; "Proactivity"—organizations try to anticipate external changes and position themselves in the direction of those changes before they occur; "Interactivity"—the organization actively interacts with external forces that generate change.

**National Bank of Romania** NBR is not a directly elected power (cf. Tucker, 2018) but an indirectly elected one, as its Board is composed of nine members appointed by the Romanian Parliament, for a period of 5 years (Law no. 312/2004, art. 33). Moreover, the governor submits annual reports to the Parliament and the fundamental objective of the NBR is to ensure and maintain price stability. The main labels used in the literature for the designation of central banks—"monetary system axis," "bankers' bank," "banks' banks"—also apply to the NBR. In addition, NBR specialists have identified over time the use of particular classifications. For example, Vasilescu (2011) appreciates that, in the years of economic growth, the NBR has often attracted "the deep dissatisfaction of the population, reprimands from banks and even from political and economic circles and was often labelled as 'orthodox' or as 'conservative'" as it limited "the penetration into our banking system of financial innovations that would prove to be toxic" (Vasilescu, 2011, p. 232).

During the analyzed period, the main debates and conflicts in which the NBR was involved in the public space can be divided into two categories: "institutions versus institutions" (NBR versus Parliament; NBR versus media; NBR versus commercial banks) and "institutions versus people" (NBR versus the general public; NBR versus lawyers, journalists, financial analysts, etc.). Some of the themes of these debates were financial stability, the right to property, the protection of depositors, and the administration of the economy.

The NBR website and traditional media, print, TV, and online, are the most important channels for external information of the NBR public. Taking into account Velthuis's (2015) definition of the ways in which central banks relate to the media, the NBR is particularly concerned with its use as a neutral transmission tool for disseminating information and sometimes as an amplifying tool for reaching audiences. In line with other central banks, the NBR also diversifies its communication channels, using its own blog (www.opiniiBNR.ro) to disseminate the opinions of the bank's representatives, but also some social media channels such as Twitter, YouTube, LinkedIn, and Instagram. In terms of communication tactics, the NBR uses the single voice, in the perspective presented by Holmes (2016), in terms of monetary communication, the messages regarding monetary policy decisions are transmitted mainly by the NBR Governor, Mugur Isărescu. Regarding nonmonetary issues, the central bank communicates in several voices, the issuers of NBR messages are representatives of the institution from various specialized departments, such as monetary policy and financial stability. Their messages are framed and transmitted by different categories of public, such as the media and the specialized public (financial analysts, bankers, representatives of academia).

**The Parliament** During and after crises, the two centers of power of capitalism, the financial markets, which represent capital, and the politicians, who represent the population, come into conflict on fundamental issues such as the administration of the economy. Simplifying, most of the time, governments pursue short-term policy goals and act pro-cyclically, pursuing the electorate, popularity, and even personal interests, unlike central banks, which pursue long-term goals, such as price stability Thus, "central banks intersect with the two centres of power on the most important issue: the administration of the economy" (Croitoru, 2012a, p. 101).

Parliament is a directly elected power, and its role is to adopt laws for the governance of the country, "Parliament is the only legislative authority of the country" (Romanian Constitution, art. 61), which gives it a strong proactive role, it is the organization setting up society for change. Depending on the legislative project at hand, it communicates in several voices and its messages are transmitted by stakeholders such as politicians, media, political analysts, economists, and lawyers. In terms of communication channels, the Parliament relies more and more on new media channels, especially social networks, rather than on traditional media. The balance of power in the analyzed period reveals two types of conflicts: "institutions versus institutions" (Parliament versus NBR) and "people versus people" (direct attack on individuals).

**Media** The Romanian Constitution guarantees journalists' freedom of expression (Romanian Constitution, art. 30), and according to the Worldwide Press Freedom Index, the Romanian media ranks 48th out of 180 countries evaluated by Reporters without borders (2020) (in the first three places are Norway, Finland, and Denmark). According to the democratic principle, the media informs the electorate and is a primary source of information for the general public regarding messages of the authorities. According to the aforementioned principle, media's news frames can influence public opinion including on state institutions such as Parliament and the central bank. "Newsrooms in Romania are underfunded, overburdened and vulnerable to economic and political pressures" (Reuters Institute, 2019, p. 104). Public information, funding, personal financial interests can become the root causes of conflicts, most taking the form of "institutions versus institutions" (media versus NBR; media versus commercial banks) and "people versus people" (attacks on individuals). The media is a proactive and an interactive actor, and uses both traditional and new media communication channels.

**Specialized Audience** Comprising commercial banks, bankers, analysts, investors, representatives of academia. This actor is the first public to which the central banks address themselves to, in the process of strategic communication, through public speeches, academic conferences, seminars, and other special events. Commercial banks participate directly in financial markets and have the role of borrowing or attracting deposits from the population and from Romanian companies. At the same time, as foreign investors in Romania, commercial banks represent the interests of their home countries. Financial, business, and personal interests can be the root causes of conflicts in which commercial banks are involved. For the period analyzed by this chapter, the conflicts of commercial banks take the form of "institutions versus institutions" (commercial banks versus Parliament, commercial banks versus NBR, commercial banks versus media) and "Institutions versus people" (commercial banks versus debtors).

Messages from commercial banks may include messages from the authorities and, in turn, are disseminated by stakeholders such as the media, financial analysts, professional associations, and clients, on traditional channels (website, media), but also on new media (official accounts on social networks). This category can be defined, according to the role in democracy, unelected (unelected power—for example, commercial banks), but also electoral power (for example, analysts, representatives of academia).

**The General Public** The role of the general public is to democratically elect (Romanian Constitution, Art. 36) its representatives who will debate and vote on the country's legislation, and vote for its leaders. For the purpose of this research, the general public consists of all categories of public who do not fall into the other categories defined above (NBR, Parliament, financial media, specialized public). The general public participates in the free market, as depositors and borrowers. The main messages communicated by public authorities, including the NBR, reach this NBR stakeholder through the traditional channel (website), through the media and through new media. Personal financial interests are the main motivation of the general public for conflicts which, during the analyzed period, take the form of "people versus institutions" (individuals against the NBR, individuals against commercial banks, individuals against the government). The general public is represented by lawyers, associations, and influencers, who transmit its messages to the media.

After 2008, the erosion of the public's trust in the NBR, but also in its stakeholders (the specialized public, the Parliament, and the media) is the common denominator of all the actors presented.

## 4.4 Research Design

Multistakeholder research of how NBR's public communication changed is built around the potential contribution of each public—specialized public (including commercial banks), general public, mass media, the Parliament—to the change in NBR's public communication. The research model adapts the operation of the frames according to the "cascading network activation" model built by Entman (2003, pp. 419–420), following the flow from the messages sent by the main actors—in this case, the NBR, but also the Parliament, the messages taken over by

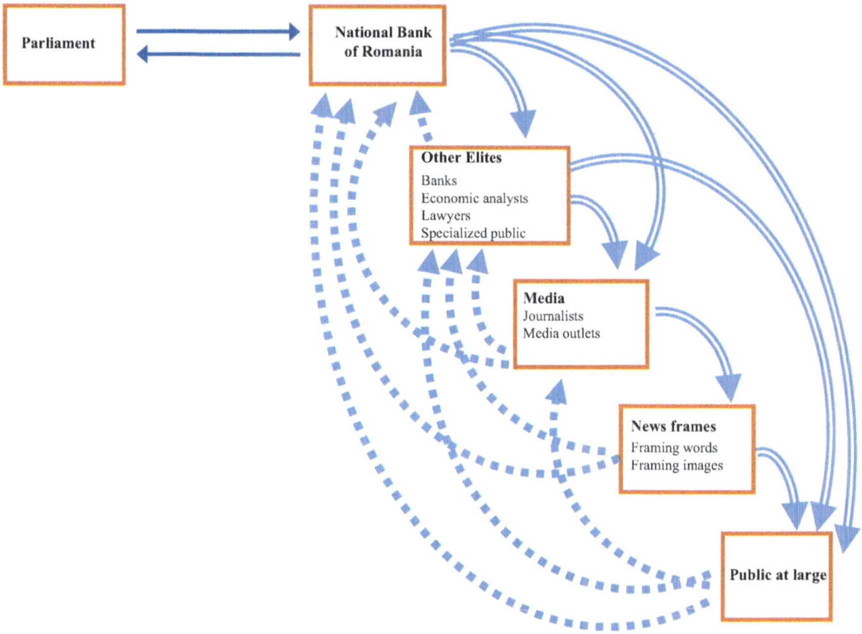


**Fig. 4.1** Research design—The second revolution in NBR communication

the elites, then by journalists, the framing of the news as it reaches the general public and then the reverse flow, in the defined post-crisis context (Fig. 4.1).

According to Entman's (2003) ranking of frames based on their intensity, this research ranks the messages sent by the NBR and Parliament as the strongest, as both organizations are primary sources of information. At the same time, between the two organizations, who are in(ter)dependent (Riles, 2018), there is, as we have shown, both a regular, regulated, inter-institutional communication, but also a spontaneous one, depending on different situations involving the NBR. The Parliament is a directly elected power, with the specific role of adopting laws, so the Parliament has a proactive role and also contributes to the change in NBR's communication environment, during the analyzed period.

First upon transmission, NBR messages reach the elite/specialized public. At the same time, one of NBR's stakeholders is the media, which frames both the messages received directly from the central bank, and the elite's messages as they are formulated based on primary sources. The frames generated by the elites (in this case, commercial banks, economic analysts, political analysts, lawyers, academia, communicators, other categories of specialized public) can coincide, support or, even contradict the messages transmitted by public authorities and institutions.

As Entman (2003) points out, the boundary between "elites" and "journalists" is difficult to draw, as journalists establish professional and social networks, formal and informal, within the industry, but also outside, through which elite frames are transmitted. Through framing process, media influences public opinion and the general public's perception of the central bank. We note that a part of the specialized public (lawyers, influencers) addressed the general public directly and took upon itself to organize and represent the general public.

Following the reverse flow of the transmission of frames, the messages of the general public are framed primarily by the media, but also by the specialized public that represents them and that transmits their frames in the media and to organizations. At the same time, the general public can address the central bank directly, by e-mail or at its information-documentation point, and the NBR provides information of public interest regarding its activities, as state in Law no. 544/2001 on the free access to public interest information. Adopting Entman's (2003) model, we observe that the media is the main channel through which the frames of the general public can reach the central bank. At the same time, the media can influence the frames and messages of the elites and thus ultimately generating changes in NBR's public communication, which we will analyze in the research.

At the same time, the research model adopts the nonlinear conceptual framework for the communication of central banks with financial markets, proposed by Muchlinski (2011), a framework that involves a dynamic relationship between three dimensions: information, interaction, and context. "This conceptual framework focuses on the interdependence between people's—and institutions'—communicative behaviour in relation to acquired knowledge and shared knowledge, or persuasion" (Muchlinski, 2011, p. 68). According to Muchlinski (2011), who uses Tversky and Kahneman's (2002) theory of information processing, the specialized public of central banks also processes information in a process of selection, perception, and adaptation, based on their own cognitive abilities and the level of understanding changes through a continuous learning process.

Therefore, in order to be able to anticipate the behavior of financial market participants, central banks must take into account how the information is accepted and understood by the public. Regarding the size of the interaction, the communication of central banks implies, in the researcher's view, that the sender, the message, and the recipient change over time, the interactivity being understood as a series of continuous changes.

Regarding the third dimension, Muchlinski (2011, p. 122) argues the following: "the context (as such) does not cause the behaviour of people, but their interaction, responses, and (re)actions within the context. In doing or acting, people will also create new contexts. Their interactions will shape or change situations." Inflationary expectations are formed in a "communicative culture" (Holmes, 2014), which influences the decisions of economic agents. Both decisions and actions of financial market participants are framed in a macro environment, influenced by action. In practice, central banks will coordinate their expectations of future developments with the expectations of financial market participants, based on the future prospects of financial market participants.

According to Muchlinski (2011), who applies the "double contingency" theory formulated by Parsons (1961):

> The central bank's context is an ingredient of the communicative interactions among agents in the financial markets. This context is also framed by the phenomenon of 'double contingency' regarding the interdependency of the agents' expectations. The term 'double contingency' emphasizes a pattern of social interaction of two interdependent persons—as a minimum. It emphasizes that communication is in no case a one-way street. (Muchlinski, 2011, p. 90)

Most of the literature dedicated to central bank communication focuses primarily on the relationship with financial market participants (monetary, foreign exchange), on informing the specialized public on the objectives, plans, and projections of these institutions, and on communication as a monetary policy tool, which, however, should not be confused with a public relations function (Holmes, 2014). This research aims to fill a gap in this literature and to bring to light new data on NBR's communication with the general public.

## 4.5 Research Elements

Empirical data was obtained by applying several methods and models of qualitative analysis (semi-structured in-depth interviews) and quantitative (sociological surveys based on questionnaires and content analysis), following which heterogeneous data series were collected. Two reasons underpinned the use of several complementary methods. On the one hand, the integrative perspective of the analytical approach, by assessing the perception of different categories of actors, required the use of different research methods adapted to their profile. On the other hand, the possibility of triangulating the results was followed, in line with the observation of Todd et al. (2004, p. 165), according to which the confirmation of the results by several methods "gives increased confidence that the results you have found are genuine, and reflect something real about the topic under study."

### *4.5.1 Research Questions*

Research questions that guided the qualitative and quantitative analysis regarding the opinion and perception of the NBR representatives, the specialized public, and the general public about the central bank's communication after 2008 were as follows:

RQ1. How were the changes in the NBR's public communication perceived after 2008?

RQ2. How did the NBR manage the communication on nonmonetary issues such as the crisis of Greek-owned banks, the Swiss francs credit crisis, and the giving in payment law?

RQ3. How was the change in public confidence in the NBR perceived as a result of the institution's public communication?

RQ4. What were the most efficient and useful communication channels of the NBR in the post-crisis period?
RQ5. What is the opinion regarding the extension of the NBR's presence on social networks?
RQ6. How was communication used as a monetary policy tool after 2008?
RQ7. To what extent are the changes in the NBR's monetary communication reversible?

In order to understand the main trends in the media coverage of one of the most visible nonmonetary topics for the NBR, we analyzed how journalists framed the "giving in payment law," using the following research questions:

RQ1. How do the Romanian general and economic media frame the "giving in payment" law in 2016?
RQ2. How do the Romanian online general and economic media differ in their use of those frames?
RQ3. What were the differences in the visibility of supporters and opponents of the "giving in payment" law during the analyzed period?
RQ4. What were the main positions of the media (editorials, comments, opinions, etc.) regarding the NBR's communication strategy in the context of the analyzed legislative change?

### 4.5.2 Research Methods

Next, the three research methods and the research universe are described, in the chronological order of their application during data collection and documentation.

The interviews and the two questionnaires used in the sociological survey were built on a theoretical framework structured around two main concepts: transparency and trust, as defined in research on central bank communication.

For example, the issue of trust in the NBR was based on the research of Ehrmann et al. (2013), which analyzes the determinants of trust in the ECB as measured by the European Commission's Eurobarometer. This research explains the decline in public confidence in the ECB on the basis of three hypotheses: the Economic Hypothesis—erosion in the context of economic evolution, the Europe Hypothesis, the global financial crisis exposed the limits of decision makers in preventing and solving global problems, and confidence in the ECB as a European institution declined, the Banks Hypothesis—in public opinion, the ECB was associated with problems in the banking sector that were unjustly helped and supported during the crisis. Ehrmann et al. (2013) focus on pre-crisis determinants, including the fact that a better knowledge of the activity of the central bank generates more confidence in normal times and can even increase it in times of financial crisis.

At the same time, the conceptual framework for defining trust in central banks is also based on the results of research focused on the financial industry (Riles, 2018; Bourne, 2011, 2016; Haldane, 2016; Tett, 2015; Owens, 2012; Wälti, 2012;

Stevenson & Wolfers, 2011; Fischer & Hahn, 2008) and barometers such as YouGov (2019), Edelman Trust Barometer (2017), INSCOP Research (2016, 2019).

To assess the transparency of central banks, two main directions were followed: on the one hand, the strategic communication of the central bank with stakeholders such as the general public, the specialized public and the media, and on the other, communication as a monetary policy tool. For the first direction, the language of the central bank was defined and evaluated, with emphasis on the clarity of the messages and the use of jargon, in line with the research of Haldane et al. (2020), Haldane (2016), and Boltanski and Chiapello (2007). For example, "communication may need to be simple, relevant and story-based to become convincing and credible to a wider audience. Traditional central bank communications tend to fail on all three fronts," according to Haldane et al. (2020, p. 36). In the same context, we evaluated the frequency of public appearances of the institution's representatives, which communication channels were used, and the diversification of communication channels.

Regarding the transparency of monetary communication, this analysis refers to research showing that monetary policy generates the best effects if it is predictable (Dincer & Eichengreen, 2013; Holmes, 2014; Jeanneau, 2009; Cournède & Minegishi, 2009; Blinder et al., 2008; Bernanke & Woodford, 2007; Woodford, 2005; Bernanke et al., 2001; Faust & Svensson, 2001). For example, Dincer and Eichengreen (2013) show, based on a transparency index, using data available for 100 countries up to 2006, that greater transparency reduces changes in inflation. In this research, we keep in line with studies that emphasize the importance of anchoring inflationary expectations of both financial market participants but also of consumers (Binder, 2017). Moreover, we take into account the opinion of the general public on the future evolution of inflation and the opinion of NBR representatives on making the decision-making process more transparent by publishing minutes of monetary policy meetings and by increasing the use of communication as a monetary policy tool after 2008.

We adapted the 2016 questions of Blinder et al. (2017), in drafting the questions regarding the frequency of NBR communication after 2008, the assessment of the future role of central bank communication and the changes toward transparency of the decision-making process, both in the interview grid and in the two applied questionnaire grids. According to the Blinder et al. (2017) questionnaire, sent to 95 central banks and to over 400 economists, over 90% of academics and over 80% of central bank governors claimed that, compared to the pre-crisis period, communication of central banks has intensified. The questionnaire of Blinder et al. (2017) also highlights the fact that the post 2008 changes in central bank communication will remain, according to the expectations of most respondents.

#### 4.5.2.1 Interviews

As there is little data in the literature on how NBR representatives perceive the change in the institution's public communication after 2008, the first stage of research consisted of a series of 20 interviews with NBR officials, conducted from February 2017 to June 2017.

The interviews were conducted following a grid of 26 questions drafted on the basis of a previously defined conceptual framework (Annex B). Most of the interviews were conducted face-to-face, with the exception of three interviews that were given in writing by e-mail. The interviewer set the agenda of the discussion and guided, in the traditional question–answer format, each interviewee, except for three situations, when the interlocutors were storytellers, rather than respondents, as described by Hollway and Jefferson (2000, p. 31), when "the agenda is open to development and change, depending on the narrator's experiences." Even in these situations, all the topics covered by the stated research questions were touched upon. The script of all the interviews generated a material of 82,000 words in Romanian (135 A4 pages, written in Times New Roman 12, with a spacing of 1 line).

The research based on the semi-structured interview method considers how NBR representatives perceived nonmonetary communication on topics such as the Greek capital bank crisis, the Swiss franc credit crisis, and the legislative changes affecting the banking system, such as the giving in payment law. It also assessed issues related to the frequency of public appearances of NBR representatives after 2008, institutional transparency, the peculiarities of the language used in addressing the general public, including jargon, the efficiency of communication channels used, the erosion of public confidence in the central bank, the media's role in reflecting nonmonetary topics of debate during the researched period (2014–2016), and changes in monetary communication.

**Sample of NBR Representatives** The sample of the 20 interviewees consisted of: a member of the NBR board, three advisers to the Governor, three strategy advisers, six directors (generals and deputies), four experts in communication and public relations, a head of service, an economist, and a former NBR advisor on financial education projects (roles that were no longer outsourced at the time of the interviews). Seniority varies from over 30 years (two of the interviewees work for the NBR since 1986) to 4 years, and the average work experience for the NBR of the interviewed subjects is 17.5 years.

More than half of the interviewees (11) were active in the media throughout the financial crisis, with statements, presentations at press conferences or seminars and opinions published on the NBR blog. The remaining nine interviewees were involved in building and implementing the communication strategy, in drafting messages disseminated during the crisis or in organizing events, seminars, and presentations, which exposed the NBR to the media or to the specialized public, on other topics than those generated by the financial crisis.

Regarding the represented departments, 35% (seven respondents) are or were part of the NBR Communication Department, between 2008 and 2017. Other departments represented in the sample are the Financial Stability Directorate, the Economic Modeling and Forecasting Department, the Legal Department, and the Secretariat and Public Relations Department. Regarding gender representation, 12 respondents are men and eight are women.

#### 4.5.2.2 Questionnaire-Based Sociological Surveys

Based on two online questionnaires aimed at different intervals, to the specialized public and to the general public, this research aims to identify the extent to which the two categories of public perceived the changes and the need for change in NBR communication in the post-crisis period. We focused on transparency (frequency of public statements, assessment of the language used by NBR's representatives or in the official reports of the central bank, communication channels, including social networks), as well as on the credibility of the institution (Annexes C and D).

**Sample of Specialized Public** Between May 2018 and July 2018, 186 responses were collected from targeted respondents via e-mail and LinkedIn. The respondents form a sample of convenience, of cluster type due to the delimitation of the population profile—the specialized public of the central banks includes bankers, analysts, investors, academia, and specialized media. The questionnaire had 48 items and was built on the isondaje.ro platform. 33% of the respondents were academia (teachers from economics universities from across the country were especially targeted), 16% from the financial-banking industry, 9% from the economics media, 9% from the public relations industry, 8% from the public sector, 6% from the services, and 15% from other professional categories (law, trade, energy industry, etc.). Of the respondents, 55% (102) were women, and the mean age was 41.6 years ($M = 41.6$, $SD = 9.13$).

**Sample of General Public** Between July 2019 and October 2019, 391 responses were collected from respondents selected through Facebook. Compared to the active population of Romania, which was, at the end of 2019, 9.033 million people (National Institute of Statistics, 2020), the sample is convenient, for a margin of error of ±5% and corresponds to an accuracy rate of 95%. The questionnaire had 32 items and was built on the isondaje.ro platform. Over 17% of the respondents were from academia, 11.7% from the IT&C industry, 8.7% from general media, 7.7% from the public relations industry, 6.9% from services, 6.4% from the health sector, 6.4% from creative industries and 12.8% were from other professional categories (construction, bar and restaurants, textile industry). Over 70% (277) were women, and the mean age was 35.9 years ($M = 35.9$, SD $= 9.59$).

#### 4.5.2.3 Content Analysis

The third methodological component of the research is content analysis, built on the articles from both the economic media and the general media in Romania regarding the giving in payment law, one of the most visible topics of nonmonetary communication that the NBR was involved in after the 2008 crisis. The general conceptual framework is the framing theory, as structured and developed over time by researchers such as Goffman (1974), Gitlin (1980), Gamson et al. (1992), Entman (1993), Pan and Kosicki (1993), Capella and Jamieson (1997), Reese (2001),

Entman (2003), Van Gorp (2007), Scheufele and Iyengar (2011), and Cacciatore et al. (2016).

For example, Robert Entman points out that selection and salience, are the main actions that "promote a particular problem definition, causal interpretation, moral evaluation, and/or treatment recommendation for the item described" (Entman, 1993, p. 52). Also, researchers Gamson et al. (1992), p. 374) consider that a "wide variety of media messages can act as teachers of values, ideologies, and beliefs and that they can provide images for interpreting the world whether or not the designers are conscious of this intent." Analyzing news related to public policy, Pan and Kosicki (1993, p. 57) argue that "we may conceive a news media frame as a cognitive device used in information encoding, interpreting, and retrieving; it is communicable; and it is related to journalistic professional routines and conventions." Capella and Jamieson (1997, p. 38) consider that similar to the structural frame of a house, the frame of a news story creates a structure on which other elements are built. Reese (2001) describes framing as an exercise of power more so as it affects our understanding of the political world.

This research is part of the sociological tradition that defines classification "as information that conveys differing perspectives on some event or issue" and considers that "This tradition can also be labelled 'emphasis' framing, since the observed framing effects represent differences in opinion that cannot be attributed exclusively to differences in presentation" (Scheufele & Iyengar, 2011, pp. 6–7).

The theory of framing was initially used to understand the role played by the media in political life. However, researchers have expanded the topic and applied this theory to the financial crisis of 2008, thus publishing studies that this research will reference (e.g., Damstra & Vliegenthart, 2018; Berry, 2016; Falasca, 2014; Zeri, 2014; Bach et al., 2013; Mylonas, 2012; Riaz et al., 2011; López & Llopis, 2010; Fuchs & Graf, 2010; and 't Hart & Tindall, 2009). The effects of the 2008 global crisis are constantly covered by local media and analyzed by communication researchers who study how they have publicized and their possible effects on audiences (Vincze, 2014; Bârgăoanu et al., 2013; Radu & Ștefăniță, 2012; Abrudan, 2009).

We analyzed how the giving in payment law was covered by the media by focusing on online articles, based on a coding grid grouping items into five sections: (A) general information about publications, (B) the actors in the articles, (C) frames, (D) subjects, (E) sources pro and against the legislative project (Annex E). Media frames were analyzed by employing the deductive approach, and using a grid that follows five frames: economic consequences, responsibility, conflict, moral interest, and human interest. This grid adapts the criteria developed by Semetko and Valkenburg (2000) when investigating media coverage of political topics by the Dutch press. Therefore, the research is part of the series of quantitative analyzes, based on predefined frames, in line with research such as those of Semetko and Valkenburg (2000), Tankard (2001), Dimitrova et al. (2005), Matthes and Kohring (2008), and Corbu et al. (2015).

**Research Corpus** The research corpus includes articles published ($N = 420$) throughout 2016 by online portals: bursa.ro, zf.ro, hotnews.ro, and adevarul.ro, based on the simultaneous search for two key phrases: "on the giving in payment law" and "National Bank of Romania." The search was performed in April 2019, and the corpus resulting from the selection of articles totaled approximately 404,000 words (1140 A4 pages, written in Romanian, in Times New Roman 12, in 1-line spacing, including illustrations). The corpus was coded by the researcher and was verified using a sample of 10% of the materials by a graduate of the National School of Political Science and Public Administration (SNSPA), trained in the coding method. Secondary coding was 80% similar to the initial coding, which validated the results of the initial coding.

The sample used during research was selected from Bursa—bursa.ro ($N = 133$ articles) and Ziarul Financiar—zf.ro ($N = 139$ articles), the website of the two most relevant financial newspapers in Romania, from adevarul.ro ($N = 59$ articles), the website of the quality newspaper Adevărul, and from hotnews.ro ($N = 89$ articles), a general news website. According to Reuters Institute (2020, p. 80), the printed financial newspaper, Ziarul Financiar (with its online website zf.ro), in continuous existence for 21 years, is the third most trusted media brand in Romania, after PRO TV and DIGI 24 TV stations. The adevarul.ro website (the online version of a 131-year-old Romanian newspaper of the same name) is in sixth place, the hotnews.ro website (exclusively online) is in seventh place; bursa.ro (the online version of the 30-year-old printed financial newspaper Bursa).

* * *

The next section of this analysis will present the results of the three complementary research methods applied—the semi-structured interviews, the questionnaire-based sociological surveys, and the content analysis—to provide a more comprehensive, current, and relevant picture that will help understand how NBR's communication changed post 2008.

## References

Abrudan, M. (2009). Quantitative and qualitative analysis of Romanian newspapers concerning the topic of global economic crisis. *Revista Română de Comunicare și Relații Publice, 11*(2), 67–80. Retrieved from http://integru.org/web/wp-content/uploads/2011/09/RJCPR_16full.pdf#page=67

Ackoff, R. (1974). *Redesigning the future*. Wiley.

Alt, M. A., Săplăcan, Z., & Berács, J. (2017). Social responsibility in Bank communication with customers before the economic crisis—The case of Swiss franc loans in Hungary and Romania. *JEEMS Journal of East European Management Studies, 22*(3), 289–317. https://doi.org/10.5771/0949-6181-2017-3-289

Asociația Parakletos. (2020). *Despre Parakletos*. Retrieved from http://www.asociatia-parakletos.ro/

Bach, T., Weber, M., & Quiring, O. (2013). News frames, inter-media frame transfer and the financial crisis. *Zeszyty Prasoznawcze, 56*(1). https://doi.org/10.4467/2299-6362PZ.13.008.1026

Balaban, G., & Ailenei, D. (2012). Inflation targeting in the Romanian banking brushwood. *Theoretical and Applied Economics, 19*(5), 19–32. Retrieved from http://store.ectap.ro/articole/718.pdf

Bârgăoanu, A., Corbu, N., & Radu, L. (2013). The role of government evaluations and EU identity in shaping economic expectations during the crisis. The case of Romania. *European Journal of Science and Theology, 9*(4), 225–241. Retrieved from https://www.researchgate.net/profile/Nicoleta_Corbu/publication/288471450_The_role_of_government_evaluations_and_EU_identity_in_shaping_economic_expectations_during_the_crisis_the_case_of_Romania/links/5a0ea7c1aca27244d2859c69/The-role-of-government-evaluations-and-EU-identity-in-shaping-economic-expectations-during-the-crisis-the-case-of-Romania.pdf

Bernanke, B. S., & Woodford, M. (Eds.). (2007). *The inflation-targeting debate* (Vol. 32). University of Chicago Press.

Bernanke, B., Laubach, T., Mishkin, F. S., & Posen, A. S. (2001). *Inflation targeting: Lessons from the international experience*. Princeton University Press.

Berry, M. (2016). No alternative to austerity: How BBC broadcast news reported the deficit debate. *Media, Culture and Society, 38*(6), 844–863. https://doi.org/10.1177/0163443715620931

Binder, C. (2017). Fed speak on main street: Central bank communication and household expectations. *Journal of Macroeconomics, 52*, 238–251. https://doi.org/10.1016/j.jmacro.2017.05.003

Blinder, A. S., Ehrmann, M., Fratzscher, M., de Haan, J., & Jansen, D. J. (2008). Central bank communication and monetary policy: A survey of theory and evidence. *Journal of Economic Literature, 46*(4), 910–945. Retrieved from https://pubs.aeaweb.org/doi/pdfplus/10.1257/jel.46.4.910

Blinder, A., Ehrmann, M., De Haan, J., & Jansen, D. J. (2017). Necessity as the mother of invention: Monetary policy after the crisis. *Economic Policy, 32*(92), 707–755. https://doi.org/10.1093/epolic/eix013

Boiciuc, I. (2015). The cyclical behavior of fiscal policy in Romania. *Procedia Economics and Finance, 32*, 286–291. https://doi.org/10.1016/S2212-5671(15)01393-3

Boltanski, L., & Chiapello, E. (2007). *The new spirit of capitalism*. Verso.

Bourne, C. (2011). *Public relations' role as trust strategist: A specialist niche evolves from turbulence*. EUPRERA Annual Conference 2011. Retrieved from http://orca.cf.ac.uk/29796/1/BourneTrust%20Strategist.pdf

Bourne, C. (2016). *Trust, power and public relations in financial markets*. Taylor & Francis.

Brown, M., Peter, M., & Wehrmüller, S. (2009). Swiss franc lending in Europe. *Aussenwirtschaft, 64*(2), 167–181. Retrieved from https://www.alexandria.unisg.ch/212832/1/Swiss%20Franc%20Lending%20in%20Europe.pdf

Cacciatore, M. A., Scheufele, D. A., & Iyengar, S. (2016). The end of framing as we know it… and the future of media effects. *Mass Communication and Society, 19*(1), 7–23. https://doi.org/10.1080/15205436.2015.1068811

Capella, J., & Jamieson, K. (1997). *Spiral of cynism. The press and the public good*. Oxford University Press.

Constitution of Romania. (2020). Retrieved from http://www.cdep.ro/pls/dic/site.page?id=339&idl=2

Contrabănci.com. (2020). *—comunitatea clienților abuzați de sistemul bancar*. Retrieved from https://contrabanci.com/?s=comunitatea+online

Corbu, N., Ștefăniță, O., Oprea, D., & Udrea, G. (2015). The European Union–From Agenda Setting and Media Frames to Citizens' Conversations. *Romanian Journal of Communication and Public Relations, 17*(1), 41–57. Retrieved from https://www.journalofcommunication.ro/index.php/journalofcommunication/article/download/114/167

Cournède, B., & Minegishi, M. (2009). *The role of transparency in the conduct of monetary policy*. OECD economics department working papers (No. 724), OECD Publishing, Paris. https://doi.org/10.1787/221128317344

CREDERE. (2020). *Care sunt obiectivele asociației CREDERE?* Retrieved from https://credere.ro/despre-noi

Croitoru, L. (2009, September 22). *Relansarea economiei mondiale şi economia României*. Business Standard. https://www.bnr.ro/Puncte-de-vedere-4011.aspx.

Croitoru, L. (2011). *Lichiditatea, atacul speculativ din octombrie 2008 şi reputația băncii centrale*. Retrieved from www.bnro.ro

Croitoru, L. (2012a). *În apărarea piețelor*. Editura Curtea Veche.

Croitoru, L. (2012b, February 15). Vom reuşi să facem din capitalism noua normalitate? Opinion published in *hotnews.ro*, *cursdeguvernare.ro*, *mediafax.ro*, *zf.ro*, *jurnalul.ro*. Retrieved from https://www.bnr.ro/Puncte-de-vedere-4011.aspx

Dăianu, D., & Murgescu, B. (2013). Which way goes Romanian capitalism-making a case for reforms, inclusive institutions and a better functioning European Union. *Romanian Journal of European Affairs, 13*, 5. Retrieved from http://rjea.ier.gov.ro/wp-content/uploads/articole/RJEA_2013_vol13_no4_dec2013_art1.pdf

Damstra, A., & Vliegenthart, R. (2018). (Un) covering the economic crisis? Over-time and inter-media differences in salience and framing. *Journalism Studies, 19*(7), 983–1003. https://doi.org/10.1080/1461670X.2016.1246377

David, D., Rai, S. K., & Paiusan, L. (2015). Appreciation of the Swiss Franc and its impact on Romania and other Central and Eastern European countries. *Studia Universitatis "Vasile Goldiş" Arad–Economics Series, 25*(4), 11–24. https://doi.org/10.1515/sues-2015-0024

Dimitrova, D. V., Kaid, L. L., Williams, A. P., & Trammell, K. D. (2005). War on the Web: The immediate news framing of Gulf War II. *Harvard International Journal of Press/Politics, 10*(1), 22–44. https://doi.org/10.1177/1081180X05275595

Dincer, N., & Eichengreen, B. (2013). Central bank transparency and independence: Updates and new measures. *International Journal of Central Banking, 10*(1), 189–253. https://doi.org/10.2139/ssrn.2579544

Dobrescu, P. (2016). *Crizele de după criză. O lume fără busolă şi fără hegemon*. Editura Litera.

Dumitru, I., & Stanca, R. (2010). *Fiscal discipline and economic growth—The case of Romania*. Munich Personal RePEc Archive. Retrieved from https://mpra.ub.uni-muenchen.de/27300/1/MPRA_paper_27300.pdf.

Edelman Trust Barometer. (2017). *Trust in crisis*. Retrieved from https://www.edelman.com/research/2017-edelman-trust-barometer

Ehrmann, M., Soudan, M., & Stracca, L. (2013). Explaining European Union citizens' trust in the European Central Bank in normal and crisis times. *The Scandinavian Journal of Economics*, 115(3), 781–807. Retrieved from: https://www.ecb.europa.eu/pub/pdf/scpwps/ecbwp1501.pdf

Entman, R. M. (1993). Framing: Toward clarification of a fractured paradigm. *Journal of Communication, 43*(4), 51–58.

Entman, R. M. (2003). Cascading activation: Contesting the White House's frame after 9/11. *Political Communication, 20*(4), 415–432. https://doi.org/10.1080/10584600390244176

European Court of Auditors. (2017). *Intervenția Comisiei în criza financiară din Grecia: însoțit de răspunsurile Comisiei*. Retrieved from https://op.europa.eu/webpub/eca/special-reports/greek-crisis-17-2017/ro/

Falasca, K. (2014). Framing the financial crisis: An unexpected interaction between the government and the press. *Observatorio, 8*(1), 01–21. Retrieved from http://www.scielo.mec.pt/scielo.php?script=sci_arttext&pid=S1646-59542014000100001

Faust, J., & Svensson, L. E. (2001). Transparency and credibility: Monetary policy with unobservable goals. *International Economic Review, 42*(2), 369–397. Retrieved from https://www.nber.org/papers/w6452.pdf

Fischer, J. A., & Hahn, V. (2008). *Determinants of trust in the European Central Bank*. SSE/EFI Working Paper Series in Economics and Finance. Retrieved from https://www.econstor.eu/bitstream/10419/56308/1/56082744X.pdf

Freeman, R.E. (1984). Strategic management: A stakeholder approach. Boston; London; Melbourne; Toronto: Pitman

Fuchs, D., & Graf, A. (2010). *The financial crisis in discourse: Analyzing the framing of banks, financial markets and political responses*. Retrieved from https://nbn-resolving.org/urn:nbn:de:0168-ssoar-344922.

Gamson, W. A., Croteau, D., Hoynes, W., & Sasson, T. (1992). Media images and the social construction of reality. *Annual Review of Sociology, 18*(1), 373–393.

Georgescu, F. (2018). *Capitalul în România postcomunistă* (Vol. 2). Editura Academiei Române.

Ghinea, R. (2015, December 3). Reacţii la legea privind "darea în plată" a imobilelor. Ce opinii au transmis cititorii ZF şi ce spune BNR. *Ziarul Financiar*. https://www.zf.ro/banci-si-asigurari/reactii-la-legea-privind-darea-in-plata-a-imobilelor-ce-opinii-au-transmis-cititorii-zf-si-ce-spune-bnr-14907021

Gitlin, T. (1980). *The whole world is watching: Mass media in the making and unmaking of the new left*. University of California.

Glassner, V., & Watt, A. (2010). Cutting wages and employment in the public sector: Smarter fiscal consolidation strategies needed. *Intereconomics, 45*(4), 212–219. https://doi.org/10.1007/s10272-010-0339-2

Goffman, E. (1986). *Frame analysis. An essay on the organization of experience*. Northeastern University Press. (Original work published in 1974).

Grupul Clienţilor cu Credite în CHF (GCCC) (Group of Customers in Swiss francs). (2020). Retrieved from https://www.facebook.com/pg/GCCCoficial/about/?ref=page_internal

Haldane, A. (2016). *The great divide*. Speech presented at the New City Agenda Annual dinner. Retrieved from https://www.bankofengland.co.uk/-/media/boe/files/speech/2016/the-great-divide.pdf.

Haldane, A. (2018). *Folk wisdom*. Speech given by at the100th Anniversary of the Bank of Estonia. Retrieved from https://www.bankofengland.co.uk/-/media/boe/files/speech/2018/folk-wisdom-speech-by-andy-haldane.pdf

Haldane, A., & McMahon, M. (2018). Central Bank communications and the general public. *AEA Papers and Proceedings, 108*, 578–583. https://doi.org/10.1257/pandp.20181082

Haldane, A., Macaulay, A., & McMahon, M. (2020). *The 3 E's of Central Bank Communication with the Public. Bank of England*. Staff Working Paper No. 847. Retrieved from https://www.bankofengland.co.uk/-/media/boe/files/working-paper/2020/the-3-es-of-central-bank-communication-with-the-public.pdf?la=enşihash=B3D34A003BB6F2B7D5653B265966DF11C8F75154

Hollway, W., & Jefferson, T. (2000). *Doing qualitative research differently: A psychosocial approach*. Sage.

Holmes, D. R. (2014). *Economy of words: Communicative imperatives in central banks*. University of Chicago Press.

Holmes, D. R. (2016). Central bank capitalism: Visible hands, audible voices. *Anthropology Today, 32*(6), 3–7.

INSCOP Research. (2016). *Barometrul ADEVĂRUL despre ROMÂNIA*. Retrieved from https://www.inscop.ro/category/2016-cercetari/

INSCOP Research. (2019). *Topul încrederii în instituţii interne şi internaţionale*. Retrieved from https://www.inscop.ro/22-martie-2019-topul-increderii-in-institutii-interne-si-internationale/

International Monetary Fund. (2009). *Financial sector coordination meeting on Romania, concluding statement by participating banks*. Retrieved from https://www.imf.org/en/News/Articles/2015/09/28/04/51/cm032609

Isărescu, M. C. (2009a). *Nine lessons from the current financial crisis*. Speech by Dr Mugur Isărescu, Governor of the National Bank of Romania and Member of the Romanian Academy, during the session titled "What lessons can be learned from the current economic crisis?", organised by the Economics, Legal and Sociology Department within the Romanian Academy, in co-operation with "Costin C. Kiritescu" National Institute of Economic Research and the "ESEN Reflection Group" Romanian National Committee, Romanian Academy. Retrieved from https://www.bis.org/review/r090508d.pdf

Isărescu, M. C. (2009b). *Criza financiară internațională și provocări pentru politica monetară din România*. Dissertation on the occasion of the awarding of the title of Doctor Honoris Causa of "Babeş-Bolyai" University. Cluj-Napoca, 26 February 2009. Retrieved from http://storage1.dms.mpinteractiv.ro/media/401/781/10376/4002028/2/r20090226guv.pdf

Isărescu, M. C. (2011, June 21). *Canalul psihologic este cel mai periculos la contagiunea crizei din Grecia. BNR e pregătită*. Interview with Xinhua news agency, published by Mediafax news agency. Retrieved from https://www.mediafax.ro/economic/isarescu-canalul-psihologic-este-cel-mai-periculos-la-contagiunea-crizei-din-grecia-bnr-e-pregatita-8513234

Jeanneau, S. (2009). *Communication of monetary policy decisions by central banks: What is revealed and why*. BIS Papers. Retrieved from https://www.bis.org/publ/bppdf/bispap47.pdf

Klingen, C. (2013). Perspectives on growth prospects for central, eastern and southeastern Europe. *Challenges and Opportunities*, 13. Retrieved from https://www.eib.org/attachments/efs/economic_report_banking_cee_turkey_en.pdf#page=17

Law no. 312/2004. (2004). *Legea nr. 312/2004 privind Statutul Băncii Naționale a României*. Retrieved from https://www.bnr.ro/apage.aspx?pid=404&actId=1

Law no. 77/2016. (2016). *Legea nr. 77/2016 privind darea în plată a unor bunuri imobile în vederea stingerii obligațiilor asumate prin credite*. Retrieved from https://lege5.ro/Gratuit/geydmnruheyq/legea-nr-77-2016-privind-darea-in-plata-a-unor-bunuri-imobile-in-vederea-stingerii-obligatiilor-asumate-prin-credite

López, A. M. R., & Llopis, M. Á. O. (2010). Metaphorical pattern analysis in financial texts: Framing the crisis in positive or negative metaphorical terms. *Journal of Pragmatics, 42*(12), 3300–3313. https://doi.org/10.1016/j.pragma.2010.06.001

Matthes, J., & Kohring, M. (2008). The content analysis of media frames: Toward improving reliability and validity. *Journal of Communication, 58*(2), 258–279. https://doi.org/10.1111/j.1460-2466.2008.00384.x

Morosan, G., & Scurtu, L. E. (2019). Regulation of the Romanian banking system. Effects on the market economy. *Ecoforum Journal, 8*(1) http://ecoforumjournal.ro/index.php/eco/article/view/939/561#

Muchlinski, E. (2011). *Central banks and coded language: Risks and benefits*. Springer.

Mylonas, Y. (2012). Media and the economic crisis of the EU: The 'culturalization' of a systemic crisis and Bild-Zeitung's framing of Greece. *tripleC: Communication, Capitalism & Critique. Open Access Journal for a Global Sustainable Information Society, 10*(2), 646–671.

National Bank of Romania. (2009a). *Comunicat de presă FMI—CE—Inițiativa de coordonare în domeniul bancar pentru România*. Retrieved from https://www.bnr.ro/page.aspx?prid=2506; https://www.bnr.ro/page.aspx?prid=1803

National Bank of Romania. (2009b). *Aranjament stand-by dintre România și Fondul Monetar Internațional, agreed by the Letter of Intent transmitted by the Romanian authorities, signed in Bucharest on 24 April 2009, and by the Decision of the Executive Board of the International Monetary Fund of 4 May 2009*. Retrieved from https://www.bnr.ro/apage-Mobile.aspx?pid=404&actid=322848

National Bank of Romania. (2015a). *Mortgage-backed loans to individuals as evidenced by the Central Credit Register as at 31 December 2015*. Retrieved from https://www.bnr.ro/Mortgage-backed-loans-to-individuals-13512.aspx

National Bank of Romania. (2015b). *Analiza creditelor în franci elvețieni*. Retrieved from www.bnr.ro

National Bank of Romania. (2015c). *Frequently asked question regarding Greek-owned Romanian banks*. Retrieved from https://www.bnro.ro/Frequently-asked-question-regarding-Greek-owned-Romanian-banks-12692.aspx

National Bank of Romania. (2015d). *Răspunsurile direcțiilor de specialitate din BNR la întrebările punctuale adresate de membrii Comisiei pentru Buget, Finanțe și Bănci din Camera Deputaților*. Retrieved from https://www.bnr.ro/Raspunsurile-directiilor-de-specialitate-din-BNR-12055-Mobile.aspx

National Bank of Romania. (2020). *Statistică monetară și financiară—indicatori agregați privind instituțiile de credit*. Retrieved from https://www.bnr.ro/StatisticsReportHTML.aspx?icid=800&table=1027&column=.

National Institute of Statistics. (2020). *Ocuparea și șomajul în anul 2019*. Retrieved from https://insse.ro/cms/sites/default/files/com_presa/com_pdf/somaj_2019r.pdf

Olescu, E. (2018, September 28). *Împrumutații în CHF au înființat o asociație pentru consumatori*. Bursa. https://www.bursa.ro/credere-imprumutatii-in-chf-au-infiintat-o-asociatie-pentru-consumatori-46814537

Owens, L. A. (2012). The polls—Trends: Confidence in banks, financial institutions, and wall street, 1971–2011. *Public Opinion Quarterly, 76*(1), 142–162.

Pan, Z., & Kosicki, G. M. (1993). Framing analysis: An approach to news discourse. *Political Communication, 10*(1), 55–75.

Parsons, T. (1961). An outline of the social system. In T. Parsons, E. Shils, K. D. Naegele, & J. R. Pitts (Eds.), *Theories of society* (pp. 30–79). The Free Press.

Popa, A. (2008, December 8). *Francii elvețieni s-au făcut dispăruți de pe piață*. Conso.ro. https://www.conso.ro/citeste-comentariu/100/imob/Francii-elvetieni-sau-facut-disparuti-de-pe-piata.html

Popovici, M. C. (2014). Romanian banking system: The degree of financial intermediation after the financial crisis. *CES Working Papers, 6*(4), 106–113.

Post, J. (1978). *Corporate behavior and social change*. Reston.

Radu, L., & Ștefăniță, O. (2012). Framing the economic crisis in the Romanian online media. *Romanian Journal of Communication & Public Relations, 14*(2), 29–46. Retrieved from https://journalofcommunication.ro/oldsite/archive2/026/26/rjcpr_26_full.pdf#page=30

Reese, S.D. (2001). Framing Public Life. A Bridging Model for Media Research. In S.D. Reese, H.G. Oscar, & E.G. August (Eds.) *Framing Public Life: Perspectives on Media and our Understanding of the Social World* (pp. 7–31). New Jersey: Lawrence Erlbaum Associates

Reporters Without Borders. (2020). *World press freedom index*. Retrieved from https://rsf.org/en/ranking

Reuters Institute. (2019). *Digital news report*. Retrieved from http://www.digitalnewsreport.org/survey/2019/romania-2019/

Reuters Institute. (2020). *Digital news report*, p. 80. Retrieved from https://reutersinstitute.politics.ox.ac.uk/sites/default/files/2020-06/DNR_2020_FINAL.pdf

Riaz, S., Buchanan, S., & Bapuji, H. (2011). Institutional work amidst the financial crisis: Emerging positions of elite actors. *Organization, 18*(2), 187–214. https://doi.org/10.1177/1350508410389630

Riles, A. (2018). *Financial citizenship: Experts, publics, and the politics of central banking*. Cornell University Press.

Roman, A., & Şargu, A. C. (2013). Analysing the financial soundness of the commercial banks in Romania: An approach based on the camels framework. *Procedia Economics and Finance, 6*, 703–712. https://doi.org/10.1016/S2212-5671(13)00192-5

Scheufele, D. A., & Iyengar, S. (2011). The state of framing research: A call for new directions. In*The Oxford handbook of political communication theories* (pp. 1–26). Oxford University Press. https://doi.org/10.1093/Oxfordhb/9780199793471.013.47

Semetko, H. A., & Valkenburg, P. M. (2000). Framing European politics: A content analysis of press and television news. *Journal of Communication, 52*(2), 93–109.

Stevenson, B., & Wolfers, J. (2011). Trust in public institutions over the business cycle. *The American Economic Review, 101*(3), 281–287.

Stoiciu, V. (2012). *Austerity and structural reforms in Romania*. International Policy Analysis, pp. 1–7. Retrieved from https://sar.org.ro/wp-content/uploads/2012/12/Austerity-and-Structural-Reforms-in-Romania.pdf.

Swiss National Bank. (2015). *Swiss National Bank discontinues minimum exchange rate and lowers interest rate to −0.75%*. Retrieved from https://www.snb.ch/en/mmr/reference/pre_20150115/source/pre_20150115.en.pdf

Tankard, J. W., Jr. (2001). The empirical approach to the study of media framing. In S. D. Reese, O. H. Gandy Jr., & A. E. Grant (Eds.), *Framing public life: Perspectives on media and our understanding of the social world* (pp. 95–106). Routledge.

Tempea, O. (2015, January 27). Trei sferturi din clienții cu credite în franci elvețieni s-au împrumutat de la Bancpost, Volksbank şi Piraeus. *Ziarul Financiar* https://www.zf.ro/banci-si-asigurari/trei-sferturi-din-clientii-cu-credite-in-franci-elvetieni-s-au-imprumutat-de-la-bancpost-volksbank-si-piraeus-13787142

Tett, G. (2015). *The silo effect: The peril of expertise and the promise of breaking down barriers*. Simon and Schuster.

't Hart, P., & Tindall, K. (2009). Understanding crisis exploitation: Leadership, rhetoric and framing contests in response to the economic meltdown. In P. 't Hart & K. Tindall (Eds.), *Framing the global economic downturn. Crisis rhetoric and the politics of recessions* (pp. 21–40). ANU E Press.

Todd, Z., Nerlich, B., McKeown, S., & Clarke, D. D. (2004). *Mixing methods in psychology: The integration of qualitative and quantitative methods in theory and practice*. Psychology Press.

Tognato, C. (2012). *Central bank independence: Cultural codes and symbolic performance*. Springer.

Tucker, P. (2018). *Unelected power: The quest for legitimacy in central banking and the regulatory state*. New Jersey: Princeton University Press

Tversky, A., & Kahneman, D. (2002). Judgment under uncertainty: Heuristics and biases. In D. J. Levitin (Ed.), *Foundations of cognitive psychology: Core readings* (pp. 585–600). MIT Press.

Van Gorp, B. (2007). The constructionist approach to framing: Bringing culture back in. *Journal of Communication, 57*(1), 60–78. https://doi.org/10.1111/j.1460-2466.2006.00329.x

Vasilescu, A. (2011). *Biletul ieşirii din criză. Bucureşti*. Editura Curtea Veche.

Velthuis, O. (2015). Making monetary markets transparent: The European Central Bank's communication policy and its interactions with the media. *Economy and Society, 44*(2), 316–340. https://doi.org/10.1080/03085147.2015.1013355

Vincze, H. O. (2014). 'The crisis' as a journalistic frame in Romanian news media. *European Journal of Communication, 29*(5), 567–582. https://doi.org/10.1177/0267323114541610

Wälti, S. (2012). Trust no more? The impact of the crisis on citizens' trust in central banks. *Journal of International Money and Finance, 31*(3), 593–605.

Woodford, M. (2005). *Central bank communication and policy effectiveness*. National Bureau of Economic Research. Retrieved from https://www.nber.org/papers/w11898.pdf

YouGov. (2019). *How clear, if at all, are you about what role the Bank of England carries out?* Retrieved from https://yougov.co.uk/topics/science/survey-results/daily/2019/04/24/12913/3

Zeri, P. (2014). Political blogosphere meets off-line public sphere: Framing the public discourse on the Greek crisis. *International Journal of Communication, 8*, 1579–1595. Retrieved from https://ijoc.org/index.php/ijoc/article/viewFile/2012/1152

# Chapter 5
# NBR Representatives About the Change of Public Communication After 2008

> *The NBR has never been in a shadow cone. But now it's under a spotlight, as all central banks are (. . .). Central banks everywhere have a big problem, and the bar for high jumps is very high, it's very difficult, and here communicators play an important role.*
> *(Interviewee no. 19)*

The NBR representatives interviewed on the post 2008 nonmonetary and monetary public communication activities of the NBR unanimously agreed that fundamental, visible, and irreversible changes took place, first of all, toward a greater transparency. The interviewees are at odds on what these changes were, what were more significant, and what effects are considered more lasting. At the same time, we consider it necessary to emphasize the tense context in which the NBR's communication took place during the interviews: in 2017, "a significant part of institutional communication focused on providing information, clarifications and analyses to debunk media attacks regarding monetary policy, market mechanisms (depreciation of the leu and the rise in interbank market rates—ROBOR), household indebtedness, the duties and actions of the National Bank of Romania in relation to banks and NBFIs, the central bank's tasks as authority for the regulation, authorisation and prudential supervision of the banking sector, the NBR's assets and the profitability of the banking system" (National Bank of Romania, 2017, p. 218).

The research based on the semi-structured in-depth interviews preserves the answers' anonymity and thus the quotes used to illustrate the research results will be assigned by mentioning the number of the interviewee. The number of interviewee was assigned based on the order of the interviews were conducted (Interviewee no. 1, Interviewee no. 2, etc.).[1]

[1] In order to maintain anonymity, the interviewees are not associated with their NBR position, as in some cases, the mentioning of the position could lead to identifying the individual respondent.

© The Author(s), under exclusive license to Springer Nature Switzerland AG 2022

R. Iacob, *Blind Spots in the Spotlight*, Financial and Monetary Policy Studies 53,
https://doi.org/10.1007/978-3-031-04067-2_5

The research questions that guided the qualitative[2] analysis refer to the opinion and perception of the NBR representatives about the central bank's communication after 2008:

RQ1. How were the changes in the NBR's public communication perceived after 2008?
RQ2. How did the NBR manage the communication on nonmonetary issues such as the crisis of Greek-owned banks, the Swiss francs credit crisis, and the giving in payment law?
RQ3. How was the change in public confidence in the NBR perceived as a result of the institution's public communication?
RQ4. What were the most efficient and useful communication channels of the NBR in the post-crisis period?
RQ5. What is the opinion regarding the extension of the NBR's presence on social networks?
RQ6. How was communication used as a monetary policy tool after 2008?
RQ7. To what extent are the changes in the NBR's monetary communication reversible?

To assess how the central bank's communication changed the perception of NBR representatives after 2008, the interview contained eight questions related to the changes toward greater transparency in the institution's strategic communication before 2008, to the frequency of public appearances, to the effects of the crisis on the NBR's public communication, and to the language used, especially jargon (See Annex B: Interview grid—Questions regarding NBR's communication, addressed to NBR's representatives).

## 5.1 Setting the Scene: Pre-crisis Communication with Stakeholders

In the first step of the analysis, we identified the general framework in which the pre-crisis public communication of the NBR took place, its main challenges and the NBR's relations with stakeholders such as the specialized public (commercial banks), media, general public.

Until 2008, the institution did not have a separate Communication Department, as the Media Relations Service was part of the Secretariat Department. "In terms of headings of NBR's institutional strategy, monetary policy communication was a very well-developed segment, but in the other areas (author's note: communication)

[2]Some of the results described on the basis of research questions 2, 3, and 7 were published in English in 2018 in the journal *Management Dynamics in the Knowledge Economy*, 6(1), 129–144, article Trust and Transparency: Perspectives upon the Communication of the National Bank of Romania during the Financial Crisis—A Qualitative Research.

there was fragmentation" (Interviewee no. 10). Interviewee no. 2 also emphasizes the existence of a monetary communication strategy, characterized by centralization and a single voice, "which I think was good, (...) the governor was the main communicator and there were very rarely other vectors of communication." In the same direction, Interviewee no. 11 considers that, on issues related to monetary policy, public interventions have been rare and made only at important times.

According to the respondents, the decision to set up the Communication Department was taken in early 2008 and implemented in August of the same year, with the mission to take over relations with the media, to manage the website, and also to manage educational projects addressed in the first phase to the academic environment. The ultimate goal of targeting the academic environment was to reach the general public, as at that time the specialized public was the main stakeholder with which the NBR constantly interacted, in conferences, symposia, and through publications: "In the first phase, you could not approach the ordinary individual, but the academia which at that time was closest to the NBR" (Interviewee no. 10). According to the NBR 2008 Annual Report (National Bank of Romania, 2008, p. 137), the general public was the first public mentioned when defining communication's objective of providing "a clear image of the policies and measures adopted by the NBR for fulfilling its tasks." The next publics mentioned in the 2008 Annual Report were the domestic and international business environment, public administration institutions, and academia.

Prior to the 2008 crisis, the NBR communicated its prudential measures,[3] however, according to Interviewee no. 10, its messages were counteracted by the reaction of the banking environment: "(...) the central bank's message was on the area of prudence and the need for tempering, not to stop some trends, but to temper and correct some excesses, while the banks had an extremely aggressive campaign. Simply said, when the central bank came up with sets of administrative measures—my phrasing was very plastic at the time—they scratched the screens with their presence at the level of all bank presidents or top officials, who said, alas (...) the NBR won't allow us to give you money."

Two respondents believe that the first episode of crisis communication came in October 2008, when specialists believed that there was a "speculative attack on the leu" (Croitoru, 2011). Referring to this episode, Interviewee no. 16 shows that "It was an action, the NBR was active in its communication, and the governor was the main communicator. Very much so. As proof, the subject did not provoke reactions until long after 2008, when the possible or so-called victims of that situation began to speak." Evaluating the communication strategy of the NBR at that time, Interviewee no. 10 emphasizes the decision of the NBR to communicate the number of operators that generated the imbalance and NBR's intervention in the foreign exchange

[3] Prior to 2008, the NBR took prudential measures, administrative barriers, and increased minimum required reserves on foreign currency liabilities from 20% in early 2002 to 40% in early 2006 to mitigate capital inflows (details in Chap. 4).

market: "Here we have caution in expression, which you must keep in mind, especially in a crisis situation. Name and shame can do worse."

In setting the stage for the NBR's post-crisis institutional communication, we also considered it useful to define the institution's relationship with the media for 10–15 years prior to the crisis, depending on the background of each respondent. Referring to the 2000s, for example, one of the respondents describes a press "much freer (…) and much more—so to speak—indulgent with the NBR than it is now. And it was like that until three years ago" (Interviewee no. 2). Two interviewees state that, until 2008, the central bank worked with certain publications, provided that they maintained a high standard of content.

The NBR's relationship with the media was characterized differently, depending on the respondents' own experiences. On the one hand, it was considered good: "we were open to understanding the need for journalists to understand what we do, to try to explain to the public what we do" (Interviewee no. 10); "I do not remember seeing malicious articles in the press about the NBR or attacks on a person at that time" (Interviewee no. 13). On the other hand, attacks were evoked regarding NBR's tasks related to banking supervision: "How did you try to make a stricter banking control, what were the attacks, press campaigns (…) Somehow, now, if I look at what the press writes, it is as if I back at the beginning of the banking system. Again, many accusations are politically motivated or have certain circles of economic interests behind them" (Interviewee no. 6).

Some of the interviewees perceived a loss of professionalism of journalists over time: "They were more willing to read, to ask questions and then come up with a result. Now they are in a hurry to publish and often make mistakes. Or they intentionally make mistakes" (Interviewee no. 2); "Just like now, the media was focused on populism and simple theories and we had to come up with complicated explanations for their simple populism, so it hasn't changed. Maybe then, the media was a bit more (…) professional, not by much, but a bit more" (Interviewee no. 3).

## 5.2 The Main Post-crisis Changes

In the questions that related to the respondents' opinions on the main changes they were aware of, in the post-crisis period, no changes were defined, so thus the results reflect only the changes considered most visible by each respondent.

The interviewees unanimously agreed that the NBR's public communication activity changed after 2008. Two of the interviewees underline the contribution of the 2008 crisis, as it highlighted the role of public communication within the central bank: "The crisis had a good effect on the NBR communication, in the sense that the role of communication has greatly increased in importance" (Interviewee no. 3); "At that moment, there were (author's note: in 2008) some press conferences and briefings and their frequency intensified, there were also hearings in the Parliament, they called us there, so it was an intensification of communication.

And maybe that thing helped us see the world (author's note: from the inside) that there is a need for communication" (Interviewee no. 18).

### 5.2.1 Frequency of NBR Communication

When asked explicitly about the frequency of public appearances, 90% of respondents answered that the NBR communicated with the public more compared to the pre-crisis period of 2008, and the remaining 10% did not evaluate or could not evaluate this indicator of public communication. The results of the present research are in line with those obtained by Blinder et al. (2017) based on a questionnaire sent to 95 central banks worldwide. According to researchers (Blinder et al., 2017), over 80% of central bank governors claimed that, compared to the pre-crisis period, central bank communication has intensified.

The most recurrent changes invoked without guidance from the interviewer were, in order of the number of respondents who reported them: multi-voice communication and diversification of communicators, diversification of topics, and changes in the elaboration and structuring of messages.

### 5.2.2 Polyphony or Cacophony?

The NBR communication on several voices was invoked by 65% of the interviewees (13). Their views are divided on the effects of nonmonetary and/or monetary communication. We mention that the evaluation of the communication on several voices is made according to the area of expertise of the respondents, both in the monetary communication and in the public one, on other subjects.

On the one hand, respondents believe that voice diversification has been an effective communication strategy. In favor of this view, they relied on the results of the responses to the attacks on the central bank (Interviewee no. 1), the fact that, in this way, the central bank was perceived as a dynamic organization (Interviewee no. 3), and that by alternating formal–informal registers, the transmission of messages to different categories of public was facilitated (Interviewee no. 16).

For example, referring to nonmonetary communication, Interviewee no. 1 considers that polyphony is beneficial for the central bank: "From the specialized and well-known voices that went out in public, it came to a close communication to the table, in the sense that many voices were taken from where they did not exist. This was a step (...) To be a polyphony. Let's not keep the communication to a few image vectors of the central bank." The same interviewee assesses that the silence, giving up the dialogue with the public, through different voices, has turned against the central bank. Polyphony is considered an asset for a central bank, as it gives the institution a human face: "(...) if an institution speaks in unison, it gives the feeling of a fake and an stiff thing. An unnatural thing (...) with this (author's note: communication in several voices), you show that you have a range of opinions, some agree others disagree, there is a range of opinions." At the same time, the diversification of voices offers the possibility to alternate the formal and informal registers for the transmission of the same information: "we have a standard communication, through several communicators approved by the bank, some more informal, like Vasilescu (Adrian Vasilescu, strategy consultant) on more informal subjects, others—more institutional, trying to explain issues in more technical terms, first of all the Governor, me (the interviewee), and two or three more, trying to professionally, like Lazea (Valentin Lazea, chief economist of the NBR), Croitoru (Lucian Croitoru, advisor to the NBR governor) or Rădulescu (Eugen Rădulescu, director of the Financial Stability Department)" (Interviewee no. 16).

The diversification of voices on monetary issues, started in 2005, when the NBR adopted the inflation targeting regime. One respondent emphasized the need for a firm choice between coherent, multi-voiced communication on a specific topic and a single voice, but one that did not contradict itself over time. The same interviewee considers that the message was better studied before being disseminated to the public and that the voices were diversified, the most relevant being "The governor in the first place, his alter-ego, Adrian Vasilescu (strategy consultant to the NBR governor), me (author's note: the interviewee), Valentin Lazea (author's note: the chief economist of the NBR). An important voice was Eugen Rădulescu (author's note: the director of the Financial Stability Department)" (Interviewee no. 2).

On the other hand, there are NBR representatives who consider that a more coherent and clearer communication is a centralized one, built on fewer voices or even a single voice, on a smaller number of topics, on better coordination of public appearances and messages, on dosage and on disengaging from "people versus people" conflicts. Three respondents emphasized the much too frequent appearances in the media (Interviewee no. 17) and the lack of coordination of public appearances (Interviewee no. 6, Interviewee no. 20): "The messages sent were not unitary, several voices sent contradictory messages and the effect was the increase in distrust of the general public" (Interviewee no. 20). Moreover, one interviewee considers that the role of spokesperson of a central bank should also belong to the governor: "It's one thing to have a PR person, or to have some people who are perceived in Romania as spokespersons for the governor, but it's another thing to have a spokesperson in a central bank. In general, the most important messages are those that come from a governor. Then the vice-governors, then, in our case, the members of the Board" (Interviewee no. 19).

### 5.2.3 *Diversification of Communication Topics*

The diversification of topics is considered by 65% of respondents as one of the major changes in the post-crisis communication of the NBR. The unanimous perception of the interviewees is that the involvement of the NBR in debates on issues not covered by the institution has negatively affected the image of the central bank to the public, even if it was necessary for the central bank to provide explanations on various topics of interest to the general public in the post-crisis period. NBR's involvement in additional subjects, raised a number of new challenges for communicators: "central banks have a big problem everywhere, and the high bar for high jumps is very high, it is very difficult, and here the communicators intervene" (Interviewee no. 19).

Regarding the controversies on nonmonetary issues, the interviewees consider that a central bank should not deal with the protection of consumers of financial services (Interviewee no. 1), and that the NBR has assumed too much by publicly showing the shortcomings of some legislative initiatives (Respondent no. 5). Communication on several topics and voices sends in the background the communication of the main objective of the NBR—ensuring and maintaining price stability (Interviewee no. 7). One respondent considers that a rethinking of the communication strategy is needed, that a greater emphasis should be put on the fundamental elements in the bank's activity (inflation, exchange rate stability, stability of the banking system, etc.), as "this was one of the bad omens of this period, because we dealt with tangential issues" (Interviewee no. 16).

More than half of the interviewees who reported the diversification of communication topics evaluate it as a necessary step in this context. For example, Interviewee no. 17 considers that, after 2008, "There was a clear need for the NBR, the supervisory authority, to go out in public and explain certain things, to be proactive in its communication, to communicate important elements. Sometimes, the NBR even had to apologize, to explain how things were during the crisis, or that we had an anti-cyclical and not pro-cyclical attitude during the economic boom." Two other respondents argued that the signals and decisions of the central bank should first be made known and explained to the public (Interviewee no. 9) and so the NBR addressed a number of topics of interest to the general public: "Once the crisis began, you needed to explain a lot more, such as financial stability, resolution, and supervision. Things that seem to affect people much faster than monetary policy decisions" (Interviewee no. 4).

The shift in focus in the NBR's communication from inflation to financial stability is considered a natural change after 2008, when focusing on controlling inflation was no longer enough. Another thematic change was observed in connection with reactions to the decisions taken by the government, "a somewhat more vocal attitude of the central banks on issues that are in the government's yard. And this is because central banks have been called upon to buy time so that governments can implement reforms" (Interviewee no. 4).

In terms of monetary communication, the NBR has been forced to face criticism of its monetary policy decisions. For example, one respondent points out that if at the beginning of the crisis, the NBR's communication was proactive, optimistic about the evolution of the crisis, in the second stage "we were overwhelmed by reality and became defensive because the accusations increased. One of the main accusations was that we reduced the interest rate too little in relation to the needs of the interest rate. We had to go out and explain that this conception is wrong" (Interviewee no. 2).

## 5.3 Jargon: A Double-Edged Sword

Respondents' comments diverge on the three questions regarding the central-bank jargon used: some focused on the challenges of language simplification for NBR communicators, while others focused on the specific needs of different audiences. In NBR representatives' opinion, the main solutions for adapting the jargon are adapting the oral communication for the general public, requesting the support of the media and the academia for turning specialized language into ordinary language, and training communicators for different audiences. Most respondents perceived visible progress in adapting the NBR language to the general public.

### *5.3.1 (Almost) Everything for Audiences*

For 40% of the interviewees, the different categories of NBR stakeholders were at the center of the comments regarding the use of jargon. For example, one respondent supports different formulations for different categories of audience: "(. . .) the audience is structured. For the public abroad you have to speak in one way, for the public here in a way, and for the non-specialized public, in another way" (Interviewee no. 2).

The respondent focused on the general public, and their opinions are divided on the adaptation of communiqués on monetary issues: on the one hand, to simplify them for the general public (Interviewee no. 17), on the other—to maintain a more elitist form of published communication, and to simplify oral communication (Interviewee no. 3).

NBR representatives describe two divergent pressures that act on the language simplification process: the pressure exerted by the example of other central banks and standards they establish: "(. . .) a certain drafting standard is internationally recognized, it is difficult for a bank to say that the other banks, talk fancy, but that it will speak to the average person on the street" (Interviewee no. 3). NBR representatives also recognize the pressure exerted by the limited attention of the general public: "it is clear that everyone is subjected to the stress of speed (. . .) And then, even in messages, the average person expects the tone to be much simpler and more understandable at first reading" (Interviewee no. 13).

With regard to the general public, respondents consider that the vectors of communication in academia (Interviewees no. 10, no. 17) or in the media (Interviewees no. 4, no. 13) can mediate, for example, the details of certain decisions of the central bank, in a more accessible language, and, for this purpose, the NBR should capitalize on events dedicated to the two categories of public (media and academia). At the same time, "the language needs to be popularized, in my opinion, so that the public understands what is being communicated to them, practically" (Interviewee no. 3).

For the specialized public, two respondents argue that it is not necessary to adapt the language, that the NBR must remain at the same level (Interviewee no. 4), or, moreover, that the language should be even more technical, focused more on educating the public (Interviewee no. 8). Another respondent points out that the public is not only reachable through speech, but also through social media (Interviewee no. 15), where the sincerity of communication is much more effective, and considers that a sincere communication is more important than a simple communication: “You speak the language of the public as long as you are aware of their needs, their illusions, and all that. When you are not, the language is already less relevant. I think it is necessary for the transparency of the central bank to be sincere and obviously applied to the benefit and interest of the many. And, if this is really the case, then the public, whether they want to or not, will feel that warmth, that protection from the institution, and then the real dialogue begins, it is the dialogue of the great ones who know how to put themselves at the service of the many” (Interviewee no. 11).

### 5.3.2 *Challenges for Communicators*

Most representatives of the NBR highlight the main challenges involved in giving up jargon for communicators: the difficulty of giving up the perspective of the specialist (Interviewee no. 4); the ability of communicators to learn new communication techniques (Interviewee no. 5); the specialist does not necessarily identify with a communicator similar to the one who represents the Central Bank’s Communication Department and who is more oriented towards the general public (Interviewee no. 2); and the communicator must cover completely different registers (Interviewee no. 14). Two NBR officials—Governor Mugur Isărescu and the governor’s strategy consultant, Adrian Vasilescu—were invoked by some of the respondents as models for their ability to adapt the language of the central bank to the general public (Interviewees no. 2, no. 7, no. 15, no. 18).

### 5.3.3 *Limits of Simplification*

NBR representatives draw attention to the dangers of excessive language simplification. Two of the interviewees use the phrase “double-edged sword” when exposing the main limitations of giving up central-bank jargon. Respondents believe that simplification can distort the meaning of messages (Interviewee no. 9) and that, in the case of crisis communication, in the absence of a common premise, “simplification can ruin things, you can sink ever deeper into the justification the accusers put forward. So I don’t know if simplification is always the right answer” (Interviewee no. 16).

The respondents highlighted the importance of both timing, especially in language simplification, but also the public's effort to understand the messages, to facilitate a meeting halfway, just as Annelise Riles (2018) considers the responsibility of the financial citizenry to take steps toward financial institutions. The line between proximity and hostility is very fragile and depends on timing: "So the public is waiting to understand what is happening in the NBR, and if you give it satisfaction in time, lowering the language to the level it needs, making certain gestures of transparency, towards the optimal levels, ie the demand meets the supply. If you do not, them in time, hostilities arise" (Interviewee no. 2). The same demarcation line depends as well on a collective effort, of the central bank and the public, at the same time: "(. . .) in the communication process both parties must be involved, ie the listener must also make an effort to understand. And, again, the press must understand" (Interviewee no. 6).

The results obtained in the RQ1 research question show that the interviewees unanimously appreciated that the NBR's public communication activity changed after 2008. The most recurrent changes mentioned by 65% of the interviewees were multi-voice communication, diversification of topics, the structure of messages. The research did not identify a consensus on the best communication strategy of the central bank in terms of multi-voice versus single-voice communication, which confirms the results of other research dedicated mainly to monetary communication of these institutions (Tutino, 2016; Marcussen, 2009; Blinder et al., 2008; Ehrmann & Fratzscher, 2005).

Respondents' comments recommending strategic silence on certain topics with crisis communication potential are in line with Smith's (2005) observations that strategic silence can shorten the duration of a crisis and that this strategy pays off when the public agrees that an organization remains silent because it is preoccupied with finding the best solutions and refuses to waste the necessary time commenting on the situation itself. Libaert (2008) also shows that organizations resort to silence when they want to avoid feeding the spiral of public controversy, when the crisis is displaced on the public agenda, by other more important topics or when organizations assess that the crisis may remain secret.

In the perception of 90% of the interviewees, after the 2008 crisis, the NBR communicated with the public more, a result in line with the one obtained by the questionnaire of Blinder et al. (2017) according to which over 80% of central bank governors claimed that, compared to the pre-crisis period, central bank communication has intensified.

Respondents' view that the NBR assumed too many responsibilities outside of its mandate, entered too much controversy on monetary and nonmonetary issues, and agreed that it has answers to everything is confirmed in the literature on how central banks became vulnerable prior to the crisis (King, 2016; El-Erian, 2016; Haldane, 2016; Ciocca, 2016; Blinder, 2013, etc.).

Summarizing the comments on language simplification, the NBR representatives consider that the central bank is part of the general efforts of central banks around the world to adapt the financial-banking jargon for the general public, a trend outlined shortly before the onset of the 2008 crisis. Giving up the jargon, defined in the financial-banking industry as Fedspeak (Greenspan, 2007) or bankspeak (Moretti & Pestre, 2015), is a concern for most NBR respondents. Interviewees call for language simplification and the use of non-elitist language for the general public, in line with the observations of specialists and central bankers (Haldane et al., 2020; Haldane, 2016). At the same time, the involvement of other categories of stakeholders (journalists, academia) to reach the general public is based on the research model proposed by Entman (2003), which posits that the frames cascade from the public administration, elites, and journalists, until they reach the general public.

## 5.4 Main Debate (2014–2016)

The time interval subjected to the qualitative analysis in this chapter (2014–2016) was intense in the communication of the central bank, and numerous debates on nonmonetary issues eclipsed the communication on the main objective of the NBR. For the evaluation of the communication strategy, we chose three situations: the crisis of Greek capital banks, the crisis of loans in Swiss francs, and the draft legislation known as the "giving in payment in law" (Law no. 77/2016) as well as some other draft laws.

In expressing their views on the NBR's communication in these three situations, respondents stressed the importance of understanding both the international and the domestic context in which the debates took place. Regarding the international context, the respondents mentioned the general erosion of public confidence in financial institutions, the external factors that contributed to the onset of these crises on the Romanian market, the sovereign debt crisis in Greece, the solutions to similar situations of debtors in countries such as Spain or the United States, and comparisons with the pressure on central banks in Hungary, Poland, Slovenia, and Croatia, which also managed the cases of debtors in Swiss francs.

In describing the internal context, four recurring issues were identified in the respondents' explanations. The electoral context and the political interests in which the legislative initiatives were voted were invoked by 35% of the respondents, secondly—pressures from some interest groups outside the political environment (lawyers, debtors, media) were underlined. A third observation regarding the internal context was the low level of financial education of both the general public and the specialized one. According to the respondents, it is important to correlate communication situations with the historical timeline of NBR's communication, as the NBR entered the public debates on these "vulnerable" issues following loud interventions on fiscal policies, according to NBR representatives.

### 5.4.1 Greek Capital Banks

All 13 respondents who commented on how they perceived the communication of the main message regarding the crisis of Greek funded banks in 2015—namely, the fact that they are "Romanian banks with Greek capital"—agree that the NBR message was received by the general public, but opinions on the implementation of the communication strategy are divided.

On the one hand, the respondents referred to the efficiency of some tools and tactics of organizational communication used in this communication situation: crisis communication cell, proactive attitude, clear messages, use of unique voice. In the respondents' perception, "we did honorably" (Interviewee no. 12), "I don't remember there being episodes of panic. I think the message reached the public" (Interviewee no. 3), "There was no panic—I speak on account of the results—and it was publicized that the NBR knew what to do and did what it had to do" (Interviewee no. 5), "The context was as such that emotion would beat any possible arguments so you had to work very carefully. I think it went well" (Interviewee no. 4). One of the factors of the success of the communication strategy was the agreements the NBR had signed with the parent banks since 2009, the fact that the banks were well capitalized (Interviewees no. 11, no. 17).

The NBR's communication strategy, which also took over the role of the communicator of the banks in question, contributed to avoiding a banking crisis in Romania (Interviewee no. 16). In the same direction, Interviewee no. 18 emphasized the use of a single voice and good internal organization in the preparation of messages: "During the Greek capital crisis I think we communicated well, on a single voice, there were some working groups with the Supervision Department, so from this point of view it communicated well."

Describing the main challenges in conveying the NBR's messages, the interviewees highlighted the efforts to change the public opinion's existing perceptions: "First, we had to fight a huge struggle to change the perception of the general public that these are not Greek banks, but banks with Greek capital. Then, we had to convince the general public that these are Romanian banks, regulated, authorized by the central bank, and that they are subject to domestic legislation and that they operate like all other banks. That was the media battle that never ended—even now this idea has not gone out of the minds of many. Three—the battle with shareholders to bring capital. Every time there was a shortfall, our supervision called the shareholders and each time they responded promptly with capital. And the result is that, now, all banks are on their feet" (Interviewee no. 1).

On the other hand, the respondents appreciate that the correct messages were not penetrating from the very beginning (Interviewee no. 2), certain messages regarding the situation of the depositors had to be sent by the credit institutions, and not by the NBR (Interviewees no. 7, no. 9). Moreover, the respondents added that more organization-wide internal training is needed and that the coordination between interdepartmental working groups can be improved (Interviewees no. 7, no. 8). For example, one respondent believes that the message did not reach the public from the beginning because it was not correctly drafted: "It is difficult to articulate a correct message from the very beginning, because of the unstable context and the lack of clear information. Later it worked and the general public forgot about these Greek banks" (Interviewee no. 2). Several respondents pointed out that, on the analyzed topics, not the central bank, but the banking community should have communicated: "In my view, the situation of depositors was not something that the NBR should have spoken on, but the banking community" (Interviewee no. 9). Evaluating the internal organization of the working groups, Interviewee no. 7 appreciates the need to set up working groups, and Interviewee no. 8 emphasizes the need for as clear crisis management procedures as possible: "so, in the end, the Greek capital banking crisis was a bit flimsy, in my view."

## 5.4.2 *The Swiss Franc Loans Crisis*

Of the 19 respondents who expressed their opinion on the NBR's communication on the Swiss franc loan crisis, more than half (11) criticized the communication strategy, and some pointed out issues related to the domestic and international context, such as the fact that the debate exceeded the powers of the central bank. Respondents disagree on the issues that affected the transmission of messages such as "loans in Swiss francs were limited and did not present a systemic risk" or "customers must negotiate with commercial banks to find customized solutions" or "NBR can not intervene on the leu—Swiss franc exchange rate."

Most of the criticisms were made in connection with the messages sent by the NBR. About 40% of the respondents described them as "non-unitary," using different statistics, lacking empathy, "were lacking in information and seemed moralizing" (Interviewee no. 15), "on Swiss francs loans we were not very consistent in our messaging" (Interviewee no. 5), the tone was "conflicting" (Interviewee no. 8): "We were very aggressive, we seemed to be the only holders of the truth. Our communication was done in a somewhat conflicting tone, and this probably stems from the fact that the drafters of these laws, in one form or another, became the enemies of the NBR" (Interviewee no. 8). Engaging in a direct conflict such as "people versus institutions" was also criticized: "Regarding the Swiss francs loans (. . .) things could have been explained, but instead we reached new heights in terms of personal accusations (. . .)" (Interviewee no. 7).

In the opinion of the NBR representatives, the communication on several voices affected the transmission of key messages: "From my perspective, it was not OK that there were several voices, but this did not depend on us. I believe that we should have published the press release and have only the PR person speak. Both, the PR person spoke and Mr. Vasilescu, each with a different number, so a different dilemma, although they had talked to each other, each cared about his number (. . .) Cacophony. You learn from that, right?" (Interviewee no. 10).

One-fifth of respondents believe that the NBR's messages were clear and the views expressed—consistent, but the interviewees criticized the public communication strategy, the lack of proactivity, the overexposure, the multi-voice communication, and the failure to connect emotionally.

Some of the positive aspects of the communication strategy were, as one respondent puts it, the coordination with commercial banks, the clear message related to direct negotiations between customers and credit institutions, holding press conferences, regular follow-ups providing new data, the use of a language accessible to the general public. "(. . .) We kept a coherent point of view. I presented in detail all the elements related to lending in francs during a public conference. We came out with regular communication as there was a change in the stock of loans in Swiss francs, and in doing so we showed that there is a dynamic process, so we kept the timing somehow, we set out to keep the timing and the score on this issue. We tried to explain, and this, again, in a fairly common language, what are the constraints in limiting lending" (Interviewee no. 16). Another interviewee is of the opinion that the message regarding the direct negotiation between customers and commercial banks has been altered or even blocked by credit institutions: "On the Swiss francs loans, when the central bank said <<Go, communicate, contact the banks, the solution is up to you and the bank, hold this discussion!>>, the banks slammed the door in the customers' face. This attitude undermined our credibility so much!"; "On the Swiss francs loans issue the first layer that had to communicate with customers were the banks, but they left us exposed and took many steps back" (Interviewee no. 10).

Regarding the transmission of NBR messages on the depreciation of the national currency against the Swiss franc, one interviewee explains that, although they were clearly formulated by the central bank, they did not reach the public (Interviewee no. 3). According to one respondent, the central bank failed to transmit its message to the general public because the content of the messages was moralizing and lacked information and because of the delay in sending the correct messages. The same interviewee considers that the NBR messages were not "strong enough" and that they were negatively framed by the media (Interviewee no. 15). Another interviewee refers to the moralizing messages of the NBR as "The message was like (. . .) a parent talking to the child. The child made a fool of himself and the father tells him so. I don't think the parent ever asked the child well, OK, look now, but what conclusion do we draw, how should we proceed?" (Interviewee no. 10). The absence of the emotional component is also observed by Interviewee no. 16: "In the case of the Swiss franc loans, from the very beginning, we missed this emotional dimension, and the subject became only an emotional one. And we, somehow naturally, did not focus on this emotional dimension, although we should have anticipated it. It was much later that we made the emotional distinction, when we recognized that there may be a fundamental problem for those who took loans in Swiss francs, and there is a real dimension there."

The perception of the NBR's communication is therefore not unitary. For example, two of the respondents consider that the NBR communicated very well on this subject (Interviewee no. 20) and that the NBR had balanced messages which were affirmed by figures (Interviewee no. 9). Additionally, in the strategic communication, the NBR must take into account all stakeholders as "It is very difficult to give a message that pleases everyone. Because in fact the great ability is to answer correctly and satisfactorily for all parties. And the parties mean: banks, and customers of banks" (Interviewee no. 9).

### 5.4.3 *Giving in Payment Law*

As we showed in Chap. 4, the main messages of the NBR regarding the legislative changes in the banking sector focused on the assessment of financial losses of credit institutions if these changes would have been applied. Other messages sent by the central bank were: "banks' losses will be passed on to all customers receiving banking services," "the NBR does not intervene in the legal relations between credit institutions and their customers," "the relationship between the bank and the consumer of financial services falls within the scope of consumer protection," "imposing financial losses through an administrative decision can be challenged in court as an unconstitutional act, based on the violation of article 44 (1-6) which guarantees the right to property" (National Bank of Romania, 2015).

#### 5.4.3.1 Stakeholder Play and Message Transmission

When conveying messages, about a third of respondents consider it very important to understand how all NBR stakeholders acted—the specialized public, the media, and the general public. They also refer to the influence of interest groups that "joined forces, published websites, assigned each other positions, some were official ideologues, like Piperea (lawyer Gheorghe Piperea), others had support in Parliament, others were in the media intimidation team" (Interviewee no. 6). In turn, Interviewee no. 5 considers that the general public was used by the elites to put pressure on the central bank, and Interviewee no. 16—that the NBR was overexposed in public discussions. Given the hostile stakeholders, one interviewee claims that the NBR could have tried more to explain the reasons of its positions: "I think the NBR should have done more to explain exactly why it got involved, but somehow I don't know if even with more explaining, given the shaming campaign of these interest groups, it would have managed to obtain a little more added value. I think that the efficiency would have been quite limited" (Interviewee no. 6).

According to the respondents, by refusing to negotiate and find solutions for customers in real difficulty, commercial banks stimulated the emergence of regulations such as the giving in payment law. Clients "ended up on various lists of known figures, mostly lawyers, who lured them by painting an extremely favorable image for resolving bank disputes or lawsuits, including by settling these issues at the level of some laws approved by the Parliament" (Interviewee no. 17).

Respondents assessed the messages sent by the central bank differently, on the one hand considering that they were clear: "We were very clear from the start, we believed that in fact, the money of the depositors is at stake, not so much of the banks, and that if the banks suffer losses or they go bankrupt because of these decisions, they will need public rescue from the taxpayers' money" (Interviewee no. 3). On the other hand, respondents believed that the first public appearances were too far from the general public: "I think that at the beginning we were off message. Our message was that". This is the contract, it needs to be followed! "After that, we ended up in a more favorable context and our messages started to be more nuanced, i.e. those who can no longer cope must be helped, not those who no longer want to" (Interviewee no. 4). As in the case of Swiss francs loans, the respondents drew attention to the fact that the NBR has no responsibilities for the protection of consumers of financial services (Interviewees no. 1, no. 17), but also to the electoral context "which made the discussion to be less coherent" (Interviewee no. 16). At the same time, the respondents consider that overcoming the banking process paradigm made a real dialogue impossible: "In fact, the big surprise was that we overcame the normal banking process paradigm (...). The issues that transcend the paradigm are much more difficult to communicate" (Interviewee no. 16).

Analyzing the NBR communicators, two respondents underline the lack of reaction of several members of the Board, and their failure to backup the governor's messages during that period (Interviewee no. 2, Interviewee no. 3). Reactivity in communication on the Swiss franc loans is explained by one respondent by the lack of a NBR justification for a press release: "You can't put together in a press release additional details to inform the public, especially when they have such an emotional and even surreal dimension (...) so to speak. And thus, willingly or unwillingly, we were reactive" (Interviewee no. 16).

Referring to the message on systemic risk, it was, according to respondents, well-articulated, but the fact that the risk did not occur attracted a new wave of criticism towards NBR: "There were several versions of the law. From the beginning, we said that there is a severe systemic risk on the first version of the law. Later on, as the crisis fail to materialize, this came back to haunt us" (Interviewee no. 16); "It was concluded that, in fact, the NBR overstated the effects of the crisis and that was it. In reality, everything was benign, nothing happened" (Interviewee no. 8).

In the description of the power relations between the stakeholders, two types of conflicts were identified which, according to the interviewees, involved the central bank in public debates: people versus institutions (debtors versus central bank) and institutions versus institutions (NBR versus Parliament), which led to attacks on individuals: "in the first communication sequence, the people versus institution one, it was obvious that we would lose some reputation, we were not empathetic to the public, but I think the loss in reputation was manageable (...). When the NBR involved itself in the communication battle, we had institution versus institution. The NBR could not have won the battle as one side was chosen by people and the NBR is chosen by the other side. So, the other institution was closer to the public than the NBR. And in this battle (...) the solution was the attack on leadership" (Interviewee no. 10).

### 5.4.3.2 NBR: Advocate of Commercial Banks?

One-third of the respondents commented on the label "NBR—banks' advocate" assigned to the central bank by media and interlocutors, during public debates on legislative changes. For the NBR representatives, this label can have two complementary explanations: on the one hand, the commercial banks withdrew from the debates, were silent, did not strengthen NBR's messages and, on the other hand, the NBR came out in many voices, said too much. Most of the interviewees explained that "commercial banks have shown that they are protected by the NBR" (Interviewee no. 1); "The NBR seemed to be vocal on this issue because the banks themselves were silent" (Interviewee no. 3); "The central bank had to take this ballast on its shoulders, which they (author's note: commercial banks) whose responsibility they avoided" (Interviewee no. 10); "We intervened late when we were supposed to intervene or the Romanian Association of Banks (ARB) should have intervened much earlier" (Interviewee no. 18).

One respondent nuances the application of the bank advocate label and explains it by analyzing the situation of the media who used it: "(. . .) not all the media used this label, but those journalists who had material or individual interests, ie journalists who happened to have taken loans or who were paid to have a certain opinion against the NBR. So, we cannot say that the entire media put this label to the NBR" (Interviewee no. 3). In turn, Interviewee no. 2 considers that "whatever we said, those who labelled us the defender of the banks were those who had suffered because of the previous behavior."

Regarding the spreading of the label "NBR—lawyer of banks", some respondents criticized the lack of solidarity in the banking system and argued that the public appearances of NBR representatives aimed to ensure financial stability: "Everything the NBR said was from the perspective of its responsibilities in terms of financial stability. The NBR alerted the general public and the politicians on the possible negative effects of the two initiatives on the banking system" (Interviewee no. 6). Referring to the way in which the media reflected the subject, Interviewee no. 11 considers that "all approaches that are in the public media are based on either group or personal interests."

The central bank needs to explain more clearly why certain practices of commercial banks in relation to customers are not acceptable, argues another respondent: "since the banking industry creates systemic risks, it must change its behavior, they can't be defended no matter their behavior (. . .) We didn't say this enough in public" (Interviewee no. 19). One-fifth of the respondents consider that the labelling was favored by the much too sustained and vocal intervention of the NBR, sometimes without the support of the specialized departments: "I think we were too exposed in the media and we made too many statements" (Interviewee no. 17), "everyone spoke on behalf of the NBR" (Interviewee no. 7).

In conclusion, more than half of the interviewees who commented on the NBR communication on the giving in payment law were critical of the communication strategy implemented by the NBR, and focused on five communication tactics, which, in their perception, were missing, but could have contributed to maintaining and increasing the trust of the general public in the institution during the analyzed period. These tactics are, in order of the number of respondents who invoked them: better coordination of public appearances, proactivity, focus on the fundamental objective of the central bank, diversification of media, and employing empathy. Most of the respondents (over a third) referred to the lack of coordination of public appearances, to the absence of a "single voice", to a "motley language" (Interviewee no. 16), to "well-developed messages between communicators, more coherence and less personal pride" (Interviewee no. 20), to the fact that, on legislative changes, "the NBR Board of Directors and the Governor did not speak on a single voice" (Interviewees no. 2, no. 3).

A third of the respondents mentioned the absence of a speedy reaction and of a proactive attitude in the NBR's communication. Some respondents believe that proactivity in communication should have been doubled by the diversification of communication channels, noting that the messages of those who drafted the legislative changes reached the general public "probably because they speculated on more efficient communication channels" (Interviewee no. 8). More than a quarter of the interviewees identified empathy as the missing element in constructing certain messages: "if empathy is an element of communication, yes, we could be more empathetic" (Interviewee no. 16), "We had no empathy in messages" (Interviewee no. 10), "the first public appearances were completely devoid of empathy towards the debtors" (Interviewee no. 12), "we were not empathetic at the beginning, which we should have been" (Interviewee no. 18).

Multi-voice communication and the high frequency of media presence are in line with the results of research by Maor et al. (2013), who showed that banking regulators choose between silence and communication depending on the possible impact of opinions outside the organization on the organization's reputation. Maor et al. (2013) show that such institutions choose to communicate about activities in which their reputation is not yet consolidated (regulations on lending conditions for individual customers), as well as in the case of extensive media coverage. Both these situations applied to NBR's communication on the giving in payment law. Regarding both empathy and the assumption of attributions that go beyond the NBR's mandate, the respondents' comments are in line with what Winkler (2000) observes in relation to monetary communication, namely: central bank communication must meet three criteria: be clear, produce effects and be honest.

By emphasizing the relationship with different categories of public in the communication strategy on the giving in payment law, the results of this analysis confirm that the NBR, part of the financial community, along with analysts and commercial banks, builds its reputation and autonomy in response to the expectations of different categories of public, like all central banks (Freeman, 1984). Interviewees also identified categories of adverse stakeholders, who stand out in times of crisis, and they even come from audiences considered allies, as defined by Fusalba (2012).

Summarizing the results of RQ2, according to the respondents, the NBR's messages regarding the Greek capital crisis, the Swiss franc credit crisis, and the legislative changes in the banking sector reached or not the general public for three main reasons: on account of how the central bank drafted and transmitted the messages (without empathy, transmitted in several voices, late, reactive in some situations), because of messages launched by other stakeholders that competed with the NBR messages, on account of how part of the media intervened in the framing process, publishing negative articles and labelling the central bank as "bank lawyer."

In line with the framing theory (Gitlin, 1980; Iyengar & Kinder, 1987; Gamson & Modigliani, 1989; Entman, 1993; Shah et al., 1996; Iyengar, 1991; de Vreese, 2002; Entman, 2003; de Vreese, 2005; Matthes & Kohring, 2008; Scheufele & Iyengar, 2011; McLeod & Shah, 2015, etc.), respondents believe that how the media framed the official statements of NBR representatives on crisis management could have had a major impact on the transmission of messages to the general public. Callaghan and Schnell (2001) argue that "in order to maximize their media coverage, successful political actors (...) must provide emotion and good quality images, to simplify the arguments (...) and to follow the conventional news thread" (Callaghan & Schnell, 2001, p. 203). Respondents' criticisms of moralizing messages and lack of empathy confirm that Callaghan & Schnell (2001) findings can be applied to central banks concerned with transmitting messages to the public through the media. Observations on competing messages and negative labelling ("NBR—Bank Advocate") are in line with researchers' observations that the public's understanding of a crisis may be influenced by competing frames ('t Hart & Tindall, 2009), and that the effects of framing on the public may be influenced by the volume (which frame is repeated most frequently) and by their strength, regardless of repetition (Chong & Druckman, 2007).

## 5.5 Trust in the NBR Post-crisis

To assess how the NBR respondents perceive the erosion of confidence in the central bank after 2008, four questions were included in the interview grid. The results of the qualitative research reflect a balance in assessing the degree of confidence erosion: in the perception of over half of the respondents (11 interviewees), the NBR was affected by a crisis of confidence after 2008. The remaining 9 respondents consider the erosion to be "quite small" (Interviewee no. 2), or that it was not a crisis of confidence, but "a battle to provoke a crisis of confidence, which I hope was not won by those who caused it" (Interviewee no. 1); there were "some attempts, they may even be shakes, that tested the solidity of the institution" (Interviewee no. 13); "I don't think the NBR suffered (author's note: a crisis of confidence), I only see a 5–10% impact, you know, like a bigger scratch" (Interviewee no. 11). For a quarter of respondents who perceived a low drop in trust, the focus shifts from the institution to its management, the crisis of confidence did not affect both the reputation of the institution and the management: "rather the credibility of the governor and the NBR leadership has been questioned" (Interviewee no. 20).

On the other hand, respondents who reported a "large" and "very large" erosion of confidence focused on stakeholders who contributed to the establishment of negative messages about the central bank. For example, one respondent considers that NBR's image suffered in 2016, a process that started under pressure from individual elites, continued with pressure from Parliament and culminated in media involvement: "you would tell someone that you work at the NBR and you would be asked "What are you doing there, do you have problems with Piperea? "There was doubt at the level of public perception, not only in some newsrooms. After a while, things calmed down at the level of public perception, but they intensified at the level of the Parliament, I am sure of this, as both I and my colleagues were met with a hostile attitude from some parliamentarians. But it was obviously a fabricated matter, maintained by certain media trusts and by certain people with a perfect cadence. This story was well staged" (Interviewee no. 17). Another respondent mentions a "demonization" of the central bank, a presentation of the institution as the "supreme evil": "We were seen, like the banking system, demonized. They demonized us and attacked us. So we had to better defend out points of view after that. When you are demonized, the human mind no longer pays attention to arguments" (Interviewee no. 2).

### 5.5.1 NBR Reputation Locally and Internationally

Interviewees offer a series of explanations for the erosion of the general public's trust in the central bank. A quarter of respondents reported a decline in public confidence in the NBR from the institution's very good reputation before the crisis and in the first years after 2008, more precisely until 2013. The erosion of trust did not occur immediately after the global crisis, as seen in barometers. For example, the INSCOP barometer (INSCOP Research, 2016) shows that, in March 2016, 44.2% of the Romanian population had "a lot and a lot of trust" in the NBR, compared to 51.3% in December 2014 Respondents referred to "extraordinary prestige," "the bank's strengths and weaknesses," and "over-sized expectations" from the public of what the central bank could do (Interviewee no. 16): "I don't think the bank realized what the public's expectations were." In the same direction, another interviewee is of the opinion that, in the first years after 2008, the public trusted the NBR because the institution had "the most rational institutional behavior (. . .) But that raised the bar, people excepted even more. You had to go down at least 2–3 steps of exposure, so that you could come to a normal level, where the wind would not blow at the first blink of an eye" (Interviewee no. 10).

The interviewees explain the erosion of trust in the NBR by referring to both the international and the local context. As the financial crisis was based in the banking sector, the erosion of trust did not bypass the NBR. As the NBR, in 2008, was at its peak in terms of public confidence the expectations were even higher, as "politicians blamed the banking system, the banking system was perceived as guilty, and we are perceived as the ones who cocoon and manage the banking system, and in a way we were, we manages this market, we regulates it and our reputation was affected. But I'd say that the erosion was quite small" (Interviewee no. 2).

One-fifth of the respondents pointed out that the erosion of trust was caused, in a local context, by the lack of reaction of commercial banks: "In the end, the NBR intervened many times because the others had a very modest attitude towards communication, they were not at all organized, and then, maybe we spoke on their behalf too and that's the reason for the bank's lawyer's stamp" (Interviewee no. 4); "The banks played a bit offside, that was obvious, the NBR cheered them to" Go explain! "but none did. In the end, I don't think we could have avoided this, it is the duty of the National Bank to say things by name when they have a more serious dimension of risk" (Interviewee no. 16). There were also interviewees who linked the erosion of confidence with the failure to hit the inflation target: "many analyze you by objective, so you did not meet the inflation target for a long time, I think only once (. . .) if we refer strictly during the mandate, this does not help our image either" (Interviewee no. 18).

### 5.5.2 *Target Audience and Financial Education*

According to the interviewees, an important cause of the erosion of trust is the low level of financial education and the low level of understanding of the general public of the fundamental objective of the central bank and the activity of the NBR in general. Specifically, 45% of the interviewees referred to the level of financial education of the public: "I said that we would not have gotten there if it were not for a lack of economic and especially financial education" (Interviewee no. 14); "Here, the public, before regaining its trust, must be educated, in the sense that its entire philosophy of life must be based on assuming responsibility" (Interviewee no. 3).

In order to regain the trust of the general public, two respondents emphasize the more intense promotion of the fundamental elements in the bank's activity: "the fundamental elements in the bank's activity must be better explained and then based on this diminished confidence must be rebuilt" (Interviewee no. 16); "There needs to be a stronger, larger-scale communication effort to explain NBR policies and policy reasons" (Interviewee no. 6). Referring to the approach of changing the mentality of the general public, one respondent claims that the main obstacle is the lack of interest of the audience (Interviewee no. 5).

### 5.5.3 *Strategic Communication*

A quarter of the interviewees referred to some tactics that were missing or, on the contrary, were used excessively after 2008, contributing, in their opinion, to eroding the general public's trust in the central bank. Interviewees consider that, to influence public opinion, a proactive communication is needed (Interviewee no. 5); "We always react, we have never been proactive" (Interviewee no. 8). Proactivity is closely linked, according to respondents, to the use of new communication channels, more accessible to the general public, and which have been used more effectively by hostile stakeholders, for example: "the messages of some people reached the general public so quickly. Probably because they speculated on some more efficient communication channels, while we published positions on opiniibnr.ro" (Interviewee no. 8).

Overexposure, communication of messages in several, sometimes contradictory, voices, and the lack of empathic messages contributed, in the opinion of NBR representatives, to the erosion of trust of the general public after 2008. To all this is added the fact that, in the opinion of the respondents, the central bank has assumed responsibilities that have exceeded its powers: "The bank has entered this game, accepting that it has answers and solutions to all problems. As you can see, things are much more complicated with the emergence of a crisis and the comet tail after the 2008 crisis, things are much more complicated and the answers are much harder to give, especially given that the NBR does not have all the tools and all the elements to answer these questions" (Interviewee no. 16).

Some interviewees who tried to estimate the time needed to regain the confidence lost after 2008 reported long intervals: "image loss, unfortunately, does not recover very easily. Once lost…, maybe even a generation must pass so that you can restore it" (Interviewee no. 9), "mentalities change very hard" (Interviewee no. 5), "In Romania it is quite difficult because distrust comes from many directions and not only related to monetary policy" (Interviewee no. 7). Other interviewees considered that the pre-crisis confidence level could not be recovered: "That confidence level was much too high and was conjunctural and based mainly on the personality of the Governor. But I never think we can return to that level of confidence" (Interviewee no. 16).

In conclusion, the third research question highlighted, relevant aspects of the way in which the NBR representatives perceived the erosion of public trust in the institution. Respondents' comments on the impact of the 2008 crisis on the NBR's reputation and credibility confirm that the erosion of confidence did not bypass the Romanian central bank either, even if Romania did not face bank failures or the need to implement unconventional, monetary policy measures after 2008. The results of this study strengthen those of local opinion barometers (INSCOP Research, 2016, 2019), which showed that after 2008, the erosion of public confidence in the central bank and the fact that the pre-crisis confidence level has not been recovered. At the same time, perceptions of declining confidence in the central bank are in line with those reflected by barometers and surveys applied in other markets (Edelman Trust Barometer, 2017; YouGov, 2019), as well as studies dedicated to analyzing this consequence of the 2008 crisis on financial institutions (Owens, 2012; Bourne, 2011).

The present study could not identify a consensus on the extent of the decline in public confidence in the NBR: in the perception of more than half of the respondents, the NBR was affected by a "large" and "very high" crisis of confidence after 2008, while the rest of the respondents consider that it was an insignificant erosion of trust or that it was a failed attempt at confidence erosion by some stakeholders. The assumption of too many responsibilities, outside of NBR's mandate, made central banks around the world vulnerable after 2008, as evidenced by numerous studies, as well as by representatives of these institutions (Blinder, 2013; El-Erian, 2016; Haldane, 2016; King, 2016). Overall, the interviewees' opinions also converge on causes and arguments related to the level of public knowledge about the activity and fundamental objective of the NBR (ensuring and maintaining price stability), validating some of the results of researchers such as Ehrmann et al. (2013) and Fischer and Hahn (2008).

In summary, according to NBR representatives, the decline in public confidence in the NBR during the financial crisis can be explained, by supporting factors which, in order of frequency of their invocation, were the following: (1) the communication strategy of adverse stakeholders who launched public attacks on the NBR and its management, commercial banks that did not communicate with the NBR on issues that affected their activity, part of the media that popularized certain negative frameworks in connection with the central bank); (2) the low level of public financial education on the Romanian market; (3) strategic communication of the central bank; (4) the very high level of credibility achieved by the NBR before 2008 and during the first part of the crisis; (5) assuming, on the basis of a high reputation, duties which have gone beyond the traditional mandate of the central bank; and (6) the widespread loss of public confidence in the main players in the global financial markets after 2008.

## 5.6 The Most Effective Communication Channels

In Romania, the online environment (including social networks) is the most important source of news for the public (83% of news consumption in 2020, 87% of news consumption in 2019), while TV channels come in second place, at 84%, an increase from the 2020 level of 80%. Social media occupies the third position (60%), while the consumption of print media reached 15% in 2020 (down from 19% in 2019), among the lowest levels in Europe (Reuters Institute, 2019, 2020). The interviews conducted for this chapter, checked the perception of the central bank's representatives regarding the transmission of NBR messages on various media channels after 2008.

Of the 17 respondents who referred to the following communication channels—print; online (including new media, such as social networks); TV, approximately 65% (11 respondents) consider that television was the most effective communication channel for the NBR. Three interviewees put the online environment first, one respondent—the print environment, and two of the interviewees limited themselves to general evaluations of the media, without considering a certain channel more efficiently.

The main arguments for respondents to put in first place TV in terms of power over public opinion and the effectiveness of NBR message transmission after 2008, were: the big audience, the ability to directly address the public, the bigger transparency, the more obvious emotional dimension compared to other media, and TV's history of proven effects and results over time for the central bank. "The subject entered a lot of screens and TV continues to be the most emotional communication mean" (Interviewee no. 16); "If you have taken action, you must have the courage to take questions (...) Publishing messages only in the online means that you are hiding (...)" (Interviewee no. 9); "The TV channel was the most efficient, had a high exposure, as Romanians are traditional TV consumers, and this, I think, helped us a lot" (Interviewee no. 12).

From the perspective of the NBR representatives, TV's efficiency is limited by the fact that it is not the most credible medium (Interviewee no. 2) and that "it is also the least clean medium" (Interviewee no. 16). NBR's efficiency in sending messages to the public through this stakeholder was affected by the lack of proactivity of the central bank and the limitation of official reactions, in situations where NBR representatives participated by telephone in TV shows: "I think of efficiency in terms of proactive transmission" (Interviewee no. 5); "Generally, NBR representatives call in TV shows, and thus their visibility is second to that of those who are in the studio" (Interviewee no. 8).

According to the majority of respondents, the impact of television on the public is currently challenged by that of the online environment, including social networks, rated more accessible and credible, especially for the new generation: "the world is informed by television but young people check these things on the internet. And the most credible source is electronic communication, through Facebook or other sources, because they can be verified on the Internet with friends, on Facebook, on chat, through messages" (Interviewee no. 2). However, opinions on the online environment remain divided, one respondent appreciates, for example, that online "is the most altered, anything can be written there" (Interviewee no. 8).

Compared to other channels, the print media was rated as more balanced and effective for a certain age group of the public: "Indeed, the print media was in decline, but I think at least for a certain segment of the population, older people, the written word weighed more" (Interviewee no. 13). Another respondent is of the opinion that, strictly from the perspective of financial stability, print was the most efficient communication channel after 2008 (Interviewee no. 4). Two of the respondents point out that, regardless of the efficiency of the channels, the central bank must use them all with care (Interviewee no. 10) and must be open to using new media as traditional media (print, TV) is no longer as effective (Interviewee no. 6).

In conclusion, over half of the NBR representatives consider that in the analyzed period, TV was the most efficient, followed by online and print. Interviewees acknowledge the role of the media as a primary source of information about central banks, as highlighted by studies such as those of Berger et al. (2006) and Böhm et al. (2012). According to respondents, after 2008, the NBR used the media to reach audiences in two of the three ways defined by Velthuis (2015): as a neutral tool for the transmission of disseminated information and as a tool for amplification (the third way defined by the researcher is as a propaganda tool for reaching audiences). At the same time, most interviewees stressed the need for the central bank to adapt to the changing media landscape, in line with the observations of researchers Haldane and McMahon (2018) and Riles (2018).

## 5.7 Should the NBR Go on Facebook?

The present research also evaluated the opinion of the NBR representatives regarding the diversification of communication channels, by opening new official accounts on social networks. Until the time of the interviews, in 2017, the NBR had a website, a blog (Opiniibnr.ro), and LinkedIn, YouTube, and Twitter accounts. In December 2019, NBR launched its official Instagram account.

The analysis regarding the NBR's presence on social networks takes into account the traffic registered on these networks in Romania, reflected by various analyzes and statistics. For example, in January 2020, in terms of market share, social media was divided, between Facebook (87.02%), Instagram (4.41%), Pinterest (4.36%), Twitter (2.43%), YouTube (1.21%), and Reddit (0.19%) (Statcounter, 2020). At the end of January 2020, there were approximately 11 million Facebook users in Romania and over 41,100 active pages, over 866,000 YouTube users, on Instagram—over 1.13 million users, while Twitter had added over 375,000 Romanian users, of which only about 15,000 are active (ZeList, 2020).

Half of the interviewees supported launching an official NBR Facebook account, but added conditions such as blocking comments, selecting topics, and carefully analyzing the public agenda of nonmonetary topics of debate involving the central bank. One-fifth of the respondents strongly opposed such a perspective in diversifying the communication channels, and one-third of the respondents considered that it could be a communication channel to be considered, but appreciated that, in the general communication context, marked by numerous crisis communication situations at the time of the interviews, such diversification would not be appropriate.

Interviewees who supported the launch of an official Facebook account raised four main arguments: the need for the central bank to reach new audience segments, the opportunity to educate the general public, direct access to topics and debates propagated exclusively on this communication channel and the need to keep up with new trends in communication. For example, one respondent believes that "Facebook creates realities, private audiences. That is, a subject can have a huge audience on Facebook, with a structure that you cannot identify unless you study the Facebook phenomenon. The bank's Facebook account must be created, new jobs will appear, others will disappear" (Interviewee no. 2). An interviewee who considers that the central bank must be present on the channels on which its public is located believes that it is time for a change in the mentality of central bankers: "the resistance to change in the mindset of central bankers who are used to communicate with specialists, but not with the disinterested general public, this type of resistance must go" (Interviewee no. 10). Some respondents believe that "Facebook would bring added value" (Interviewee no. 4), that the presence on the social network would humanize the institution: "we are perceived as closed here, we do not know what is with the world, we look seem aloof and disconnected. And it's not really like that" (Interviewee no. 17).

Of those who supported a NBR Facebook account, one respondent assessed asked for the blocking of comments "On Facebook, and not only on Facebook, blogs in general have one big disadvantage: from dark courtyards throw stones at illuminated streets. Usually, those online use their real names and publicly assume their identity and positions. On Facebook, you can have Stefan the Great and Dracula and other pseudonyms who from dark courtyards, throw stones, boulders even at those who pass" (Interviewee no. 1). Another interviewee sees a NBR Facebook account as a necessary compromise, a change forced exclusively by pressure from the general public: "Unfortunately, I think so. If only for the fact that those under 30 don't even watch anything else, they don't even watch TV, not to mention newspapers. In order to talk to them, you have to get on social media" (Interviewee no. 3).

Regarding the appropriate content for this communication channel, some of the favorable respondents, but also among those who consider that it was not yet appropriate at the time of the interviews, consider that it should be selected, in a first stage, from the area of financial education and the history of the NBR, on capitalizing the Central Bank Museum: "for communication campaigns, you can start with the Museum, with financial education, with what is unique (...) And then, taking advantage of the fact that you are unique and you have a lot of values, you can attract your audience and then send them the messages you want them to receive" (Interviewee no. 18); "I would recommend it for education, museum, financial education and I would open up Facebook only for taking online questions during press conferences" (Interviewee no. 10). Another interviewee is of the opinion that the presence on social networks is necessary and emphasizes "an impeccable communication behavior, as the NBR has been doing for some time. From messages written correctly from a grammatical point of view and to their content" (Interviewee no. 15).

Respondents who considered a Facebook presence, but not in the near future, unanimously pointed out to the unfavorable communication context, marked by many episodes of crisis communication: "I think it will be like a battle here, a melee, because you will have to respond to every comment and especially the negative ones" (Interviewee no. 13). The respondents add the difficulty of establishing a real dialogue with the general public, the absence of a common background with the public, human resources, but also limited content to respond to each message: "you have little in common. Plus, social media has this fundamental problem that there is no defined common platform to base a dialogue on. So what are we talking about? It's not clear. And if we don't start from some common points, this dialogue, which is still complicated in social media, can't really be organized" (Interviewee no. 16); "(...) there are a lot of crazy discussions. Now what, we intersperse in these discussions, we become protagonists, what do we do? I think it's a big mistake. Big mistake. There is the big problem of fake news, which affects us, but here it is a quasi-general problem, it also concerns governments" (Interviewee no. 19).

All four respondents who strongly rejected the launch of a NBR Facebook account motivated their opinion by evaluating the institution's profile, a limited dialogue on this communication channel, exposure and interaction with a hostile public, the absence of a common background (knowledge), context generally unfavorable, the mandate of the central bank, all generating, in the opinion of the interviewees, a small impact on the public. One interviewee refers to the hostile publics and to the exit from the traditional mandate of the NBR, militating for the use of the social network exclusively with a personal account, for expressing their own opinions (Interviewee no. 7). Three other interviewees evaluate the usefulness of the Facebook channel rather to capture the messages, but not to transmit them, as the social network is not considered appropriate to the profile of the institution (Interviewees no. 9, no. 11, no. 14).

In conclusion, half of the NBR representatives recognize the importance and relevance of Facebook as a communication channel and are in favor of the immediate launch of an official account of the institution, and 30% of respondents would accept it but not in the current period, marked by crises. The main favorable argument identified—reaching new segments of the audience—confirms that the central bank is trying to connect with the general public and is considering new communication channels, as recommended by specialists and researchers such as Haldane et al. (2020), Haldane and McMahon (2018), and Riles (2018). On the other hand, interviewees are skeptical about entering into a direct dialogue with the general public, a challenge for all categories of organizations confirmed by research such as that of Carr and Hayes (2015). NBR representatives are not optimistic about the interactivity with the public and the ability to send messages to this category of the institution's stakeholders, in line with the observations and research results on the limited effects on audiences generated by the adoption of new media channels by central banks (Haldane et al., 2020; Binder, 2017; Haldane, 2017; Shin, 2017; Bjelobaba et al., 2017; Vardy, 2015). According to one respondent, after 2008, given the crisis and the rise of social networks, the entire public communication is fundamentally reconfigured, including for central banks: "We have completely parted from the textbook. Moreover, I argued that, after the crisis, textbooks would be rewritten, including those on economics. And this is likely to happen, some have already begun to be rewritten (. . .) and communication books are being rewritten from cover to cover, because the public communication system has changed completely. First of all, Facebook and social networks in general killed the written press" (Interviewee no. 1).

## 5.8 Monetary Communication After 2008

### *5.8.1 Evaluating Communication as a Monetary Policy Tool*

The NBR included communication in its arsenal of monetary policy tools in 2005, with the adoption of the inflation targeting regime, therefore, shortly before the outbreak of the financial and economic crisis. The correct transmission of NBR messages regarding inflation, the evolution of prices of goods and services, to different categories of public has an important role in reaching the inflation target, as public expectations about the future, including those regarding future monetary policy decisions, influence current economic behavior. Thus, four questions from the interview grid aimed at evaluating monetary communication after 2008.

Three-quarters of respondents estimate that, after 2008, in terms of monetary communication, the central bank "adapted as well as possible" (Interviewee no. 1); the communication was "quite clear" (Interviewee no. 3); "It was good, clear enough" (Interviewee no. 5); "It was appropriate, given that we had no experience in crisis communication. It was trial and error" (Interviewee no. 4); "We were moderate" (Interviewee no. 9). One interviewee, who believes that inflation reports addressed to the general public have been simplified in recent years, emphasizes the importance of communication and transparency for the effectiveness of monetary policy: "other mechanisms work in vain (...) if the financial sector does not know what it is behind your decisions, what are your motivations, if you do not explain to them why you are making those decisions it is quite difficult to gain their trust, you make them more cautious" (Interviewee no. 7).

Shortcomings in the public information channel occur, according to respondents, either because of the media that sometimes distorts them (Interviewee no. 1) or because of hostile stakeholders, who challenge monetary policy decisions, ignoring the rational arguments put forward by the central bank ("When you are demonized, the human mind no longer pays attention to arguments. And if the key messages are not very well crafted, your arguments won't matter to people as they were already told that the NBR protects the banks so they'll resonate to what they expect to hear"—Interviewee no. 2). Another respondent has a more nuanced opinion and evaluates differently the efficiency of monetary communication, depending on the category of target audience—less accessible to the general public, but clearer for the specialized public: "Let's not be naive and believe that monetary policy can be debated in the public sphere and be understood by more than a few hundred people. But for the specialized public? Yes, I think things have improved here, including on the communication side, and the press releases are more accessible, I have gone beyond the Greenspanian saying (e.g., based on deliberate ambiguity as promoted by A. Greenspan, former Fed governor) that «If you understood more than a certain percentage of what I said, then I was wrong». It is clear that things are changing, that the paradigm has changed, that we need to tell people more simply what we have to say" (Interviewee no. 17).

The comments of the respondents, who consider that the general public's trust in the central bank and in the NBR governor is always efficient: "No one in Romania can, or can claim to be able to, communicate better than him (author's note: the governor)"; In the first years after 2008, "people were looking at the NBR to see what the governor was saying," whose statements were not yet "interpreted" by televisions (Interviewee no. 15).

Opinions are divided on the role of the TV channel in framing NBR messages about inflation. For example, one respondent considers that the objectives of monetary communication have been achieved, but not necessarily due to the use of basic tools, such as the Inflation Report, but rather through the massive use of television (Interviewee no. 16). In the opinion of the same interviewee, the NBR messages were very well interpreted by the specialized public due to the line of communication, "a wooden language, if you will, which was translated quite well and these repetitive communications from one month to another, with little change, they started to be understood quite well." In terms of content, "the in-house message was studied much better, before going to the public, and the voices were diversified" (Interviewee no. 2).

Three interviewees considered either that the central bank did not effectively manage monetary communication after 2008, or that the governor's public appearances were too frequent on other topics or that the central bank is not connected to what the public thinks and expects: "The NBR has not worked enough on monetary policy and our mandate. Then, the minute could have been published earlier, before being requested, it would have been very good" (Interviewee no. 18); "Monetary policy should be guided by what we expect to happen in the future. Or I have not seen this type of speech in the public space from our representatives. In our country, monetary policy decisions are always based on current economic factors, and very little on what they should be based on. And that's why I say that the public doesn't have very clearly fixed landmarks, what to look for" (Interviewee no. 8).

The main challenges for the future monetary communication of the NBR are within the limits of the explanations provided to the public ("the problem is how much you give information, how you explain the given information, how you make it accessible, if you give it in raw form or if you try to explain better certain indicators, parameters"—Interviewee no. 6). Other challenges are revisiting the models and concepts with which the central bank operates (Interviewee no. 19), maintaining coherence when messages are communicated in several voices (Interviewee no. 2), as well as the correct understanding of the significance of inflation targeting: "What was not understood here and somehow wrongly transmitted was the understanding of the inflation target, ie the target was understood as a stationary point, if you hit it, it's fine, if not—you missed it. This is a problem of message transmission that must be understood rather as a trend, than as a point" (Interviewee no. 16).

In conclusion, according to the results obtained in RQ6, three-quarters of the respondents consider that, after 2008, the monetary communication was transparent, clear, and efficient. The opinions of the NBR representatives are in agreement with the studies on the transparency of central banks, which show that monetary policy generates the best effects if it is predictable (Dincer & Eichengreen, 2013; Holmes, 2014; Jeanneau, 2009; Cournède & Minegishi, 2009; Blinder et al., 2008; Bernanke & Woodford, 2007; Woodford, 2005; Bernanke et al., 2001; Faust & Svensson, 2001). Some respondents appreciate that progress has been made toward simplifying and making messages more transparent, especially for the specialized public. The role of the media in transmitting NBR messages is assessed differently: on the one hand, it distorts and simplifies the central bank's messages, looking for "sensationalism" or "more popularly formulated messages", on the other—the media, and especially television, are appreciated for the role played in the efficiency of monetary communication.

### 5.8.2 Are Changes Toward Greater Transparency Reversible?

After 2008, the NBR continued its efforts toward greater transparency of monetary communication, which is currently manifested by the publication of the calendar of monetary policy meetings of the Board of Directors, the publication of monetary policy decisions and their presentation by the governor in press briefings, the presentation, in regular conferences, of the Inflation Report and of the Stability Report. The transparency process included, in 2016, a new communication practice of publishing the minutes of monetary policy meetings. In the same year, the central bank decided to make public the incomes of the members of the NBR Board. Through this research, we assessed the extent to which the NBR representatives consider that the steps taken toward greater transparency will remain.

Three-quarters of respondents (15) consider that the publication of the minutes—the most recent decision towards transparency—is not reversible post the 2008 economic and financial crisis. Two respondents considered that this measure could be reversible in the long-term putting the explanation in historical perspective: "History tells me so (…): Nothing won is definitely won. So the process of transparency will depend on how society will evolve" (Interviewee no. 13); "In principle, I do not think it is something irreversible" (Interviewee no. 4). Three interviewees did not respond or found it difficult to assess the prospects of monetary communication: "I do not know where the communication will go, I have no idea if there will be less transparency. It is difficult to say, there are many factors to take into account, and political, not only financial and banking factors" (Interviewee no. 3).

Estimating that the NBR will not give up the transparency measures, the interviewees characterize the publication of the minutes as progress (Interviewee no. 2); a decision that reduces "the volatility of expectations and uncertainties" (Interviewee no. 4); "Information that is as complete as possible contributes to market regulation" (Interviewee no. 5); a measure that brought the NBR "into a select company" (Interviewee no. 8); a practice of the big central banks (Interviewee no. 19); an evolution in monetary communication—"we have very good standards of transparency" (Interviewee no. 16). Moreover, one interviewee appreciates that the efficiency of transparency would increase if the minute would include the names of decision makers, because, in his opinion, the minute should make you accountable, and knowing that you are accountable and transparent you become more careful in what you do" (Interviewee no. 7).

Some of the interviewees believe that publishing the minutes is an irreversible change in the context of profound changes in society ("No. The world has changed its style. And no one on the planet discusses the return to the old lifestyle"—

Interviewee no. 1), and based foreseen negative reactions of the public (Interviewee no. 14).

Even if they anticipate the preservation of transparent practices, the interviewees also exposed some limitations and criticisms, either referring to the reactive nature of certain decisions and reactions, or—to the perception that, in the political context at the time of interviews, the transparency of communication is altered: "It's more and more the atmosphere that you don't have to talk, you started to be afraid to talk. So if we are afraid to talk, it means that our communication will be altered, that is, it will not be as clear, it will be influenced by the idea that we must not upset anyone. So society has changed and communication will change. I don't think we will regress in technical terms, but in terms of climate we will not be able to practice what we learned. Basically, we have already returned to hiding. We have reduced transparency" (Interviewee no. 2). One respondent drew attention to the debates on the independence of the central bank and the possible impact on transparency: "I see, an interesting discussion about the status of the bank, and the independence of the bank. And then, yes, many things can change. As soon as the subject of central bank independence changes, then ... but let's just say it's not acute yet. But in the future this will be the discussion" (Interviewee no. 16).

Regarding the publication of the earned incomes of NBR Board members, two of the respondents consider that by publishing them late and only upon request, another stone was set for the erosion of the general public's trust in the central bank (Interviewees no. 2 and no. 10), and one interviewee considers that another important step towards transparency would be to publish salary bands similar as the ECB does (Interviewee no. 7). The interviewees also point out a series of negative effects of wage transparency, with an impact on certain NBR stakeholders. For example, one respondent argues that the publication of such a grid generates competition from other institutions to reach the same salary thresholds (Interviewee no. 4). At the same time, the importance of the media reaction and the context of crisis communication at the time of the transparency decision was emphasized: "Is the press ready to understand the type of transparency or what we mean? And we have to build that training. At this moment, as we are under attack, it is very difficult to prepare something like that" (Interviewee no. 16).

Two of the respondents claim that the publication of revenues is a decision that is not part of the transparency required by the central bank: "Transparency must be within the responsibilities and roles of the bank (...) It seems to me an excess of mandate" (Interviewee no. 9); "Who is it useful to? In the end, as every human being must have his own intimacy so does an institution, it must have privacy" (Interviewee no. 11).

Summarizing the results obtained on RQ7, three-quarters of the NBR representatives are of the opinion that the publication of the minutes—the most recent decision toward transparency, taken in 2016—is not reversible post the 2008 crisis. The answers of the 20 representatives of the central bank confirm some of the results of the Blinder et al. (2017) showing that over 70% of central bank governors estimate that changes in institutions' communication will remain or further develop even after the effects of the 2008 crisis have ended, and that, in terms of using forward guidance—59% of governors considered that it will remain a communication tool.

## 5.9 Post-crisis Communication Lessons

During the qualitative research, the interviewees were challenged to formulate the main lessons learned after 2008 following the public communication activity. Without being guided in their answers, three-quarters of the respondents (15) referred to improving relations with different categories of NBR stakeholders (specialized public, general public, media). Regarding the specialized public, the respondents considered that it is necessary to cultivate partnerships with certain professional organizations for the transmission of NBR messages. Respondents also identified gaps in the financial education of the specialized public and appreciate that it is important to understand the motivations of different segments of the public.

Referring to the relationship with the general public, respondents point out that the rational arguments of the central bank do not work in an emotional context, during a crisis, or in front of a hostile public, that it is necessary to change the mentality of central bankers towards greater openness to the public. At the same time, the respondents underlined NBR's need to better inform and educate. The interviewees consider that, after 2008, given the crisis and the technological advance, the relationship of the central bank with the media changed towards verbal communication through press releases, and moved away from written communication through press releases (Interviewee no. 1), it changed toward a constant dialogue (Interviewee no. 19). The respondents highlighted the increased importance of a common background for the objective transmission of messages on certain topics (Interviewee no. 16).

Regarding the communication strategy, the interviewees referred to the importance of issues such as preparing communication before the emergence of crisis communication situations, fighting planned misinformation, being proactive, diversifying communication channels, using empathy and sincerity in messages to the public. Two of the respondents stressed the need for better organization and internal communication, and one-fifth of the respondents made general recommendations around some keywords: caution, prevention, empathy.

### *5.9.1 New Strategies in Stakeholders' Communication*

The challenges of the 2008 crisis, over which technological advancement overlapped, required the central bank to be more transparent, including counter attacks by hostile audiences and the fake-news phenomenon. According to one respondent: "the crisis plus the media (...) have forced greater transparency, more frankness, and a quasi-permanent dialogue. Because the online, which replaced the print, is more demanding and it is always on, as the markets are open 24 hours a day (...) The challenges of communication as a function of the central bank are incomparably greater than they were now 10–15 years. You have technological evolutions and the impact of the financial and economic crisis, you have evolutions in the banking system. From all this arises a burden for communicators" (Interviewee no. 19).

Respondents also believe that the main vector of central bank communication is the media, and that after 2008, amid the crisis and the rise of social networks, public communication has changed fundamentally, the importance of written communication has decreased and social networks "killed the written press"; "And the crisis came and then the whole communication system of the central bank changed, the direct dialogue was in the forefront, the verbal communication without communiqués came to the forefront" (Interviewee no. 1). Interviewee no. 1 considers that the central bank is still far from "textbook communication": "I always understood that one day will come when the NBR's communication will textbook. This day has not come yet. A central bank should not face the problems facing the NBR. Communication should be done differently in a system where the legislation is clear, where legal issues are well understood and discussed in a separate department, where laws apply."

Some of the interviewees appreciate that the limits of "classic" communication, as shown after 2008, can be overcome with the help of new means of communication, whose impact is increasing (Interviewee no. 4). At the same time, the respondents emphasize the limits of rational, objective arguments, in an emotional context and on assuming a smaller number of responsibilities (Interviewees no. 2, no. 3). And Interviewee no. 6 focuses on the NBR's relationship with hostile audiences and considers that, in order to correct the information misrepresented by the media, the NBR should build "a site to expose alternative facts (...) It is true that we are a central bank and we cannot get involved in disputes that others can bring to the lowest level (...), but somewhere you have to do something with those in bad faith."

One of the respondents summarizes lessons learned as proactive communication, in good times, alliances with various stakeholder groups to convey central bank messages in times of crisis communication, rational arguments that cannot be imposed on emotional ones, the importance of sincerity and acknowledging one's mistakes: "So it is important, when you are wrong, and sometimes you will be, to be fair and to acknowledge this. Something that almost no central bank in the world does, to be honest" (Interviewee no. 3). And Interviewee no. 17 also supports communication vectors outside the central bank.

Another interviewee emphasized the proactivity in communication, the preparation of certain topics, but also the common background with various stakeholders (population, media, other audiences), the preparation of communication before episodes of crisis communication: "I think that in calm times, the communication strategy should define topics on which to rely when crises occur" (Interviewee no. 16). For another respondent, the lessons are maintaining the ethical–legal framework, having a firm reaction on formal channels, maintaining informal communication, drawing attention to the messages of leaders and influencers

(Interviewee no. 5). For the Interviewee no. 11, the 2008 crisis showed that "this specialized public is very slippery, because it is enslaved", and gives the example of the relations between the NBR and the commercial banks: "the barricade between the two camps, so to speak, is, has been and will be forever, because the interests are different, you want the risk to be as low as possible (...) they want the profit to be as high as possible."

For Interviewee no. 10, the essence of the post-crisis lessons is the central bankers' change in mentality, a greater openness toward the general public, and meeting the general public on new communication channels. Interviewee no. 18 sees as main lessons post 2008 crisis, the proactivity in public communication, the diversification of communication channels with a more pronounced online presence and greater empathy in the messages transmitted on certain topics.

The interviewees focused on informing the general public, but also the specialized one (authorities, judges, etc.), in connection with the banking financial market instruments and the NBR regulations: "financial education must be done not only at the level of ordinary consumers, but also at the level of authorities and entities responsible for certain segments, including those who provide solutions in cases of violations of regulations, abuses and so on" (Interviewee no. 9). Another interviewee refers to the approach of the specialized public, but this time—of the one represented by the bankers—as "the crisis is caused not first of all by the citizens' ignorance of finance, of the financial system, but was essentially caused by bad practices in the financial-banking industry and some errors of central banks. Large central banks. We are talking about the need for financial education. Well, bankers need financial education. That is, to give up bad practices" (Interviewee no. 19).

### 5.9.2 *Internal Communication*

The post-crisis period highlighted, in the opinion of two interviewees, some dysfunctions in the internal communication of the institution. They consider that the lesson of the crisis "is simple: we need to re-transform the NBR into an institution as I don't think it's an institution right now. It is a group of Directorates that work together occasionally for a common goal and, most of the time, they probably do their job, but they are not taken into account" (Interviewee no. 8). A second lesson touches upon how the Directorates are run ("you must realize that only together with others can you achieve the purpose for which you are paid"). And a third lesson concerns the internal consultation of specialists in more technical issues. In turn, another interviewee said that, during the crisis, the need for greater support from internal communication for external communication was highlighted: "without internal communication you cannot have external communication (...) What will you communicate if you are not supported?" (Interviewee no. 18).

### 5.9.3 *Caution and Prevention*

From the series of lessons and general recommendations, we note caution and prevention. For example, two respondents consider that, after 2008, the main lesson is that of caution: "what we had in 2008 globally is something we had not had for 80 years (...) it is a unique event, and although we cannot say that we should be much, much, much more cautious because the same thing could happen every year, I'd say that we need to be little more cautious" (Interviewee no. 7); "I believe that, in Romania, and given the reporting of the NBR to the Romanian society, prudence, combined with well-calculated initiatives, is what we should learn from the crisis and apply in our communication. And it is clear that we do not communicate in general, we communicate on particular issues using specific tools" (Interviewee no. 13). According to another respondent, the first post-crisis lesson is prevention, anticipating mistakes, "you have to be more symmetrical, in the sense that you realize that once the banking industry creates systemic risks it has to change its behavior, you can't defend them no matter what they do. Such a thing is not acceptable. And we didn't say it enough to the public" (Interviewee no. 19).

## 5.10 Conclusions

The interpretation of the 20 semi-structured interviews highlighted the way in which the NBR representatives perceived the changes in the institution's public communication after 2008. The interviewees' opinion regarding the nonmonetary and monetary public communication activities of the institution is unanimous in supporting that fundamental, visible and irreversible changes have taken place towards greater transparency, both against the background of the economic and financial crisis, but also in the context of technological advancement and the rise of new media.

First of all, compared to the pre-crisis period, the central bank communicated more with various categories of public, according to the perception of a large majority of respondents. Communication in several voices, diversification of topics, drafting, and structuring of messages were the most invoked changes in the NBR communication by two-thirds of the respondents. However, the research did not identify a consensus on the central bank's best communication strategy in terms of multi-voice versus single-voice communication, and some respondents believe that strategic silence on certain topics with potential crisis communication can help shorten the duration of their exposure to the media. The interviewees are of the opinion that the NBR has assumed too many responsibilities compared to the duties conferred by its mandate, has entered too much into controversies on monetary and nonmonetary issues and hinted that it has answers to all questions, which increased its vulnerability.

Jargon adaptation is a concern for most NBR respondents. Respondents have seen visible progress in simplifying the language for the general public and believe that the NBR is part of the general efforts of central banks around the world to adapt financial-banking jargon, a trend outlined before the 2008 crisis. Respondents also take into account the involvement of other categories of stakeholders (journalists, specialists in academia), in addition to simplifying language, and using correct and clear messages to the general public.

Regarding the three communication situations analyzed in this chapter—the crisis of Greek banks, the Swiss franc loans crisis and the legislative changes in the banking sector—respondents believe that the NBR messages were difficult to convey to the general public or that they even lacked entirely because of how the central bank drafted and transmitted the messages (without empathy, transmitted in several voices, late, reactive in some situations), because of the competing messages of other stakeholders, and because the media intervened in the framing process, printing negative articles and labelling the central bank as "bank lawyer." Respondents believe that the way in which the media framed the official statements of NBR representatives on crisis management could have had a major impact on the transmission of information to the general public.

The present research also highlights relevant aspects of the way in which the NBR representatives perceived the erosion of the public trust in the institution. Respondents' comments on the impact of the 2008 crisis on the NBR's reputation and credibility confirm that the erosion of confidence has not bypassed the Romanian central bank, even if this market has not faced bank failures or the need to implement unconventional monetary policy measures. The magnitude of the decline in public confidence in the NBR is assessed differently by respondents: in the perception of more than half of respondents, the NBR was affected by a "big" and "very high" confidence crisis after 2008, while the rest of the interviewees consider that it was an insignificant erosion of trust or that it was a failed attempt at erosion by some stakeholders. The decline in public confidence in the NBR during the financial crisis can be explained, in the perception of central bank representatives, by complementary factors: (1) the communication strategy of opposing stakeholders (interest groups that launched public attacks on the institution and management, commercial banks did not communicate with the NBR on common topics, a part of the media having aired certain negative frameworks in connection with the central bank); (2) the low level of public financial education on the Romanian market; (3) strategic communication of the central bank; (4) the very high level of credibility achieved by the NBR before 2008 and in the first part of the crisis; (5) assuming, on the basis of a high reputation, duties which have gone beyond the traditional mandate of the central bank; and (6) the widespread loss of public confidence in the main players in the global financial markets after 2008.

Interviewees acknowledge the role of the media as a primary source of information for the general public about central banks and stressed the need for the NBR to adapt to changing media. In the opinion of the NBR representatives, the most efficient communication channel in the post-crisis period for transmitting messages to the public was the TV, followed by online and print. According to the respondents, to reach various categories of public, the NBR used the media mainly as a neutral tool for the transmission of disseminated information and as a tool for amplifying messages.

Half of the interviewed NBR representatives favorably evaluate the consolidation of the presence in the online environment, on social networks, recognize the importance and relevance of Facebook as a communication channel and are in favor of the immediate launch of an official account of the institution. Almost a third of respondents believe that the launch should be considered in a period not marked by crisis communication situations. The main favorable argument identified—reaching new segments of the audience—confirms that the central bank is trying to connect with the general public and is considering new communication channels. At the same time, some of the interviewees are skeptical about entering into a quasi-permanent direct dialogue with the general public and about the effectiveness of this channel.

Regarding monetary communication, three-quarters of respondents consider that, after 2008, it was transparent, clear, and efficient, and the views of NBR representatives are in line with studies on the transparency of central banks, which show that monetary policy is most effective if it is predictable. Some respondents appreciate that progress has been made towards simplifying and making messages more transparent, especially for the specialized public. The role of the media in transmitting NBR messages is assessed differently: on the one hand, it distorts and simplifies the central bank's messages, looking for "sensationalism" or "more popularly formulated messages," on the other—the media, and especially television, are appreciated for the role played in the efficiency of monetary communication. According to 75% of respondents, the publication of the minutes, the most recent decision toward transparency, taken by the NBR in 2016, does not represent a reversible change after the end of the effects of the 2008 economic and financial crisis.

This analysis foretells a reconfiguration of the NBR's relations with all categories of stakeholders for better transmission of messages. The main directions announced are the diversification of communication channels, the simplification of language, the concern for the financial education of the public. To these are added changes in content, with an emphasis on empathy and the formulation of arguments depending on the emotional context in which public debates take place, but also tactical, toward a more proactive attitude. We believe that this study paves the way for future research to reflect the extent to which changes in NBR public communication will continue in the new crisis context generated by the COVID-19 pandemic and how these changes will contribute to the efficient transmission of messages to different categories of the public and, finally, to regain public confidence in the central bank.

## References


Berger, H., Ehrmann, M., & Fratzscher, M. (2006). *Monetary policy in the media*. ECB Working Paper No. 679. https://doi.org/10.2139/ssrn.931350

Bernanke, B. S., & Woodford, M. (Eds.). (2007). *The inflation-targeting debate* (Vol. 32). University of Chicago Press.

Bernanke, B., Laubach, T., Mishkin, F. S., & Posen, A. S. (2001). *Inflation targeting: Lessons from the international experience*. Princeton University Press.

Binder, C. (2017). Fed speak on main street: Central bank communication and household expectations. *Journal of Macroeconomics, 52*, 238–251. https://doi.org/10.1016/j.jmacro.2017.05.003

Bjelobaba, G., Savic, A., & Stefanovic, H. (2017). *Analysis of central banks platforms on social networks*. UBT International Conference. Retrieved from https://knowledgecenter.ubt-uni.net/cgi/viewcontent.cgi?article=1223&context=conference.

Blinder, A. S. (2013). *After the music stopped: The financial crisis, the response, and the work ahead*. Penguin.

Blinder, A. S., Ehrmann, M., Fratzscher, M., de Haan, J., & Jansen, D. J. (2008). Central bank communication and monetary policy: A survey of theory and evidence. *Journal of Economic Literature, 46*(4), 910–945. Retrieved from https://pubs.aeaweb.org/doi/pdfplus/10.1257/jel.46.4.910

Blinder, A., Ehrmann, M., De Haan, J., & Jansen, D. J. (2017). Necessity as the mother of invention: Monetary policy after the crisis. *Economic Policy, 32*(92), 707–755. https://doi.org/10.1093/epolic/eix013

Böhm, J., Král, P., & Saxa, B. (2012). The Czech National Bank's monetary policy in the media. *European Journal of Political Economy, 28*(3), 341–357. https://doi.org/10.1016/j.ejpoleco.2012.01.004

Bourne, C. (2011). *Public relations' role as trust strategist: A specialist niche evolves from turbulence*. EUPRERA Annual Conference 2011. Retrieved from http://orca.cf.ac.uk/29796/1/BourneTrust%20Strategist.pdf

Callaghan, K., & Schnell, F. (2001). Assessing the democratic debate: How the news media frame elite policy discourse. *Political Communication, 18*(2), 183–213.

Carr, C. T., & Hayes, R. A. (2015). Social media: Defining, developing, and divining. *Atlantic Journal of Communication, 23*(1), 46–65. https://doi.org/10.1080/15456870.2015.972282

Chong, D., & Druckman, J. N. (2007). A theory of framing and opinion formation in competitive elite environments. *Journal of Communication, 57*(1), 99–118. https://doi.org/10.1111/j.1460-2466.2006.00331.x

Ciocca, P. (2016). *Stabilising capitalism. A greater role for central banks*. Palgrave Macmillan.

Cournède, B., & Minegishi, M. (2009). *The role of transparency in the conduct of monetary policy*. OECD Economics Department Working Papers, No. 724. OECD. https://doi.org/10.1787/221128317344

Croitoru, L. (2011). *Lichiditatea, atacul speculativ din octombrie 2008 şi reputaţia băncii centrale*. National Bank of Romania. Retrieved from www.bnro.ro

de Vreese, C. H. (2002). *Framing Europe: Television news and European integration*. Aksant Academic.

de Vreese, C. H. (2005). News framing: Theory and typology. *Information Design Journal and Document Design, 13*(1), 51–62. Retrieved from https://asset-pdf.scinapse.io/prod/2089363775/2089363775.pdf

Dincer, N., & Eichengreen, B. (2013). Central bank transparency and independence: Updates and new measures. *International Journal of Central Banking, 10*(1), 189–253. https://doi.org/10.2139/ssrn.2579544

Edelman Trust Barometer. (2017). *Trust in crisis*. Retrieved from https://www.edelman.com/research/2017-edelman-trust-barometer

Ehrmann, M., & Fratzscher, M. (2005). Communication by central bank committee members: Different strategies, same effectiveness? *Journal of Money, Credit and Banking, 39*(2–3), 509–541.

Ehrmann, M., Soudan, M., & Stracca, L. (2013). Explaining European Union citizens' trust in the European Central Bank in normal and crisis times. *The Scandinavian Journal of Economics, 115*(3), 781–807.

El-Erian, M. A. (2016). *The only game in town: Central banks, instability, and avoiding the next collapse*. Random House.

Entman, R. M. (1993). Framing: Toward clarification of a fractured paradigm. *Journal of Communication, 43*(4), 51–58.

Entman, R. M. (2003). Cascading activation: Contesting the White House's frame after 9/11. *Political Communication, 20*(4), 415–432. https://doi.org/10.1080/10584600390244176

Faust, J., & Svensson, L. E. (2001). Transparency and credibility: Monetary policy with unobservable goals. *International Economic Review, 42*(2), 369–397. Retrieved from https://www.nber.org/papers/w6452.pdf

Fischer, J. A., & Hahn, V. (2008). *Determinants of trust in the European Central Bank*. SSE/EFI Working Paper Series in Economics and Finance. Retrieved from https://www.econstor.eu/bitstream/10419/56308/1/56082744X.pdf

Freeman, R. E. (1984). *Strategic management: A stakeholder approach*. Pitman.

Fusalba, T. (2012). *Managementul crizei*. Editura C.H.Beck.

Gamson, W. A., & Modigliani, A. (1989). Media discourse and public opinion on nuclear power: A constructionist approach. *American Journal of Sociology, 95*(1), 1–37.

Gitlin, T. (1980). *The whole world is watching: Mass media in the making and unmaking of the new left*. University of California.

Greenspan, A. (2007). *The age of turbulence: Adventures in a new world*. Penguin Press.

Haldane, A. (2016). *The great divide*. Speech presented at the New City Agenda Annual dinner. Retrieved from https://www.bankofengland.co.uk/-/media/boe/files/speech/2016/the-great-divide.pdf.

Haldane, A. (2017). *A little more conversation. A little less action*. Speech at the Federal Reserve Bank of San Francisco. Retrieved from https://www.bis.org/review/r170403e.pdf

Haldane, A. & McMahon, M. (2018). Central Bank Communications and the General Public. *AEA Papers and Proceedings, 108*, 578–583. https://doi.org/10.1257/pandp.20181082

Haldane, A., Macaulay, A., & McMahon, M. (2020). *The 3 E's of central bank communication with the public*. Staff Working Paper No. 847. Bank of England. Retrieved from https://www.bankofengland.co.uk/-/media/boe/files/working-paper/2020/the-3-es-of-central-bank-communication-with-the-public.pdf?la=enșihash=B3D34A003BB6F2B7D5653B265966DF11C8F75154

Holmes, D. R. (2014). *Economy of words: Communicative imperatives in central banks*. University of Chicago Press.

Iacob, R. (2018). Trust and transparency: Perspectives upon the communication of the National Bank of Romania during the financial crisis—A qualitative research. *Management Dynamics in the Knowledge Economy, 6*(1), 129–144. https://doi.org/10.25019/MDKE/6.1.08

INSCOP Research. (2016). *Barometrul ADEVĂRUL despre ROMÂNIA*. Retrieved from https://www.inscop.ro/category/2016-cercetari/

INSCOP Research. (2019). *Topul încrederii în instituții interne și internaționale*. Retrieved from https://www.inscop.ro/22-martie-2019-topul-increderii-in-institutii-interne-si-internationale/

Iyengar, S. (1991). *Is anyone responsible? How television frames political issues*. University of Chicago Press.

Iyengar, S., & Kinder, D. R. (1987). *News that matters: Agenda-setting and priming in a television age*. University of Chicago Press.

Jeanneau, S. (2009). *Communication of monetary policy decisions by central banks: What is revealed and why*. BIS Papers. Retrieved from https://www.bis.org/publ/bppdf/bispap47.pdf

King, M. (2016). *The end of alchemy: Money, banking, and the future of the global economy*. Little, Brown.

Law no. 77/2016. (2016). *Legea nr. 77/2016 privind darea în plată a unor bunuri imobile în vederea stingerii obligațiilor asumate prin credite*. Retrieved from https://lege5.ro/Gratuit/geydmnruheyq/legea-nr-77-2016-privind-darea-in-plata-a-unor-bunuri-imobile-in-vederea-stingerii-obligatiilor-asumate-prin-credite

Libaert, T. (2008). *Comunicarea de criză*. Bucureşti: Editura C.H. Beck.

Maor, M., Gilad, S., & Bloom, P. B. N. (2013). Organizational reputation, regulatory talk, and strategic silence. *Journal of Public Administration Research and Theory, 23*(3), 581–608. https://doi.org/10.1093/jopart/mus047

Marcussen, M. (2009). Scientization of central banking: The politics of a-politicization. In K. Dyson & M. Marcussen (Eds.), *Central banks in the age of the Euro: Europeanization, convergence, and power* (pp. 373–390). Oxford University Press.

Matthes, J., & Kohring, M. (2008). The content analysis of media frames: Toward improving reliability and validity. *Journal of Communication, 58*(2), 258–279. https://doi.org/10.1111/j.1460-2466.2008.00384.x

McLeod, D. M., & Shah, D. V. (2015). *News frames and national security. Covering big brother*. Cambridge University Press.

Moretti, F., & Pestre, D. (2015). Bankspeak: The language of World Bank reports. *New Left Review, 92*(2), 75–99.

National Bank of Romania. (2008). *Annual report—2008*. Retrieved from https://www.bnr.ro/PublicationDocuments.aspx?icid=6874

National Bank of Romania. (2015). *Răspunsurile direcţiilor de specialitate din BNR la întrebările punctuale adresate de membrii Comisiei pentru Buget, Finanţe şi Bănci din Camera Deputaţilor*. Retrieved from https://www.bnr.ro/Raspunsurile-directiilor-de-specialitate-din-BNR-12055-Mobile.aspx

National Bank of Romania. (2017). *Annual report (2017)*. Retrieved from https://www.bnro.ro/Regular-publications-2504.aspx

Owens, L. A. (2012). The polls—Trends: Confidence in banks, financial institutions, and wall street, 1971–2011. *Public Opinion Quarterly, 76*(1), 142–162.

Reuters Institute. (2019). *Digital News Report*, p. 103. Retrieved from http://www.digitalnewsreport.org/survey/2019/romania-2019/

Reuters Institute. (2020). *Digital News Report*, p. 80. Retrieved from https://reutersinstitute.politics.ox.ac.uk/sites/default/files/2020-06/DNR_2020_FINAL.pdf

Riles, A. (2018). *Financial citizenship: Experts, publics, and the politics of central banking*. Cornell University Press.

Scheufele, D. A., & Iyengar, S. (2011). The state of framing research: A call for new directions. In*The Oxford handbook of political communication theories* (pp. 1–26). Oxford University Press. https://doi.org/10.1093/oxfordhb/9780199793471.013.47

Shah, D. V., Domke, D., & Wackman, D. B. (1996). "To thine own self be true": Values, framing, and voter decision-making strategies. *Communication Research, 23*(5), 509–560.

Shin, H. S. (2017). *Can central banks talk too much?* Speech at the ECB conference on "Communications challenges for policy effectiveness, accountability and reputation". Retrieved from https://www.bis.org/speeches/sp171114.pdf

Smith, R. D. (2005). *Strategic planning for public relations*. Lawrence Erbaum Associates.

Statcounter. (2020). *Social media stats Romania*. Retrieved from https://gs.statcounter.com/social-media-stats/all/romania

't Hart, P., & Tindall, K. (2009). Understanding crisis exploitation: Leadership, rhetoric and framing contests in response to the economic meltdown. In P. 't Hart & K. Tindall (Eds.), *Framing the global economic downturn. Crisis rhetoric and the politics of recessions* (pp. 21–40). ANU E Press.

Tutino, A. (2016). Central bank communication must overcome the public's limited attention span. *Economic Letter, 11*(6), 1–4. Retrieved from http://www.dallasfed.org/assets/documents/research/eclett/2016/el1606.pdf

Vardy, J. (2015). *Reputational risk management in central banks* (No. 2015–16). Bank of Canada. Staff Discussion Paper.

Velthuis, O. (2015). Making monetary markets transparent: The European Central Bank's communication policy and its interactions with the media. *Economy and Society, 44*(2), 316–340. https://doi.org/10.1080/03085147.2015.1013355

Winkler, B. (2000). *Which kind of transparency? On the need for clarity in monetary policymaking*. ECB Working Paper, No. 26. European Central Bank (ECB). Retrieved from https://www.econstor.eu/bitstream/10419/152460/1/ecbwp0026.pdf

Woodford, M. (2005). *Central bank communication and policy effectiveness*. National Bureau of Economic Research. Retrieved from https://www.nber.org/papers/w11898.pdf

YouGov. (2019). *How clear, if at all, are you about what role the Bank of England carries out?* Retrieved from https://yougov.co.uk/topics/science/survey-results/daily/2019/04/24/12913/3

ZeList. (2020). *Overview social media in Romania—January 2020*. Retrieved from https://www.zelist.ro/blog/overview-social-media-in-ro-ianuarie-2020/

# Chapter 6
# Public Perception of the NBR Communication After 2008

The general objective of this chapter is to analyze the perception of two categories of NBR stakeholders—the specialized public and the general public—in connection with the changes toward greater transparency of public, monetary, and nonmonetary communication of the central bank in the post-crisis period. The questions focused on transparency, frequency of public appearances, evaluation of the language used by the institution's representatives or in the official reports of the central bank. At the same time, the level of public confidence in the central bank and the expectations regarding the changes in the NBR communication were assessed, following the seven research questions that guided the qualitative analysis of this research.

The sociological surveys based on questionnaires were carried out between May and July 2018, for the specialized public ($N = 186$), and between July and October 2019, for the general public ($N = 391$). The questions regarding the frequency of NBR communication after 2008, the assessment of the future role of central bank communication and the changes toward transparency of the decision-making process were adapted from the section dedicated to central bank communication on monetary issues in the 2016 questionnaire launched by Blinder et al. (2017). All other questions were built on the conceptual framework presented above, the specific context of the Romanian financial market after 2008 and the topics of debate that put the central bank on the public agenda. The collected data were processed with the SPSS Statistics program, version 17. The complete list of items can be consulted in the questionnaires in Annexes C and D.

## 6.1 Samples

Regarding the specialized public, reached exclusively through e-mail and LinkedIn, the respondents make a sample of convenience, cluster type due to the delimitation of the population profile—the specialized public of central banks being composed of bankers, analysts, investors, representatives of academia, the specialized media, etc.

---

The original version of this chapter was revised: Some changes have been made in the text now. The corrections to this chapter can be found at https://doi.org/10.1007/978-3-031-04067-2_9

© The Author(s), under exclusive license to Springer Nature Switzerland AG 2022, corrected publication 2022

R. Iacob, *Blind Spots in the Spotlight*, Financial and Monetary Policy Studies 53,
https://doi.org/10.1007/978-3-031-04067-2_6

About a third of the respondents represent academia (teachers from universities with an economic profile from across the country were targeted), 16% represent the financial-banking industry, 9%—media (the survey was sent to economics journalists), 9%—public relations industry, 8%—public sector, 6%—services, and 15%—other professional categories (law, trade, energy industry, etc.). In terms of gender, 55% (102) were women, and the mean age was 41.6 years ($M = 41.6$, SD $= 9.13$).

The sample of the general public, targeted through Facebook, is one of convenience, with a margin of error of ±5% and corresponds to a 95% accuracy, by reference to the active population of Romania. Over 17% of respondents were in the field of education, 11.7% represent the IT&C industry, 8.7%—media (the survey was distributed to general journalists), 7.7%—public relations industry, 6.9%—services, 6.4%—healthcare system, 6.4%—creative industries, and 12.8%—other professional categories (construction, bars and restaurants industry, textile industry, etc.). In terms of gender, over 70% (277) were women, and the mean age was 35.9 years ($M = 35.9$, SD $= 9.59$).

## 6.2 Research Results

### 6.2.1 The NBR Communicated More, but Not by Much

We adapted the five variants question on the Likert scale from the survey of Blinder et al. (2017): "How do you think the NBR communicated with the public in recent years, compared to the period before 2008?" to assess the perception of both the specialized public and the general public regarding the frequency of NBR's post-2008 public communication, on monetary and nonmonetary issues. The results show that 39.8% of the specialized public and 38.6% of the general public believe that the central bank communicated more and somewhat more after 2008. However, approximately 30% of the specialized public did not perceive any change while over a quarter of the general public respondents could not make an assessment (hard to say) (Table 6.1). The Chi-square test identified statistically significant differences depending on the public profile in assessing the frequency of NBR communication in the post-crisis period ($\chi 2 = 17{,}841$, $p < 0.01$, $N = 577$).

The results of this question reflect a difference between the perception on the one hand of the two categories of public, and, on the other hand, the perception of the NBR representatives, expressed in the analyzed interviews. According to 90% of NBR respondents, the central bank communicated more with the public compared to the pre-crisis period of 2008. The responses of the specialized public are not in line with the conclusions of Blinder et al. (2017), according to which 90% of the 159 respondents in academia estimated that central banks communicated more on monetary issues, while only about 3% rated a similar frequency.

Regarding the importance of the messages, over 85% of the specialized public rated NBR's messages as important and very important, while 56.8% of the general public gave them the same degree of importance (Table 6.2).

**Table 6.1** NBR communication after 2008

| Compared to before 2008, the NBR communicated with the public … | Specialized public ($N = 186$) | General public ($N = 391$) | Chi-sq. |
|---|---|---|---|
| A lot less | 1.6 | 2.8 | 17.84[a] |
| Somewhat less | 14.5 | 7.9 | |
| No change | 29.6 | 23.3 | |
| Somewhat more | 31.7 | 32.5 | |
| A lot more | 8.1 | 6.1 | |
| Difficult to tell | 14.5 | 27.4 | |

Note: Figures represent percentages of respondents
[a]Denotes significant differences at the level of 5%, calculated using Chi-square tests for the independence of the answers of the general public and of the specialized public. $\chi 2 = 17{,}841$, d.f. = 5, $N = 577$, $p < 0.01$

**Table 6.2** Importance of NBR messages for the public

| How important are NBR messages? | Specialized public ($N = 186$) | General public ($N = 391$) | Chi-sq. |
|---|---|---|---|
| Not important at all | 1.1 | 3.1 | 74.13[a] |
| Somewhat important | 2.7 | 13.3 | |
| Neutral | 10.2 | 23.8 | |
| Important | 55.9 | 49.1 | |
| Very important | 29.6 | 7.7 | |
| Difficult to tell | 5.0 | 3.1 | |

Note: Figures represent percentages of respondents
[a]Denotes a significant test at the level of 5%, calculated using Chi-square tests for the independence of the answers of the general public and the specialized public. $\chi 2 = 74{,}138$, d.f. = 5, $N = 577$, $p < 0.01$

The Chi-square test highlighted statistically significant differences depending on the public profile in assessing the importance of NBR messages ($\chi 2 = 74{,}138$, $p < 0.01$, $N = 577$). The result confirms that the specialized public, participating in financial markets, and as the first public to which central banks address in the field of strategic communication, through public speeches, academic conferences, seminars, and other special events, is much more interested in NBR's messages, compared with the general public.

The answers to the question regarding the assessment of the frequency of messages at the time of the questionnaires were of the same nature: almost a fifth of the specialized public estimated that they often and very often receive messages from the NBR, while only 74% respondents from the general public agreed. Over 55% of the general public answered that the messages received from the central bank are rare and very rare, while 43% of the specialized public evaluate them at this frequency. The results confirm that the NBR's attention to the general public intensified in the post-crisis period, a trend identified by central bank communication researchers (Haldane et al., 2020; Haldane & McMahon, 2018; Riles, 2018; Binder,

2017; Haldane, 2016), who emphasize the importance of anchoring inflationary expectations not only for financial market participants but also for consumers. However, the difference in perception between the public and the NBR representatives on the changes in the central bank's public communication demonstrates that the NBR must continue and intensify the communication activity, especially that aimed at the general public.

Regarding monetary communication, about a third of the respondents of the specialized public estimate that the NBR communicated with higher visibility about the evolution of prices, compared to the pre-crisis period, almost on a par with those who did not identify any change. The approximately 18% of those who felt that visibility was lower had an optional question available in which they assessed what they thought could have attenuated the visibility of the central bank's inflation messages after 2008. According to the results, 15, 9% indicated jargon, 14.4%—communication on several voices, through several representatives, in the same time interval. Next, were the parallel approach to several topics and the involvement of the NBR in public debates on issues which, in their view, should not have been the subject of a central bank communication. The assessment of the specialized public is in line with the observations of the NBR representatives, as the adaptation of the specialized language is among the main concerns for improving the communication process. At the same time, the NBR's multi-voice communication and the diversification of communication topics, including involvement in debates that go beyond the institution's object of activity, were considered by some central bank representatives among the most visible changes after 2008, but also among the most toxic in terms of negative effects for the entire public communication activity, first of all because they eclipsed the communication of the main objective of the NBR—ensuring and maintaining price stability—and negatively affected the image of the central bank.

In summary, the answers to the first research question show that both the general and the specialized public perceived that the central bank communicated more after 2008, compared to the pre-crisis period, on both nonmonetary and monetary issues. However, there is a difference in perception between the two categories of public and NBR representatives: while between 30 and 40% of survey respondents considered that the NBR communicated more, 90% of NBR officials agreed. This difference demonstrates that the NBR must continue the series of changes in communication and intensify the communication activity, especially that aimed at the general public.

### *6.2.2 Messages on Prominent Topics: Clear or Not?*

The respondents of the specialized public assessed the clarity of the statements made by the NBR after 2008, on a series of 16 monetary and nonmonetary communication topics, using a five-step Likert scale (from very clear to very unclear) (Table 6.3; Fig. 6.1). The interpretation of the results shows that the clearest messages are on the

**Table 6.3** Clarity of NBR messages on monetary and nonmonetary issues, specialized public assessment (descending order)

| Topics | Mean | SD | *N* |
|---|---|---|---|
| Inflation evolution | 3.75 | 0.902 | 164 |
| Banking system | 3.50 | 1.023 | 162 |
| Lending activity | 3.46 | 0.999 | 164 |
| Monetary policy decisions | 3.43 | 0.980 | 161 |
| Economic crisis | 3.37 | 1.049 | 165 |
| Gold reserve | 3.27 | 1.119 | 157 |
| Giving in payment law | 3.21 | 1.086 | 161 |
| Swiss francs loans | 3.20 | 1.179 | 162 |
| Euro adoption | 3.16 | 1.125 | 160 |
| IMF loans | 3.15 | 1.082 | 156 |
| Greek capital banks crisis | 3.10 | 0.998 | 154 |
| Changes to the Fiscal Code | 3.09 | 1.022 | 151 |
| Fiscal policy | 3.06 | 1.051 | 148 |
| Brexit | 2.99 | 1.045 | 143 |
| National Committee for Macroprudential Oversight | 2.62 | 1.152 | 135 |
| Revenue of NBR board members | 2.50 | 1.218 | 147 |

evolution of inflation, on the banking system, on credit, on monetary policy decisions, and on the economic crisis.

Practically, the topics directly related to the object of activity of the NBR were considered the most clearly communicated messages in the analyzed period, confirming the results of the qualitative research. Three-quarters of NBR respondents said that, after 2008, in terms of monetary communication, the central bank's messages were clear, appropriate, contextualized, balanced, and temperate.

The first half of the ranking also included the messages sent by the NBR on the administration of the gold reserve, the giving in payment law and on Swiss franc loans. On the last positions are, in the perception of the specialized public, the messages regarding taxation, but also the role of the National Committee for Macroprudential Oversight, established in 2017 and whose members are the NBR, the Financial Supervisory Authority and the Government. The messages about the incomes of the NBR Board members were the most unclear, according to the respondents.

The results are in line with the views expressed by NBR representatives.

Some of the interviewees believed that the late and only on-demand disclosure of the incomes of the NBR Board members contributed to the erosion of the public trust in the central bank. Also, in the opinion of the representatives of the central bank, the repeated positions on the amendments to the Fiscal Code and on fiscal policy, in general, contributed to the increase in the vulnerability of the institution.

According to the respondents, the messages on the giving in payment law and on the Swiss francs credit crisis were clearer than those about the situation of the banks with Greek capital.

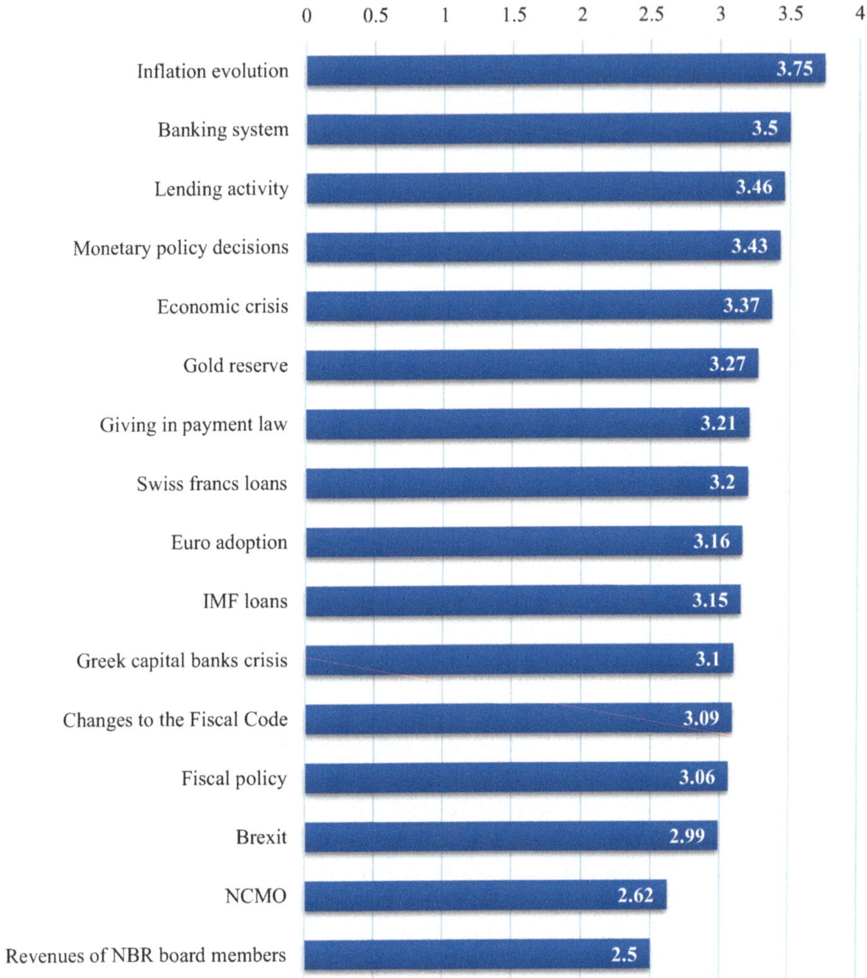


**Fig. 6.1** Hierarchy of clarity of NBR messages on monetary and nonmonetary issues, specialized public assessment. NCMO National Committee for Macroprudential Oversight

The results confirm, but not with the same intensity, the observations of the NBR representatives, who appreciated that the messages on these topics were difficult to convey to the general public or that they even lacked entirely because of how the central bank drafted and transmitted the messages (without empathy, transmitted in several voices, late, reactive in some situations), because of the competing messages of other stakeholders, and because the media intervened in the framing process, printing negative articles, and labelling the central bank as "bank lawyer." As stated by approximately 27% of the respondents of the specialized public, the most unclear messages (assessed unclear and very vague) sent by the central bank were those related to the Swiss francs credit crisis, followed by those on the giving in payment

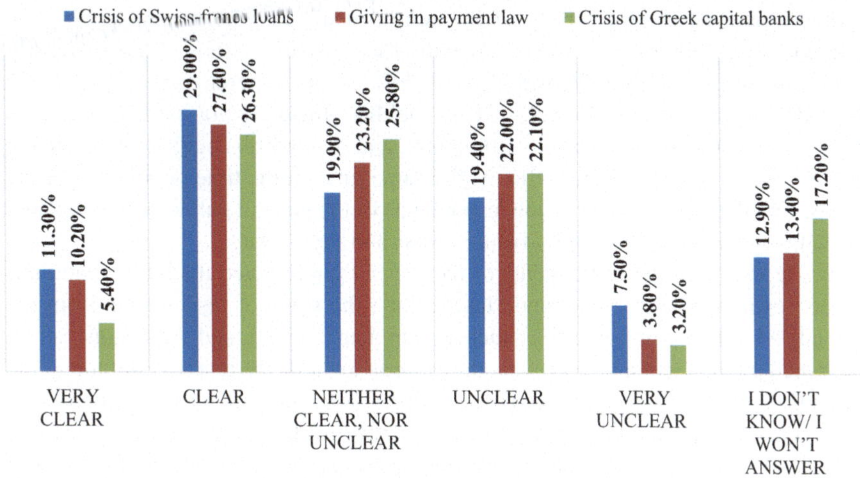


**Fig. 6.2** How clearly the NBR communicated about the Swiss francs credit crisis, the giving in payment law, and the Greek capital bank crisis—the perception of the specialized public (percentages)

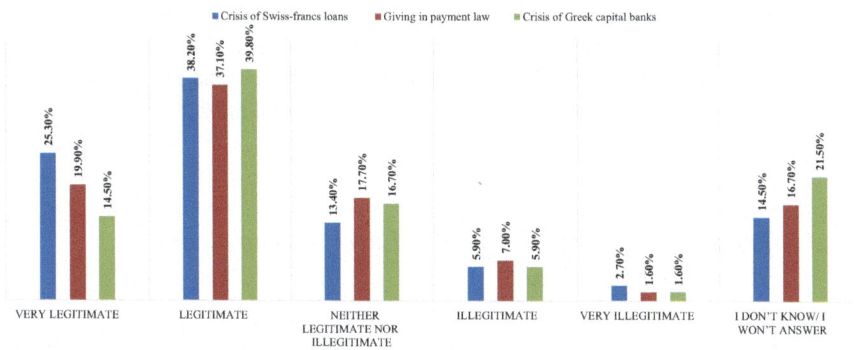


**Fig. 6.3** How justified were the public interventions of the NBR on the Swiss francs credit crisis, the giving in payment law and the Greek capital bank crisis—the perception of the specialized public (percentages)

law (25.8%) and about Greek capital banks (25.3%). On all three topics, however, the largest share of the specialized public considered that the NBR communicated clearly and very clearly. In percentages between 40.3% (Swiss francs credit crisis) and 31.7% (Greek capital banks), the specialized public deemed the messages of the central bank to be clear and very clear (Fig. 6.2).

Over 35% of the same category of public is of the opinion, that NBR's intervention was justified on all three topics (Fig. 6.3).

Respondents of the general public assessed the efficiency of the NBR's communication after 2008, defined on the basis of the clarity of the messages for the target audience and the reaction speed of the central bank. For the general public, the question was built on a Likert scale with five answer options, from extremely inefficient to extremely effective. Almost 29% of the general public opined that the NBR communicated efficiently, 30%—neither efficiently nor inefficiently, 15% considered that it communicated inefficiently, and over a fifth could not evaluate the public communication of the NBR. At the same time, at the time of completing the survey, in 2019, almost 44% of the respondents of the general public considered that the language used by the central bank is clear and very clear.

While 18.2% of the respondents of the general public rated the NBR communication "extremely inefficient" and "inefficient", the share of respondents from the specialised public who rated it as such was higher (27.4%), and the results can be explained by the fact that they reflect the opinion towards the reactive attitude of the institution, to which some of the representatives of the central bank also referred.

In conclusion, according to the results obtained in RQ 2, the public assessed that the messages on monetary and nonmonetary issues closer to the object of activity of the central bank were also most clearly communicated in the post-crisis period, the perceived level of clarity decreased as the topics moved farther away from the mandate of the NBR (Fig. 6.1).

About 30% of both the specialized public and the general public consider that the central bank's messages on nonmonetary issues, in the post-crisis period, were clear. The results confirm, but not to the same degree, the observations of the NBR representatives that the NBR messages on certain nonmonetary topics such as the giving in payment law, Swiss francs credit crisis, and the situation of the Greek capital banks reached the public with difficulty or not at all after 2008.

### 6.2.3 Trust and Clarity Versus the Level of Knowledge of the NBR Activity

The 2019 survey of the general public shows that 41.4% of respondents trusted the central bank to a very great degree (very much), and 5.4%—to a great degree (a lot), while the survey applied to the specialized public in 2018 shows that over half of the specialists evaluated BNR as credible, very credible and extremely credible during the post-crisis period. The results of both polls confirm that the NBR was not bypassed by the erosion of confidence in the post-crisis period, but the degree of distrust of the central bank is lower than that expressed in national opinion barometers. For example, INSCOP Research (2019) reflects the fact that, in March 2019, only 35.6% of Romanians had a high and very high confidence in the central bank. The generalized confidence deficit facing central banks around the world is highlighted by numerous barometers and specialized papers (Bergbauer et al., 2020; YouGov, 2019; Edelman Trust Barometer, 2017; Owens, 2012; Bourne, 2011).

The results of the quantitative research conducted for this chapter confirm those of the qualitative research, which identified a balance in assessing the degree of erosion of confidence. In the perception of more than half of central bank representatives, the NBR was affected by a crisis of confidence after 2008, while the rest of the interviewees believe that the erosion was insignificant.

The results of the two questionnaires reflected significant correlations between the level of trust in the NBR and the degree of assessment of the clarity of central bank messages after 2008. For the general public, the Pearson correlation was applied between trust ("How much do you trust the NBR?") and NBR communication efficiency ("How would you assess NBR's communication after 2008?") and both questions, with five steps on the Likert scale, show that a significant negative average correlation is established ($r = -0.508$, $N = 292$, $p < 0.01$); therefore, the less clear and reactive the communication is assessed, the lower the public's trust in the NBR. A significant weak positive correlation was also identified between the general public's trust in the central bank and the perceived clarity of the NBR language at the time of completing the questionnaire ($r = 0.167$, $N = 147$, $p < 0.05$).

For the specialist public, the same correlation applied between the institution's credibility ("How would you assess the NBR's credibility during the crisis?") and the effectiveness of communication—a seven-step Likert scale assessment for both questions—shows that a strong positive correlation is established ($r = 0.830$, $N = 186$, $p < 0.01$), therefore, the more efficient the communication is perceived to be, the more confidence the public has in the central bank.

The Chi-square test shows that there are statistically significant differences between the level of confidence and the level of knowledge of the NBR's activity for the general public ($\chi2 = 43{,}163$, df. $= 24$, $p = 0.01$, $N = 313$) (Table 6.4). Thus, it is observed that 66.9% of the respondents who correctly consider that the main objective pursued by the NBR is to ensure and maintain price stability, have a lot of trust in the central bank. On the other hand, over 57% of respondents who mistakenly consider that the NBR makes fiscal decisions in Romania have little and very little trust in the institution, and half of those who believe that the NBR lends money to the Romanian state have little confidence in the bank. Over 30% of the respondents of the general public correctly identified the object of activity of the NBR. A quarter of respondents believe that the NBR sets the exchange rate, 14.5%—that it sets interest rates on loans and deposits, and 16.6% did not make any assessment. The fewest were of the opinion that the NBR sets taxes and duties (2%) and that it lends money to the Romanian state (1.5%).

In the case of the specialized public, over half of the respondents (51.6%) correctly indicated the NBR mission, approximately 16% consider that the central bank sets the exchange rate and 11.3%—that it sets the interest rates on loans and deposits. No respondent chose setting the country's fiscal policy as an answer. The highest percentage of those who consider the NBR to be extremely credible, very credible, and credible (59.4%) are among the respondents who correctly assessed NBR's main mission. The highest percentage of respondents who rated the institution extremely not credible, moderately not credible, not credible (50%) are among the respondents who considered that the objective of the NBR is to lend to the Romanian state. However, the Chi-square test did not reveal a statistically significant association between the degree of credibility of the NBR assessed by the specialized public and the level of knowledge of NBR's mission ($\chi2 = 45{,}278a$, df. $= 30$, $p = 0.03$, $N = 171$) (Table 6.5).

**Table 6.4** The relationship between trust and knowledge of the object of activity of the NBR—general public

| Trust in the NBR | Which is NBR's main objective? | | | | | | | Total (%) |
|---|---|---|---|---|---|---|---|---|
| | Sets interest on loans and deposits (%) | Ensures and maintains price stability (%) | Sets the exchange rate (%) | Protects customers in relation to banks (%) | Sets taxes (%) | Lends money to the government (%) | Lends money to commercial banks (%) | |
| Very much | 3.6 | 8.9 | 2.1 | 8.3 | 0 | 16.7 | 16.7 | 6.1 |
| A lot | 41.1 | 58.0 | 41.7 | 41.7 | 28.6 | 33.3 | 33.3 | 46.6 |
| Neutral | 19.6 | 23.2 | 25.0 | 33.3 | 14.3 | 0 | 16.7 | 23.0 |
| A little | 26.8 | 6.3 | 21.9 | 16.7 | 42.9 | 50.0 | 33.3 | 18.2 |
| Very little | 8.9 | 3.6 | 9.4 | 0 | 14.3 | 0 | 0 | 6.1 |

**Table 6.5** The relationship between credibility and knowledge of the NBR's main mission—specialized public

| | Which is NBR's main mission? | | | | | | |
|---|---|---|---|---|---|---|---|
| NBR credibility | Sets interest on loans and deposits (%) | Ensures and maintains price stability (%) | Sets the exchange rate (%) | Protects customers in their dealings with banks (%) | Lends to the Romanian Government (%) | Other (%) | Total (%) |
| Extremely credible | 4.8 | 5.2 | 3.3 | 0 | 0 | 7.1 | 4.7 |
| Very credible | 9.5 | 27.1 | 16.7 | 0 | 16.7 | 14.3 | 21.1 |
| Credible | 23.8 | 27.1 | 30.0 | 50.0 | 16.7 | 14.3 | 26.3 |
| Neutral | 23.8 | 18.8 | 30.0 | 0 | 16.7 | 28.6 | 21.6 |
| Not credible | 14.3 | 19.8 | 6.7 | 50.0 | 16.7 | 21.4 | 17.5 |
| Moderately not credible | 19.0 | 2.1 | 6.7 | 0 | 0 | 7.1 | 5.3 |
| Extremely not credible | 4.8 | 0 | 6.7 | 0 | 33.3 | 7.1 | 3.5 |

The statistically significant correlations established between the assessments of the level of trust and the clarity of the messages established for the two categories of public show that trust in the central bank can be recovered through the institution's efforts toward greater clarity, streamline, and accessibility of messages.

Researchers concerned with reducing uncertainty through communication have shown the importance of accessibility of central bank messages to the public, on monetary and nonmonetary issues (Haldane & McMahon, 2018; Coenen et al., 2017; Haldane, 2016; Bulíř et al., 2013, etc.). The results reconfirm another important cause of the erosion in public confidence in the central bank—the level of public knowledge about the activity and fundamental mission of the NBR (ensuring and maintaining price stability), thus validating some of the results of researchers such as Bergbauer et al. (2020), Ehrmann et al. (2013), and Fischer and Hahn (2008).

The results obtained at RQ3 confirm that the NBR was not bypassed by the erosion of confidence in the post-crisis period. The proportion of those who expressed confidence in the central bank is lower than the level of confidence reported in national opinion barometers, but similar to the results of qualitative research on this topic. Based on the results, we believe that the trust in the NBR can be improved both by the institution's efforts toward greater clarity in communication and information on the main purpose and objectives, but also by intensifying communication on its mandate, which is to maintain price stability.

### *6.2.4 Who Informs the Public?*

Online media and TV are the main sources of information on NBR's messages, both for the general public and for the specialized public. The data analysis shows that, for the specialized public, the NBR website is the third most useful source of information, while for the general public it comes in fifth place (Tables 6.6 and 6.7; Figs. 6.4 and 6.5). For the general public, the difference between online media and TV is insignificant, while the responses of the specialized audience reflect a difference between the frequency of choosing online media ($M = 0.82$, $SD = 0.37$) compared to TV ($M = 0.71$, $SD = 0.45$). The results were obtained by analyzing the answers to multiple-choice questions from 15 proposed answer options, coded with 1 (chosen variant) or 0 (unchosen variant).

For the general public, Facebook ranks third as a source of information about decisions and other information provided by central bank representatives, while for the specialized public, this social network is ranked sixth in importance after radio and NBR events.

For the specialized public NBR's blog is the seventh most important source of information, while for the general public is the tenth most important source, following print, NBR events, other events, and email. In terms of usefulness as information source, the written press is ranked sixth by the general public, and eighth by the specialized public. The results of the two surveys confirm those of the Reuters Institute studies (2019, 2020), according to which, in Romania, the online

**Table 6.6** Main sources of information about the NBR for the general public

| Sources and channels | Mean | SD | *N* |
|---|---|---|---|
| Online mass media | 0.70 | 0.455 | 278 |
| TV | 0.69 | 0.460 | 272 |
| Facebook | 0.30 | 0.460 | 119 |
| Radio | 0.29 | 0.458 | 118 |
| NBR website | 0.28 | 0.453 | 113 |
| Printed press | 0.08 | 0.278 | 33 |
| NBR events | 0.07 | 0.270 | 31 |
| Other events | 0.05 | 0.220 | 20 |
| Email | 0.04 | 0.209 | 18 |
| NBR blog | 0.03 | 0.179 | 13 |
| LinkedIn | 0.02 | 0.165 | 5 |
| Informal meetings | 0.02 | 0.158 | 10 |
| YouTube | 0.01 | 0.100 | 4 |
| Twitter | 0.002 | 0.050 | 1 |
| No answer | 0.03 | 0.186 | 14 |

**Table 6.7** Main sources of information about the NBR for the specialized public

| Sources and channels | Mean | SD | *N* |
|---|---|---|---|
| Online mass media | 0.82 | 0.378 | 154 |
| TV | 0.71 | 0.452 | 133 |
| NBR website | 0.45 | 0.498 | 84 |
| Radio | 0.35 | 0.479 | 66 |
| NBR events | 0.27 | 0.447 | 51 |
| Facebook | 0.20 | 0.404 | 38 |
| NBR blog | 0.18 | 0.387 | 34 |
| Printed press | 0.16 | 0.373 | 31 |
| Email | 0.16 | 0.368 | 30 |
| Other events | 0.12 | 0.336 | 24 |
| Informal meetings | 0.09 | 0.296 | 18 |
| LinkedIn | 0.08 | 0.273 | 15 |
| YouTube | 0.04 | 0.203 | 8 |
| Twitter | 0.03 | 0.190 | 7 |
| Other channels | 0.005 | 0.073 | 1 |

environment (including social networks) is the most important source of news for the public (83% of news consumption in 2020, 87% of news consumption in 2019), while TV channels are in second place, with 76%, decreasing in 2020 compared to the previous year (80%). According to the aforementioned source, social media comes in third position (60%), while print media consumption reached 15% in 2020 (down from 19% in 2019), among the lowest levels in Europe.

At the top of the ranking of information sources, the quantitative analysis is separated from the results of the qualitative analysis. Both categories of the public consider that the online media is the main source of information, while over half of the NBR representatives interviewed considered that TV was the most efficient in the

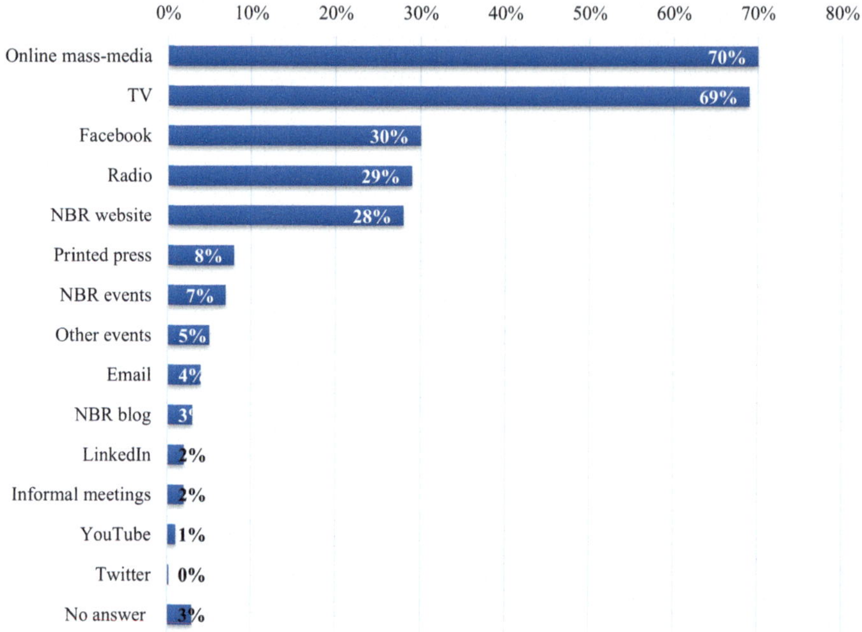


**Fig. 6.4** Hierarchy of information sources for the general public

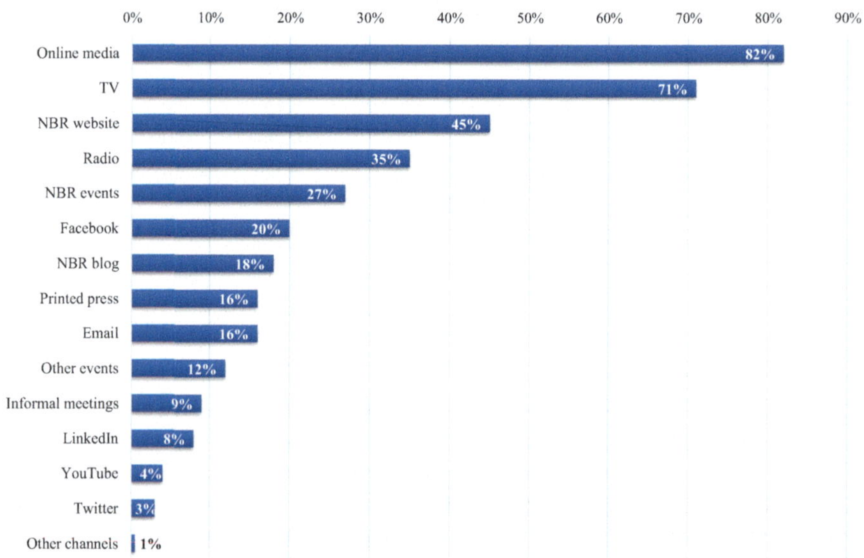


**Fig. 6.5** Hierarchy of information sources for the specialized public

period analyzed, followed by the online and print media. A communication channel that was not mentioned in the qualitative analysis—radio—was appreciated by both categories of public as being more relevant than the written press.

Both categories of public downgraded the other social networks on which the NBR was present, at the time of applying the questionnaires. LinkedIn had the same frequency ($M = 0.08$, $SD = 0.27$), followed by YouTube and Twitter. The results of the two questionnaires confirm some of the observations and research results regarding the limited effects on audiences generated by the adoption of new media channels by central banks (Haldane et al., 2020; Binder, 2017; Haldane, 2017; Shin, 2017; Bjelobaba et al., 2017; Vardy, 2015).

In conclusion, the results of the RQ4 show that both the general public and the specialized public primarily watch online and TV to keep informed on the NBR. Radio is also one of the most favorably evaluated sources, with a higher relevance compared to the print media for both audiences. The analysis of this quantitative research shows that, for the efficient transmission of messages to the general and specialized public, the central bank should focus its online communication efforts, with emphasis on its website and Facebook. At the same time, we believe that the NBR could focus on radio as well.

The answers also highlighted the importance of the events organized by the NBR, both for the specialized public and for the general public. As for the other social networks (LinkedIn, YouTube, Twitter), on which the central bank had official accounts at the time of the two questionnaires, they have an insignificant impact on audiences and do not represent communication channels through which BNR messages reach the public.

### 6.2.5 *The Public Is Waiting for NBR on Facebook*

At the time of applying the two questionnaires, the NBR has accounts on Twitter, LinkedIn, and YouTube, and maintained a blog, OpiniiBNR.ro. In December 2019, the central bank expanded its online presence and launched its official Instagram account, with the stated aim of attracting "new segments of the public, in order to increase the general level of information on the activity of the central bank" (National Bank of Romania, 2019). As of June 2020, the NBR has over 38,000 followers on LinkedIn, almost 4200 followers on Twitter, over 1750 followers on YouTube, and over 1200 followers on Instagram.

We found out that both categories of public feel the need for an NBR Facebook account. More than 58% of the general public and about 78% of the general public consider that such a presence would be useful in finding out more quickly the information transmitted by the central bank. The category of those who do not consider an NBR Facebook account useful is better represented as a percentage of the specialized public (over 30% of respondents) compared to the general public (11.5%), and the difference is significant ($\chi 2 = 33{,}401$a, df $= 1$, $N = 516$, $p < 0.01$) (Table 6.8).

**Table 6.8** NBR—on Facebook or not?

| Would an NBR Facebook account be useful for faster information? | Specialized public ($N = 186$) | General public ($N = 391$) | Chi-sq. |
|---|---|---|---|
| Yes | 58.1 | 78.0 | 33.40 |
| No | 30.6 | 11.5 | |
| I don't know/I won't answer | 11.3 | 10.5 | |

Note: Figures represent percentages of respondents. Chi-square tests for the independence of responses from the general public and the specialist public show significant differences of 1%. $\chi 2 = 33.401a$, d.f. $= 1$, $N = 516$, $p < 0.01$

The results confirm social media as being one of the most relevant sources of information for the public, including in relation to central bank messages. As we have shown, according to Statcounter (2020), in terms of market share, social media was divided, in January 2020, between Facebook (87.02%), Instagram (4.41%), Pinterest (4.36), Twitter (2.43%), YouTube (1.21%), and Reddit (0.19%), and at the end of January 2020, there were approximately 11 million Facebook users in Romania and over 41,100 active pages (ZeList, 2020).

The specialized public also expects an NBR Facebook account, even if the NBR addresses it through a series of publications and periodical reports (economic bulletins, reports on inflation, on stability, etc.), press releases, reports, research, minutes of policy meetings monetary policy. The answers of the specialized public are in accordance with the evaluations of the NBR representatives: half of the interviewees acknowledged the importance and relevance of Facebook as a communication channel and were in favor of the immediate launch of an official account. 30% of respondents considered this communication channel in a period not marked by crisis communication situations.

In summary, the main result of RQ5 shows that both the specialized and the general public have high expectations regarding the presence of the central bank on Facebook. In this context, and taking into account the traffic and activity registered on Facebook in Romania, we believe that the distance between the public and the central bank could be reduced, through an active presence on Facebook. However, the main concerns expressed by both researchers and NBR representatives regarding the constant interactivity with the public and the ability to send messages to these categories of stakeholders of the institution remain to be resolved.

### 6.2.6 *Monetary Communication*

As highlighted by the results on previous research questions, the communication on monetary issues and other issues that are close to the NBR objectives were assessed by both audiences as being clearer in the post-crisis period compared to the messages on issues that went beyond NBR's mandate. This confirms the comments made by the interviewees in the qualitative analysis.

The specialist has assessed the extent to which the language used by the NBR in periodicals, such as Annual Reports, Inflation Reports, Financial Stability Reports,

Monthly Economic Bulletins, and Minutes of Monetary Policy Meetings, is easy for the public to understand using a five step Likert scale (from very small to very large) (Table 6.9). Inflation Reports come in the first place, with more than a third of the specialized public estimating that the language is largely easy to understand by the public. Financial Stability Reports come in second (32.8% consider them easy and very easy to understand), then Monthly Bulletins (32.2%), the Annual Reports (31.7%), and in the last place—the minutes of the meetings on monetary policy (22.1%).

Regarding the size of the periodic reports (Table 6.10), almost a third of the specialized public is of the opinion that the Annual Reports are long and very long, a quarter thus evaluating the Financial Stability Reports, followed by the Inflation Reports (22.6%), and in the last place is the Minutes, which 6.5% of respondents consider long (no respondents rated them as very long).

These results show that, from the perspective of the specialized public, there is still room for simplification of the language and reduction of the number of pages in the specialized reports of the NBR, while three-quarters of the NBR interviewees estimated that, after 2008, the monetary communication was transparent, clear and efficient. Some of the respondents who took part in the qualitative research considered that the Inflation Reports addressed to the specialized public are more simplified. At the same time, over 65% of the respondents of the specialized public consider that the central bank must move to the next level of communication after overcoming the economic crisis. Approximately 12% were of the opinion that the NBR should remain at the current level, and 2.7% of the respondents opted to return partially or completely to the previous communication level. Specialists who responded to the questionnaire applied in this research were less conservative about entering a new stage of communication with the central bank compared to those who answered the same question from Blinder et al. (2017). More than half of

**Table 6.9** Clarity of NBR language in periodic reports—specialized public

| Language clarity | | Annual reports | Inflation reports | Financial stability reports | Monthly bulletins | Minutes of monetary policy meetings |
|---|---|---|---|---|---|---|
| *N* | Valid | 161 | 165 | 163 | 157 | 145 |
| | Missing | 25 | 21 | 23 | 29 | 41 |
| **Mean** | | **2.91** | **2.99** | **2.93** | **2.97** | **2.66** |
| Standard deviation | | 1.198 | 1.171 | 1.218 | 1.216 | 1.277 |

**Table 6.10** Size of periodic reports—specialized public

| Size of reports | | Annual reports | Inflation reports | Financial stability reports | Monthly bulletins | Minutes of monetary policy meetings |
|---|---|---|---|---|---|---|
| *N* | Valid | 131 | 136 | 134 | 131 | 118 |
| | Missing | 55 | 50 | 52 | 55 | 68 |
| **Mean** | | **3.51** | **3.24** | **3.32** | **3.03** | **2.78** |
| Standard deviation | | 0.788 | 0.765 | 0.762 | 0.712 | 0.668 |

the academic respondents to the Blinder et al. (2017) questionnaire considered that changes in communication should remain after the end of the crisis, and almost 22% estimated that they should move to the next level.

The results of the quantitative research are in line with the comments made by NBR representatives regarding the publication of the minutes of monetary policy meetings—three-quarters of respondents consider that the publication of the minutes—the latest decision of the NBR towards transparency—is not reversible.

In conclusion, the NBR public considers it necessary for the central bank to move to the next level of communication after the 2008 crisis, and not to return to pre-crisis communication. In the opinion of the specialized public, the NBR can improve the communication on monetary issues through a clearer language in the specialized reports and by reducing their size.

### *6.2.7 Post-crisis Communication Lessons*

Based on multiple-choice questions, as well as the option to express their own recommendations, the two audiences indicated what they thought should be the current changes in the NBR's communication. The results were obtained by analyzing the answers to multiple-choice questions from 11 proposed answer options (general public) and 10 answer options (specialized audience), coded with 1 (chosen option) or 0 (unchosen option).

Except for video productions as an additional answer included in the questionnaire addressed to the general public, the results of the two questionnaires show that both audiences have the same expectations regarding changes in NBR communication (Tables 6.11 and 6.12; Figs. 6.6 and 6.7).

**Table 6.11** The main changes expected by the general public

| Sources and channels | Mean | Standard deviation | *N* |
|---|---|---|---|
| Channel diversification | 0.59 | 0.490 | 234 |
| More public appearances | 0.59 | 0.492 | 231 |
| Language adaptation | 0.54 | 0.498 | 213 |
| Using info graphs | 0.47 | 0.500 | 186 |
| Video productions | 0.43 | 0.497 | 172 |
| More communicators | 0.26 | 0.443 | 106 |
| Larger reports | 0.12 | 0.331 | 49 |
| Smaller reports | 0.06 | 0.249 | 26 |
| Other changes[a] | 0.02 | 0.141 | 9 |
| Fewer communicators | 0.01 | 0.132 | 7 |
| Fewer public appearances | 0.01 | 0.100 | 4 |

[a]Other changes proposed by respondents: "Flexible and up-to-date communication style"; "Proactive, not reactive communication"; "Promoting young communicators"; "Concrete examples to support technical communications"

**Table 6.12** The main changes expected by the specialized public

| Sources and channels | Mean | Standard deviation | *N* |
|---|---|---|---|
| Channel diversification | 0.70 | 0.457 | 131 |
| More public appearances | 0.66 | 0.472 | 124 |
| Language adaptation | 0.62 | 0.484 | 117 |
| Using info graphs | 0.48 | 0.501 | 91 |
| More communicators | 0.29 | 0.457 | 55 |
| Larger reports | 0.16 | 0.368 | 30 |
| Smaller reports | 0.06 | 0.246 | 12 |
| Other changes[a] | 0.05 | 0.236 | 11 |
| Fewer communicators | 0.02 | 0.162 | 5 |
| Fewer public appearances | 0.01 | 0.103 | 2 |

[a]Other changes proposed by respondents: "Use of forward guidance"; "Modern means of communication"; "Single voice"; "Financial education"

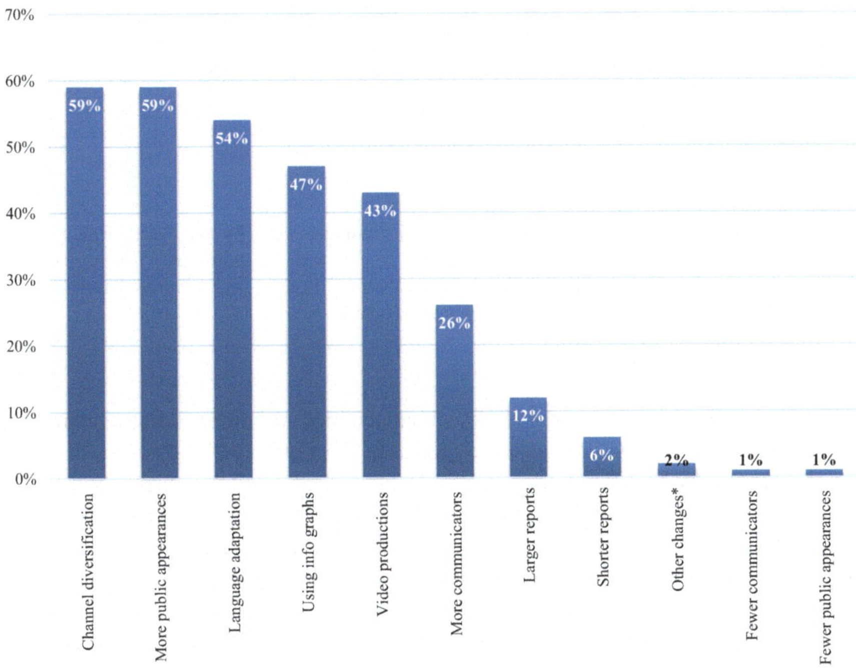


**Fig. 6.6** Hierarchy of changes in NBR communication expected by the general public. (Asterisk) Other changes proposed by respondents: "Flexible and up-to-date communication style"; "Proactive, not reactive communication"; "Promoting young communicators"; "Concrete examples to support technical communications"

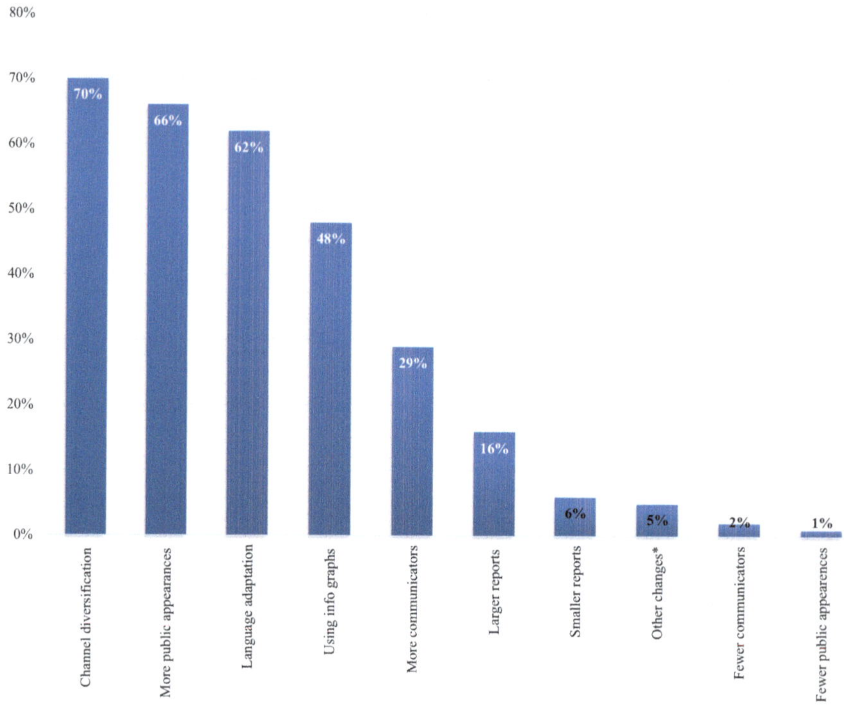


**Fig. 6.7** Hierarchy of changes in NBR communication expected by the specialized public. (Asterisk) Other changes proposed by respondents: "use of forward guidance"; "Modern means of communication"; "Single voice"; "Financial education." Source: Calculations based on the online questionnaire applied in 2018 to the specialized public

The diversification of communication channels, more public appearances, and the adaptation of specialized language are the three most anticipated changes in NBR communication by both categories of stakeholders. The results confirm some of the observations of the central bank interviewees who are concerned with adapting the jargon, although they would not adopt the language for the specialized audience, aim for better coordination of public appearances and included in the list of post-2009 learned communication lessons, the diversification of communication channels. Opinions expressed by the public are in line with the central bankers' comments that there is currently a need for a greater concern about the nature of communication, for a simplification of communication, and for the use of non-elitist language in a format that is closer to the requirements and expectations of various audiences (Haldane et al., 2020; Haldane, 2016).

In conclusion, both the general public and the specialized public believe that the central bank needs to take strategic communication steps toward a greater diversification of communication channels and a greater presence in the public space through more public appearances and the diversification of communicators, including young communicators within the institution. At the same time, the public is interested in adapting the specialized language and in the use of graphic and video support in disseminating information.

## 6.3 Conclusions

The results of the two sociological surveys based on questionnaires provide the perspective of the general public and of the specialized public on central bank communication after 2008. At the same time, these results represent feedback that complements the perspective expressed in the qualitative research by NBR representatives. However, we draw attention to the limitations of this quantitative research, which consists mainly of convenience samples and the exclusive distribution of questionnaires online, via e-mail and social networks. We also consider that a longitudinal study, on exclusively representative samples, can provide a more relevant picture in terms of stakeholders' perception of the NBR's public communication efforts.

Both categories of the public believe that the central bank communicated more after 2008, compared to the pre-crisis period, on both nonmonetary and monetary issues. However, the two categories of public on the one hand and the NBR representatives on the other hand, diverge on whether the central bank must continue the series of changes in communication and intensify communication activity, especially toward the general public.

Both the general public and the specialized public agreed that the messages on monetary and nonmonetary issues that are closer to the mission of the central bank were most clearly communicated in the post-crisis period. The perceived level of clarity decreased as the topics proposed for evaluation moved further away from the mandate of the NBR. The results confirm, to some degree the observations of the NBR representatives that NBR messages on certain nonmonetary issues such as the giving in payment law, the Swiss franc credit crisis, and the Greek-owned banks crisis reached the public with difficulty or not at all after 2008.

Our analysis confirms that the trust of both categories of the public in the NBR was eroded in the post-crisis period. Based on the significant correlations identified between the level of confidence in the NBR and the degree of clarity of central bank messages after 2008, as well as between the level of confidence and the level of knowledge of the NBR's mission, we believe that confidence in the NBR can be restored through greater clarity in communication.

Regarding the most followed sources of information about the NBR, the data points to online channels (online media, central bank website, Facebook). Radio is one of the most favorably evaluated sources, with a higher relevance compared to the print media for both categories of audiences. Public responses suggest that the central bank should continue its online communication efforts, with an emphasis on communication on its website and on Facebook, as well as paying more attention to the use of radio. The results of the quantitative research show that both the specialized and the general public have high expectations regarding the presence of the central bank on Facebook, but also the fact that the presence of the NBR on other networks (LinkedIn, YouTube, Twitter) has an insignificant impact on audiences.

The NBR's specialized public considers it necessary for the central bank to move to the next level of communication after the 2008 crisis, and not to return to pre-crisis communication, including monetary communication. The two categories of public are of the opinion that the central bank needs to take strategic communication steps, first of all, toward a greater diversification of communication channels, a greater presence in the public space, but also through the diversification of communicators. At the same time, the public is interested in adapting the specialized language and in the use of graphs and video.

We believe that the perspective of NBR stakeholders on changes in communication in the post-crisis period, on formulating expectations regarding future changes, and on assessing how NBR messages were received can help strengthen the bridges between the institution and its audiences and identify new ones.

## References


Bergbauer, S., Hernborg, N., Jamet, J. F., Persson, E., & Schölermann, H. (2020). *Citizens' attitudes towards the ECB, the euro and Economic and Monetary Union*. ECB Economic Bulletin, Issue 4/2020. Retrieved from https://www.ecb.europa.eu/pub/economic-bulletin/articles/2020/html/ecb.ebart202004_01~9e43ff2fb2.en.html#toc8

Binder, C. (2017). Fed speak on main street: Central bank communication and household expectations. *Journal of Macroeconomics, 52*, 238–251. https://doi.org/10.1016/j.jmacro.2017.05.003

Bjelobaba, G., Savic, A., & Stefanovic, H. (2017). *Analysis of central banks platforms on social networks*. UBT International Conference. Retrieved from https://knowledgecenter.ubt-uni.net/cgi/viewcontent.cgi?article=1223&context=conference

Blinder, A., Ehrmann, M., De Haan, J., & Jansen, D. J. (2017). Necessity as the mother of invention: Monetary policy after the crisis. *Economic Policy, 32*(92), 707–755. https://doi.org/10.1093/epolic/eix013

Bourne, C. (2011). *Public relations' role as trust strategist: A specialist niche evolves from turbulence*. EUPRERA Annual Conference 2011. Retrieved from http://orca.cf.ac.uk/29796/1/BourneTrust%20Strategist.pdf

Bulíř, A., Čihák, M., & Jansen, D. J. (2013). What drives clarity of central bank communication about inflation? *Open Economies Review, 24*(1), 125–145. https://doi.org/10.5089/9781463931148.001

Coenen, G., Ehrmann, M., Gaballo, G., Hoffmann, P., Nakov, A., Nardelli, S., Persson, E., & Strasser, G. (2017). *Communication of monetary policy in unconventional times*. Frankfurt: ECB Working Paper, No. 2080. https://doi.org/10.2866/72507

Edelman Trust Barometer. (2017). *Trust in crisis*. Retrieved from https://www.edelman.com/research/2017-edelman-trust-barometer

Ehrmann, M., Soudan, M., & şi Stracca, L. (2013). Explaining European Union citizens' trust in the European Central Bank in normal and crisis times. *The Scandinavian Journal of Economics, 115*(3), 781–807.

Fischer, J. A., & Hahn, V. (2008). *Determinants of trust in the European Central Bank*. SSE/EFI Working Paper Series in Economics and Finance. Retrieved from https://www.econstor.eu/bitstream/10419/56308/1/56082744X.pdf

Haldane, A. (2016). *The great divide. Discurs susținut la the New City agenda annual dinner*. Retrieved from https://www.bankofengland.co.uk/speech/2016/the-great-divide

Haldane, A. (2017). *A little more conversation. A little less action*. Speech at the Federal Reserve Bank of San Francisco. Retrieved from https://www.bis.org/review/r170403e.pdf

Haldane, A., & McMahon, M. (2018). Central bank communications and the general public. *AEA Papers and Proceedings, 108*, pp. 578–583. https://doi.org/10.1257/pandp.20181082.

Haldane, A., Macaulay, A., & McMahon, M. (2020). *The 3 E's of central bank communication with the public*. Bank of England, Staff Working Paper No. 847. Retrieved from https://www.bankofengland.co.uk/-/media/boe/files/working-paper/2020/the-3-es-of-central-bank-communication-with-the-public.pdf?la=enşihash=B3D34A003BB6F2B7D5653B265966DF11C8F75154

INSCOP Research. (2019). *Topul încrederii în instituții interne și internaționale*. Retrieved from https://www.inscop.ro/22-martie-2019-topul-increderii-in-institutii-interne-si-internationale/

National Bank of Romania. (2019). *Press release on the NBR launching an Instagram social media account*. Retrieved from https://www.bnro.ro/page.aspx?prid=17199

Owens, L. A. (2012). The polls—Trends: Confidence in banks, financial institutions, and wall street, 1971–2011. *Public Opinion Quarterly, 76*(1), 142–162.

Reuters Institute. (2019). *Digital news report*, p. 103. Retrieved from http://www.digitalnewsreport.org/survey/2019/romania-2019/

Reuters Institute. (2020). *Digital news report*, p. 80. Retrieved from https://reutersinstitute.politics.ox.ac.uk/sites/default/files/2020-06/DNR_2020_FINAL.pdf

Riles, A. (2018). *Financial citizenship: Experts, publics, and the politics of central banking*. Cornell University Press.

Shin, H. S. (2017). *Can central banks talk too much?* Speech at the ECB conference on "Communications challenges for policy effectiveness, accountability and reputation". Retrieved from https://www.bis.org/speeches/sp171114.pdf

Statcounter. (2020). *Social media stats Romania*. Retrieved from https://gs.statcounter.com/social-media-stats/all/romania

Vardy, J. (2015). *Reputational risk management in central banks* (no. 2015–16). Bank of Canada. Staff Discussion Paper.

YouGov. (2019). *How clear, if at all, are you about what role the Bank of England carries out?* Retrieved from https://yougov.co.uk/topics/science/survey-results/daily/2019/04/24/12913/3

ZeList. (2020). *Overview social media in Romania—January 2020*. Retrieved from https://www.zelist.ro/blog/overview-social-media-in-ro-ianuarie-2020/

# Chapter 7
# Framing the Giving in Payment Law by Online Media (2016)

The third methodological component of this research approach is the analysis of the content of articles in the economic and general media in Romania regarding the giving in payment law, one of the most visible topics of nonmonetary communication that the NBR was involved within the post-crisis period. The general conceptual framework is set by the framing theory, as structured and developed by researchers such as Goffman (1974), Gitlin (1980), Gamson et al. (1992), Entman (1993), Pan and Kosicki (1993), Capella and Jamieson (1997), Reese (2001), Entman (2003), van Gorp (2007), Scheufele and Iyengar (2011), Cacciatore et al. (2016).

The present research is part of the sociological tradition that defines framing as "as information that conveys differing perspectives on some event or issue" and considers that "this tradition can also be labeled 'emphasis' framing, since the observed framing effects represent differences in opinion that cannot be attributed exclusively to differences in presentation" (Scheufele & Iyengar, 2011, pp. 4–5).

In order to capture the main trends in the media coverage of one of the most visible nonmonetary topics for the NBR and which frames reached the general public, we analyzed the way in which journalists framed the "giving in payment law," using the following research questions[1]:

RQ1. How do the Romanian general and economic media framed the "giving in payment" law in 2016?

RQ2. How do the Romanian online general and economic media differ in their use of those frames?

RQ3. What were the differences in the visibility of supporters and opponents of the "giving in payment" law during the analyzed period?

---

[1] Parts of this chapter, concerning the results described on the basis of research questions 1 and 2, were published in English in 2020 in the journal Mediální studia/Media studies, 14 (1), pp. 126–146, Blind Spots in the Spotlight: Media Reporting on the National Bank of Romania's answers to Financial Crisis Aftershock.

© The Author(s), under exclusive license to Springer Nature Switzerland AG 2022

R. Iacob, *Blind Spots in the Spotlight*, Financial and Monetary Policy Studies 53,
https://doi.org/10.1007/978-3-031-04067-2_7

RQ4. What were the main positions of the media (editorials, comments, opinions, etc.) regarding the NBR's communication strategy in the context of the analyzed legislative change?

## 7.1 Research Methodology

The research body includes articles published ($N = 420$) throughout 2016 by the online portals: bursa.ro, zf.ro, hotnews.ro, and adevarul.ro, based on the simultaneous search for two main keywords: "giving in payment law" and "National Bank of Romania." The sample to be researched was selected from two online portals of the two most relevant financial newspapers in Romania: Bursa—bursa.ro ($N = 133$ articles) and Ziarul Financiar—zf.ro ($N = 139$ articles), the online portal of the quality newspaper Adevărul—adevarul.ro ($N = 59$ articles), and from the generalist portal hotnews.ro ($N = 89$ articles). According to Reuters Institute (2020, p. 80) the 21 years old, printed financial publication, Ziarul Financiar (and its online version zf.ro), is the third most trusted media brand in Romania, after the TV channels PRO TV and DIGI 24. The adevarul.ro portal (the online version of a 131-year-old Romanian publication) ranks sixth, and the generalist portal hotnews.ro (exclusively online) ranks seventh in the trust top; bursa.ro is the online version of the printed financial newspaper Bursa, which reaches its 30th anniversary in 2020.

The selected timeframe (January first, 2016–December 31st, 2016) includes important events for the legislative initiative, such as proposed amendments sent by the NBR to the Parliament, a European Commission report on Romania's economic perspectives, the Swiss franc debtors' protest, the February Senate vote on the giving in payment law, various press conferences and public debates organized by lawyers, journalists, bankers, academia, and the central bank, as well as debates in the Chamber of Deputies (March 2016). The research also includes the central bank's official warning about the risks to economic stability, the adoption of the law by Parliament and its publication (April 2016), the entry into force of the giving in payment law (May 2016), negative reactions against the law addressed in the open letter to the Government by the credit institution Raiffeisen Bank (August 2016), the second protest of the debtors in Swiss francs (September 2016), the decision of the Constitutional Court of Romania on the objections of unconstitutionality raised by commercial banks on the giving in payment law (October 2016) and a new warning from the NBR (December 2016).

In 2016, the most publicized topics related to the NBR were monetary policy decisions, credit policy developments, and economic and financial legislative amendments. The topics were identified by the analysis of over 13,000 articles on the NBR in the central media and local press (print, radio-TV, and online), according to the NBR Annual Report for 2016. Most articles were published online, 6335 or 48% of the total (National Bank of Romania, 2016). According to the 2016 NBR annual report, more than 70% of the articles that debated the giving in payment law had a balanced tone, 8% used a positive tone and 22% used a negative tone.

The online search for the articles analyzed in this research was conducted in April 2019, and the corpus resulting from the selection of articles totalled approximately 404,000 words (1140 A4 pages, written in Romanian in Times New Roman 12, 1 line spacing, including illustrations). The corpus was coded by the researcher, and was verified by a secondary sampling of 10% of the materials by a graduate of the National School of Political and Administrative Studies (Bucharest), trained in coding. Secondary coding was 80% similar to the initial coding, which validated the initial coding results.

The method used to analyze the media coverage of the giving in payment law was the analysis of the content, with registration unit and context of the online article, based on a coding grid in which the items were grouped into five sections: (A) general information about publications, (B) the actors presented in the articles, (C) the frames, (D) the subject, and (E) the sources for and against the legislative project (Annex E).

Framing analysis consists of a deductive approach, using a grid that quantifies five frames: economic consequences, responsibility, conflict, ethics/moral interest, and human interest, based on criteria developed by Semetko and Valkenburg (2000). Therefore, the research is part of the series of quantitative analyzes, based on predefined frames, in line with research such as those of Semetko and Valkenburg (2000), Tankard (2001), Dimitrova et al. (2005), Matthes and Kohring (2008), and Corbu et al. (2015), etc.

To measure the five generic frames, the present analysis uses 19 questions grouped in sets of 3–5, coded with "1" for "Yes" and "0" for "No," where "Yes" means that the frame is found in the news topic, in the special dimension reflected by each question. The intensity of the framing was calculated as the average of the values of all the items in a framing. The average intensity of the frames revealed important differences from one frame to another and differences in the hierarchy of dominant frames depending on the online portal.

For example, by adapting sets of questions from the Semetko and Valkenburg (2000, p. 100) to which the respondent had to answer "Yes" (1) or "No" (0), the questions used in this analysis to assess the conflict frame are as follows:

- Does the article reflect the disagreement/conflict between the NBR and other institutions, companies, consumer groups, lawyers, etc. related to the debates on the giving in payment law?
- Does the article contain any reproaches addressed to the NBR by other parties involved in the debate (such as other institutions, companies, consumer groups, and lawyers)?
- Does the article include both perspectives or all aspects of the situation/problem?
- Does the article refer to winners and losers?

Thus, the framing of the conflict "highlights the conflict between individuals, groups or institutions in order to capture the interest of the audience" (Semetko & Valkenburg, 2000, p. 95).

The economic framework focuses on the economic repercussions of events or problems (Semetko & Valkenburg, 2000, p. 96) and was assessed in the present research by applying three questions in the coding of materials: "Does the article mention financial repercussions (losses, gains) for other institutions/companies/ consumer groups generated by the decision/action of the NBR?"; "Does the article mention costs/costs for consumers/institutions/companies?"; "Does the article refer to the economic consequences of NBR actions/decisions/inactions?".

"The framing of responsibility presents an issue or a problem in such a way as to assign responsibility for its production or to offer the solution either to the government or to an individual or a group" (Semetko & Valkenburg, 2000, p. 96) and was assessed with the help of four questions: "Does the article blame the NBR for this situation/problem?"; "Does the article suggest that the NBR can improve the situation for consumers/institutions/companies?"; "Does the article propose solutions to the situation/problem?"; "Does the article suggest that the issue calls for urgent action by the NBR?"

For the evaluation of the moral framework, from an ethical or religious perspective, the questions used were: "Does the article contain a moral message?"; "Does the article refer to morality, God, or other religious precepts?"; "Does the article include specifications on how NBR representatives should behave?"

The framing of the human interest "involves the human side or an emotional approach in presenting an event/situation/problem" (Semetko & Valkenburg, 2000, p. 95) and was established using the following questions: "Does the article emphasize whether institutions/consumers are affected/affected of situation?"; "Does the article present case studies or give a human face to the problem?"; "The article uses adjectives, metaphors, etc. which can generate feelings of anger, empathy, sympathy or compassion for those affected by the situation?"; "Does the article contain images that could generate anger, empathy, sympathy, or compassion for those affected by the situation?"

## 7.2 Competition Between Frames

The analysis of the most visible frames and of the differences between the frames used by the four online portals is based on the average values of the identified frames, as they measure the intensity of each frame. The results indicate that the economic and conflict frames are dominant, to the detriment of the moral and the human interest frames. The main classification used was the economic one, with an average registered value of 0.35, an intuitive result considering the economic nature of the analyzed subject. The classification of the conflict reached the value of 0.29, and the moral one—0.06 (Table 7.1).

The quantitative analysis of the ratings reveals an obvious difference between the two online financial portals analyzed. The mainframe used intensively by bursa.ro was that of the conflict, registering the highest average of all publications (0.40). However, the economic situation reached the second position, at an insignificant distance (0.39). At the same time, zf.ro focused on the economic consequences (average of 0.34), and the conflict rate reached an average of 0.22. In quantitative

**Table 7.1** The intensity of frames by Romanian online media for news stories about the NBR's official statements and actions regarding the "giving in payment" law

| Media frames | | Giving in payment law (2016) | | | | |
|---|---|---|---|---|---|---|
| | | Economic | Conflict | Responsibility | Human interest | Moral |
| bursa.ro | Mean | **0.39** | **0.40** | **0.20** | **0.15** | **0.10** |
| | *N* | 133 | 133 | 133 | 133 | 133 |
| | Std. deviation | 0.30 | 0.36 | 0.27 | 0.21 | 0.19 |
| zf.ro | Mean | **0.34** | **0.22** | **0.08** | **0.02** | **0.01** |
| | *N* | 139 | 139 | 139 | 139 | 139 |
| | Std. deviation | 0.16 | 0.28 | 0.16 | 0.09 | 0.06 |
| hotnews.ro | Mean | **0.34** | **0.21** | **0.07** | **0.06** | **0.06** |
| | *N* | 89 | 89 | 89 | 89 | 89 |
| | Std. deviation | 0.15 | 0.27 | 0.19 | 0.16 | 0.19 |
| adevarul.ro | Mean | **0.30** | **0.33** | **0.02** | **0.05** | **0.09** |
| | *N* | 59 | 59 | 59 | 59 | 59 |
| | Std. deviation | 0.11 | 0.32 | 0.11 | 0.16 | 0.20 |
| Total | Mean | **0.35** | **0.29** | **0.11** | **0.07** | **0.06** |
| | *N* | 420 | 420 | 420 | 420 | 420 |
| | Std. deviation | 0.21 | 0.32 | 0.21 | 0.17 | 0.16 |

Source: Calculations based on the coding of online articles ($N = 420$) published in 2016 by bursa.ro, zf.ro, hotnews.ro, adevarul.ro, regarding the giving in payment law

terms, the coverage of the subject was the same, but the two financial websites framed the conflict differently. This result contradicts the expectations that all financial publications present economic issues much more intensely than the conflict frame and to a greater extent than generalist newspapers, due to their economic profile. Moreover, bursa.ro reflected the conflict more strongly than the generalist portal adevarul.ro. Major differences regarding the classification of responsibility, human interest, and moral interest can be observed by analyzing the intensity of the classification in the reports of bursa.ro and of the three other websites. Therefore, the Romanian public had access, in the same period, to different perspectives and interpretations of the same subject.

The popularity of the frames calculated based on the number of articles in which the frame appears (Fig. 7.1) reveals similarities between the four online publications: the economic consequences and the conflict were the most publicized frames in both financial and general media. The responsibility frame comes in third only in the financial press. In the general press, the framing of the human interest (hotnews.ro) and the moral one (adevarul.ro) were presented more frequently.

During the analyzed period, the economic frame was the most visible, a result easily anticipated taking into account the impact of the law that was researched in various studies (e.g., Morosan & Scurtu, 2019; Petrescu & Stan, 2017; Badiu & Niță, 2016). The result can also be explained by the fact that the economic consequences were the most recurring arguments invoked both by the promoters of the law and by its opponents. The frame recorded the highest values in correlation with the financial

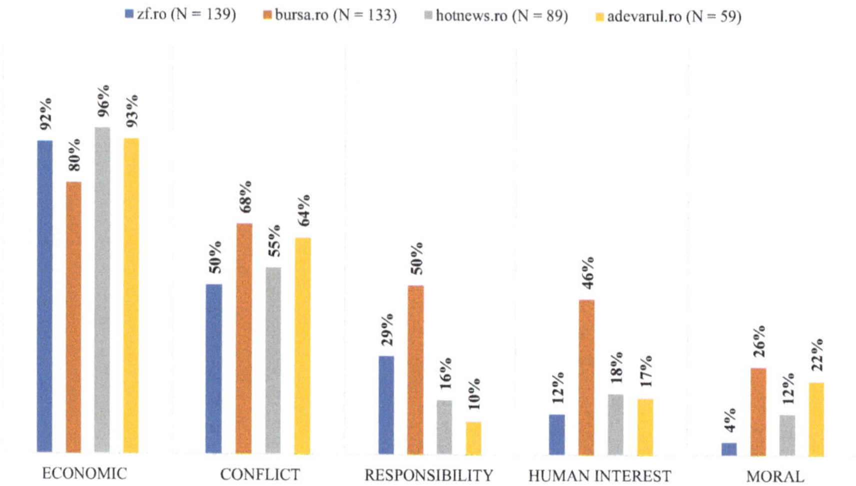


**Fig. 7.1** Frames presence by the online portal ($N = 420$)

losses of debtors, of the banking sector, and of other commercial activities, as the initiators of the law and the NBR made different official assessments:

> "The giving in payment law is consequential not only for the tens of thousands of desperate people who are despised by the NBR and the banking lobby, but also for future borrowers. The increase in interest rates in the next period will also lead to an increase in the rate of non-performance in the Prima Casă program", said the lawyer Gheorghe Piperea. (Oncu, 2016, February 28)

> At the request of the NBR, the European Central Bank issued an opinion on the giving in payment law, warning that it threatens legal certainty, may cause payment delays, and may also affect the confidence of foreign investors and the stability of the banking system. (Manu, 2016, January 7).

Some opinion articles presented the general economic consequences, which would have been favored even by the central bank: "it seems that the core of the European Union has thrown its garbage on the shoulders of the citizens of the periphery, and our Central Bank seems to be doing everything it can to keep the situation, with the help of the European Union, behind the Parliament" (Make, 2016c, March 15).

The focus on economic consequences confirms the results of researchers who analyzed how the financial crisis was framed (e.g., Damstra & Vliegenthart, 2018; Falasca, 2014; Mylonas, 2012). The qualitative research conducted in this chapter showed that, in the opinion of NBR representatives, the messages about the consequences of systemic risk were well articulated, but the fact that the risk did not occur generated a new wave of criticism of the NBR.

The media analysis identified three types of conflicts. The mainframe was on the conflict between the NBR and the commercial banks, on the one hand, and the debtors and supporters of the law—on the other. The other secondary divergences that emerged during the period under review focused on the conflict between the central bank and lending institutions and the conflict between the NBR and

Parliament. These results confirm the comments made by central bank officials regarding the description of the power relations between the stakeholders, according to which two types of conflicts involved the central bank in public debates and led to personal attacks: people versus institutions (debtors versus central bank) and institutions versus institutions (NBR versus Parliament):

> The giving in payment law (...) has caused a real war between the banking system (including the NBR), on the one hand, and initiators and consumers, on the other. (Olescu, 2016a, January 5)

> It seems like, two football teams are fighting: a well-established team with 11 stars, but completely disconnected and annoyed by the persistence of their opponents, and the other—a team made up of amateurs who play the match of their lives. And the public is definitely interested in amateurs, writes economics professor Bogdan Glăvan (...) In this disproportionate fight with the promoters of the law, the banking representatives are still visibly suffering—and this is due to the bad image that the banks have. They should do something in this direction. Possibly hire a PR professional. (Popa, 2016d, March 8)

Journalists used terms that came from the semantic area of conflict, such as "battle," "war," "attack," and the most used word was "conflict" (20 times in the articles published by bursa.ro, 10 times in zf.ro; 7 times in hotnews.ro; and once in adevarul.ro). During the debates, the NBR governor, Mugur Isărescu, and other NBR representatives explained the role of the central bank ("I must say it very clearly for all Romanians to hear: NBR is not the lawyer of any bank. The NBR is protective, and it protects Romanians' money") (Popa, 2016c, March 7) and pointed the finger at lending institutions ("He (author's note: Mugur Isărescu) mentioned that banks and the Romanian Association of Banks are largely to blame because they <<completely>> forgot what the bases of banking are"—Ghinea, 2016, February 25). The intensity of the conflict frame highlights once again the similarities between the approach of financially focused bursa.ro and of the generalist adevarul.ro, since in the two online publications this classification prevails.

The media has consistently portrayed the NBR as a defender of commercial banks against the initiators and debtors, or they took this label from hostile stakeholders:

> A few days ago, Governor Isărescu complained that the public has been informed that he would play the role of "bank lawyer", but the defiance of the current parliamentarians leaves no room for interpretation. (Make, 2016c, March 15)

> Lawyer Piperea, on Facebook: "The war, although not officially over, was obviously lost by the delinquent banks with loans in Swiss francs and, in particular, by their anachronistic general and ex-officio lawyer, the NBR". (Popa, 2016a, January 15)

According to central bank officials, the label "defender of the bank" released in 2016 could have the following explanations: NBR intervened too vocal and repeatedly in debates because of the frames launched by other stakeholders (elites, media) that competed against the frames of the NBR, and commercial banks did not react adequately.

According to Capella and Jamieson (1997), the conflict frame is most intensely used in political news, during election periods. In the context of the eroded confidence in the central bank in the post-crisis period, the question posed by the authors may broaden the perspective, including for future research on the process of building frames in relation to economic news and institutional actors:

> Is the lack of public trust in institutions justified? If leaders are motivated exclusively or at least primarily by self-interest and if there is an intrinsic conflict between self-interest and the public good, then media reports of self-interest political action are not cynical, but only realistic, and growing distrust of leaders and institutions represent a rejection of Pollyannaism. This conclusion is supported by the findings that cynicism can be based on the experience of those who are more active and more informed—more cynical. (Capella & Jamieson, 1997, pp. 19–20)

The results of this research are in line with previous studies that highlight that both conflict and controversy rank second among news values (Shoemaker & Reese, 2014) or Harcup & O'Neill's analysis (2017, p. 1471) which show that negative news is "news from the negative spectrum, such as conflict or tragedy."

All other financial and general portals placed the responsibility frame in third place, while in adevarul.ro it came in last. The central bank and lending institutions have been held accountable by the promoters of the law for the financial losses suffered by borrowers and at the same time have been criticized for not supporting the law and being asked to find solutions. According to the liability frame, the regulator relaxed the lending conditions and the credit institutions lured the population with low interest rates. At the same time, commercial banks have been accused of overpromoting new financial products in Swiss francs, and credit officers have been considered responsible for not clearly exposing the risks associated with the Swiss francs products.

The responsibility frame indicated possible solutions to the given situation, but also some shortcomings of the NBR's actions both before and during the financial crisis:

> Some parliamentarians asked the NBR several questions, including: "Where was the NBR when the loans were given and the real estate appraisals made? Why did the NBR chose to not intervene when foreign currency loans suffered because of the exchange rate? I guess there are well-paid people out there (author's note: in the NBR) who can predict what's going on in the foreign exchange market. Banks are now trying to cover up the mistake of making assessments on the fly. The BNR had to intervene then". (Olescu, 2016d, March 31)

From the perspective of responsibility, the central bank and lending institutions were held accountable by the initiators of the law for the financial losses of indebted Romanians and, at the same time, were criticized for not supporting the law and were asked to find solutions:

> "I have frequently seen our "glorious" governor of the NBR, Mr. Isărescu, give lessons on prudential banking policies and monetary policies, but never assuming a trace of responsibility for the drama of those who took out loans and are now unable to pay them. People have become poorer than when they hoped to get the loan, but they are the only ones responsible", Băsescu (author's note: Traian Băsescu, a Romanian politician and President of Romania from 2004 to 2014) wrote on a social media page. (Popescu, 2016, March 3)

The results confirm some of the results regarding the European economic crisis obtained by Radu and Ștefăniță (2012), showing that, in hotnews.ro and ziare.com, in intervals from 2009 to 2011, the media framed the topics mainly from the perspective of responsibility, followed by conflict and conspiracy.

The human interest frame ranked fourth among all publications. Although the frame of human interest is frequently used in social news, this analysis highlights, surprisingly, that bursa.ro, a publication with a financial profile, recorded the highest intensity (average of 0.15) of all online publications.

Journalists gave a human face to the situations presented and exposed life stories of indebted people, organized in associations or groups who took part in public debates on the law and who protested against the banking sector and the central bank several times in 2016:

> The NBR cannot and does not have the right to legitimize abuses, it cannot bail out those who are guilty of the dramas of Romanians who wanted to own a three-room apartment and who ended up ending their days because of the financial crisis, the abusive clauses in the contracts, the loans in exotic currencies with which they were lured by the banks, without being explaining the enormous risks to which they were exposed. (Vasiescu, 2016, March 15)

Some news framed from the perspective of human interest also referred to the loss of human lives:

> Daniel Zamfir, initiator of the giving in payment law: (...) We have the case of a client who will be pursued by the bank until he is 104 years old, for a loan. I will present this case to you immediately, his house was taken away, he paid as much as he could pay. There were 32 people who committed suicide because of the banks (...) But who will give anything back to those who committed suicide? (Popa, 2016b, February 17)

> The banners carried by the protesters read "NBR without immunity" or "We want the conversion on the date of granting". At the NBR headquarters, protesters left a wreath on the steps and lit candles. (Vlad, 2016, September 25)

Referring to the communication on this topic, more than a quarter of the NBR representatives interviewed stated that empathy toward debtors was the missing element in the construction of certain messages.

The results confirm what Shoemaker & Reese (2014, p. 171) highlighted when they opened the list of predictable values of news with prominence and importance: "The importance of an event is measured by its impact; how many lives it affects. Deaths are more important than property destruction. The actions of those in power are the subject of news because they have the ability to influence the general public." Several researchers (e.g., Alicandro et al., 2019; Economou et al., 2013; Fountoulakis et al., 2014) have studied the influence of the recession on mental health and the advance of the idea of suicide among those facing financial difficulties. Alicandro et al. (2019, p. 794) show that "the suicide rate has fallen in most countries, but in some states there was an increase in 2008 during the financial crisis, and in others the downward trend registered before the crisis was interrupted." Between 2008 and 2015, rising unemployment in Greece, the Netherlands, Italy, and Spain was linked to an increase in suicide deaths in Greece and the Netherlands and an interruption in a declining trend in Italy and Spain (Alicandro et al., 2019). The same researchers found that in the 2000s, in Eastern European countries, including Romania, there was a declining trend, remaining, however, at the top of the suicide death rate.

Although the "human interest" classification is often used in social news, the analysis shows that, out of the evaluated online press, the highest average of intensity of this classification was registered by the financial publication bursa.ro. Damstra and Vliegenthart (2018, p. 994) consider that "the inclusion in the system of moral values provided a distinctive image of the crisis. The diagnosis of the crisis was found in the shortcomings of the financial system and in close connection with humanity in general."

In the moral frame, which was, as expected, the frame least frequently represented, journalists most often exposed the official statements of the initiators of the law and their continued "labelling" of the NBR ("blackmail," "lies," "manipulation," "lobbying"):

> The initiator of the law, Daniel Zamfir, a PNL deputy, said that during the legislative procedure, the banks and the NBR carried out a real manipulation campaign: "It is an ordinary manipulation to say that the giving in payment law blows up the banking system". The parliamentarian asked the NBR governor to stop this manipulation. (Olescu, 2016e, April 13)

> "Let's clarify the mafias we work with," said Anghel (Cristiana Anghel, senator), insinuating that behind every parliamentarian who tried to take on an amendment to the NBR is the banking lobby. (Popa, 2016b, February 17)

The moral frame was also found by researchers who analyzed the framing of the financial crisis—for example, the greed frame (Bach et al., 2013) and the moral frame (Damstra & Vliegenthart, 2018). Although the moral frame has almost the same frequency in bursa.ro, zf.ro and hotnews.ro, in terms of intensity—bursa.ro and adevarul.ro are much closer, with an average of 0.10, respectively, 0.09, in hotnews.ro it reached 0.06, while in zf.ro it had the weakest average, of 0.01. The intensity of the frame indicates a similarity between the financial leaning bursa.ro and the generalist adevarul.ro.

Regarding the clarity of the NBR's messages, the specialized public questioned in the sociological survey by questionnaire, believe that the messages on the giving in payment law and about the credit crisis in Swiss francs were clearer than those about the situation of Greek-owned banks, but less clear compared to monetary information.

Summarizing the conclusions for RQ1 and RQ2 based on the content analysis of the articles, in 2016, the online press in Romania reported on the giving in payment law in a relatively similar way compared to the use of the five frames: conflict, economic repercussions, responsibility, human interest, and moral values. The preponderance of the conflict frame and that of the economic consequences reveals a similarity between the four online publications analyzed, considering that these frames were the most popular both in the economic and financial press and in the general press. The economic frame was the most visible, which was easy to anticipate given the economic impact of the law and the economic arguments used by both the initiators and opponents of the law. Regarding the financial press, the third most used frame was the responsibility frame while in the general press, the most used frames were the human interest frame (hotnews.ro), and the moral frame (adevarul.ro).

On the other hand, the analysis of the intensity of the frames indicates a clear difference between the two financial portals included in the evaluation, zf.ro and bursa.ro. Although coverage was the same, the two websites framed issues differently and counterintuitively, given their financial profile, the financial news they published were not more intense than the articles in the general media. In fact, the framing of the conflict, which put the central bank in a very difficult position during debates, was even more intensely reported in bursa.ro, than in adevarul.ro.

Although the framing of human interest is frequently used in social news, the analysis indicates another unexpected result: the highest intensity of framing, among all online publications, was recorded by the financial leaning bursa.ro. In all the online press analyzed, the moral framework was used the least and with the smallest intensity. At the same time, the use of the moral framework once again reflected the differences between the two newspapers with a financial profile, the averages registered by bursa.ro and zf.ro being at opposite poles. These results indicate a homogeneous presence of the five analyzed frames and a heterogeneous intensity in the online financial press. Differences in the way financial framing were used may suggest the existence of a split in this media segment. The results pave the way for future research on the elements that influenced the construction process in each case, on the perceptions, background, and education of journalists and, on the other hand, on the differences in the profiles of readers of the two financial publications.

## 7.3 The Most Visible Pros and Cons: Readers' Reaction

In identifying the most visible actors in the analyzed articles, the present study referred to the most visible individuals, institutions, client groups, or professional associations, giving statements and other official positions (press releases, reports, notifications, petitions, etc.) regarding the giving in payment law, in 2016. Thus, in the category of supporters, eight recurring actors were noted: Daniel Zamfir (senator, initiator of the law), Gheorghe Piperea (lawyer, representative of debtors), the Association of Romanian Financial Services Users, various groups of clients with loans in Swiss francs, individual clients, representatives of political parties, tax consultants, and specialists. On the other hand—the NBR, through the voice of several officials, was followed by The Council of Banking Employers in Romania, Romanian Association of Banks, credit institutions, the presidency, politicians, European institutions (ECB, EC), consultants, specialists, Superior Council of Magistracy, and the Ministry of Justice.

The data analysis reflects the fact that the NBR was closely followed by commercial banks (with a presence in 34% of the analyzed news) and European institutions (ECB, EC) (18%). In the category of supporters, in the first position was, in 2016, Senator Daniel Zamfir, with a presence of 38%, followed by lawyer

**Table 7.2** Presence in articles of supporters and detractors of the giving in payment law

| Actors | Pro or against | Mean | Std. deviation | Percentage |
|---|---|---|---|---|
| NBR (representatives) | Against | 0.95 | 0.213 | 95 |
| Daniel Zamfir | Pro | 0.38 | 0.487 | 38 |
| Commercial banks | Against | 0.34 | 0.474 | 34 |
| Gheorghe Piperea | Pro | 0.20 | 0.404 | 20 |
| European institutions (European Central Bank, European Commission) | Against | 0.18 | 0.385 | 18 |
| Presidency | Against | 0.15 | 0.359 | 15 |
| Politicians | Pro | 0.15 | 0.357 | 15 |
| Romanian Association of Banks (RAB) | Against | 0.12 | 0.335 | 12 |
| Consultants, analysts | Against | 0.11 | 0.321 | 11 |
| Consultants, analysts | Pro | 0.10 | 0.306 | 10 |
| The Council of Banking Employers in Romania (CBER) | Against | 0.10 | 0.300 | 10 |
| Client groups | Pro | 0.06 | 0.253 | 6 |
| Swiss franc debtors | Pro | 0.05 | 0.227 | 5 |
| Association of Romanian Users of Financial Services (ARUFS) | Pro | 0.04 | 0.208 | 4 |
| Politicians | Against | 0.04 | 0.202 | 4 |
| Superior Council of Magistracy (SCM) (consultative role) | Against | 0.04 | 0.197 | 4 |
| Ministry of Justice (MoJ) (consultative role) | Against | 0.02 | 0.144 | 2 |

Gheorghe Piperea (20%) and politicians in favor of the project (15%) (Table 7.2; Fig. 7.2). The results confirm the perception of central bank representatives who pointed out in interviews that the NBR was considered the bank's lawyer because it communicated in many voices, communicated too much (a 95% presence in the news), but also because commercial banks withdrew from the debates, were silent, did not strengthen the messages of the NBR (34%).

Regarding the distribution of the main supporters and detractors of the legislative initiative (Fig. 7.3), we can see that the NBR registered the highest averages in adevarul.ro (98% of articles) and bursa.ro (95%) (this result could be explained by taking into account the keywords used in the selection of the coded articles). Daniel Zamfir was more present in bursa.ro (in 43% of articles), followed by zf.ro (37%), the representatives of commercial banks were more present in bursa.ro (in over half of the articles) and zf.ro (29%), and the lawyer Gheorghe Piperea was more present in bursa.ro (in 29% of the articles) and adevarul.ro (23%), whereas in zf.ro he was mentioned in 10% of the articles. Once again, similarities can be observed between the financial website bursa.ro and the general adevarul.ro in covering the NBR's and Piperea's messages, as well as a difference in the dissemination of Daniel Zamfir's messages by the two financial publications, confirming the results obtained at RQ1 and RQ2.

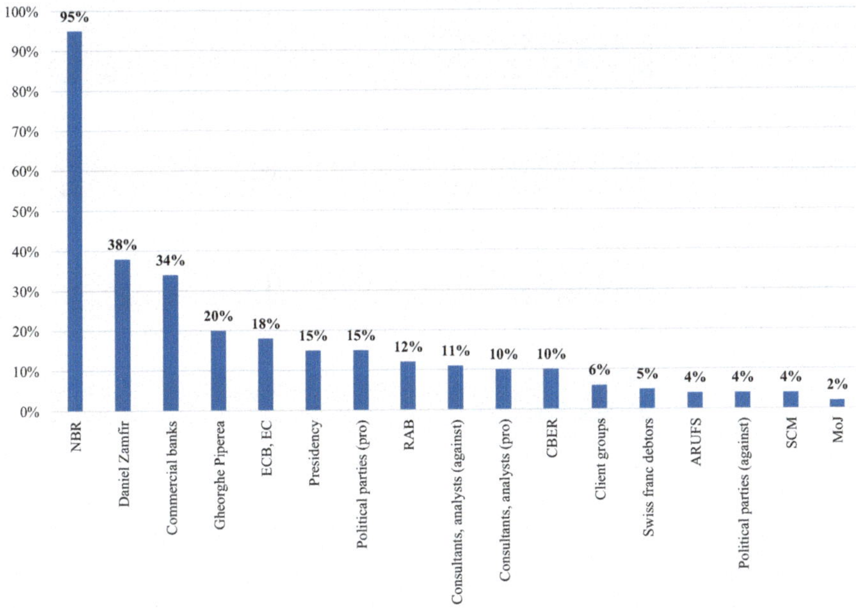


**Fig. 7.2** Ranking of the most visible supporters and detractors of the giving in payment law ($N = 420$). *ECB* European Central Bank, *EC* European Commission, *RAB* Romanian Association of Banks, *CBER* The Council of Banking Employers in Romania, *ARUFS* Association of Romanian Users of Financial Services, *SCM* Superior Council of Magistracy, *MoJ* Ministry of Justice

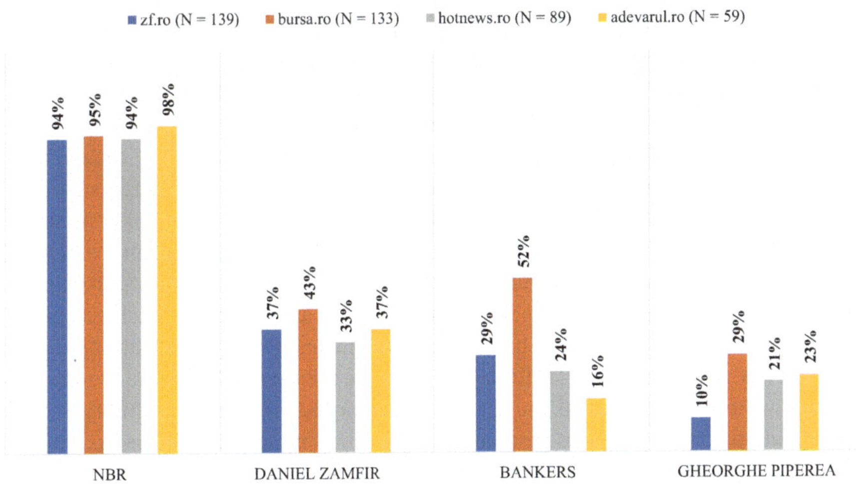


**Fig. 7.3** Presence of the four main supporters and detractors of the giving in payment law

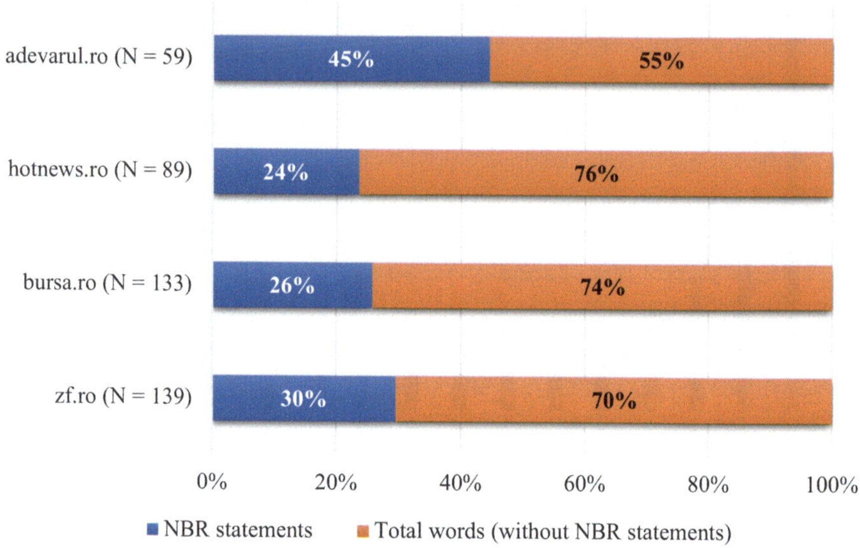


**Fig. 7.4** The share of statements of NBR representatives in total number of words

The statements of all visible NBR representatives on this subject (Mugur Isărescu, Adrian Vasilescu, Bogdan Olteanu, Eugen Rădulescu, Nicolae Cinteză, Liviu Voinea, Daniel Dăianu, Florin Georgescu) quantified in the analyzed materials had the largest share of the number of words in the adevărul.ro (44.50%), followed by zf.ro (29.50%), bursa.ro (25.70%), and hotnews.ro (23.50%) (Fig. 7.4).

Quantitative analysis of several indicators regarding the visibility of the content and the interest, and the reactions and engagement of the audiences, such as the number of views and the number of comments, shows that, on average, hotnews.ro articles had over 8900 views, and those of zf.ro—over 3100. Regarding the engagement of readers in comments on articles, the most intense activity was registered by the bursa.ro portal, with almost 6500 total comments (an average of 40 comments/article), followed by hotnews.ro (with a total of 3092 comments and an average of 34 comments/article) and adevarul.ro (with an average of 4.5 comments/article). In the absence of the same indicators for all publications, a comparative analysis cannot be performed, but we note that hotnews.ro has made the subject of the giving in payment law prominent, a fact reflected both by the number of views and comments. However, the financial portal bursa.ro had the largest number of comments, and counterintuitively, adevarul.ro generated a very small number of comments.

The results of RQ3 reconfirm that the NBR was, disproportionately compared to the other actors, the most visible actor against the giving in payment law in the analyzed media. The representatives of commercial banks come in a distant second place, a fact which could have attracted the label of "lawyer of the banks" for the NBR. At the same time, the data reflect new similarities between the financier bursa.ro and the generalist adevarul.ro in reflecting the messages sent by the central bank and the lawyer Gheorghe Piperea, as well as a difference in the dissemination of the messages of the initiator of the law by the two financial newspapers.

## 7.4 NBR's Public Communication, Under the Magnifying Glass of the Editorialists

The main sub-themes of the giving in payment law were, in 2016, the possible effects generated by the application of the legislative initiative (48% of the total evaluated materials), the steps for the adoption of the draft law (31%), aspects related to the implementation of the giving in payment law (11%) and communication of commercial banks and of the National Bank of Romania (10%) (Fig. 7.5).

Regarding the quantitative evaluation of the materials related to the communication of the NBR and of the credit institutions, most of them were published by the financial profile portals—bursa.ro (21) and zf.ro (17), followed by hotnews.ro (6) and adevarul.ro (4). Over 45% of them (23 articles) were opinions expressed by the editorial directors, presidents, and directors of the press groups or by the journalists who constantly documented the subject. Most of them were expressed by Make (Florian Goldstein, editorialist, founder, and chairman of the Bursa press group), Cristian Hoştiuc (editorial director, Ziarul Financiar), Dan Popa (coordinating editor, finance—banks, HotNews), Cristian Dogaru (Bursa journalist). To these were added comments expressed by public figures (analyst Lucian Isar, lawyer Gheorghe Piperea, etc.), taken up in full by the publications. Along with the opinions, the news articles signed by Emilia Olescu (publisher, finance—banks, stock exchange), Claudia Medrega (publisher, Ziarul Financiar), Liviu Popescu

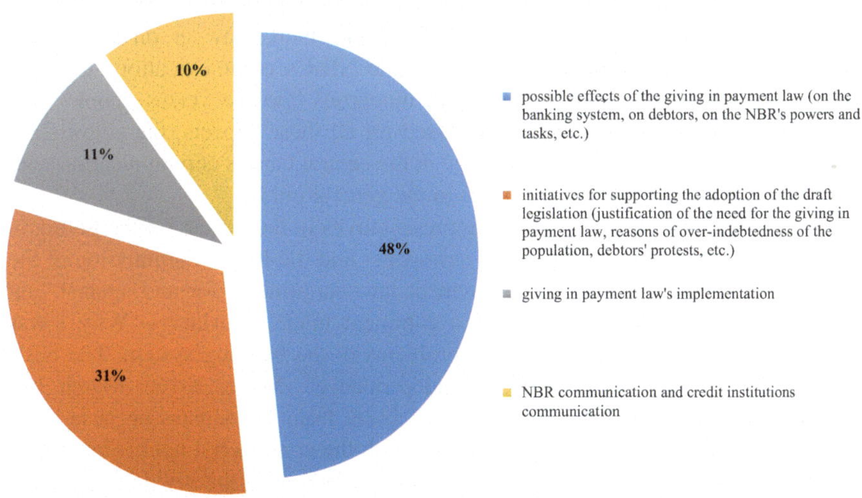


**Fig. 7.5** The giving in payment law—the main sub-themes

(editor of Ziarul Financiar), Dan Popa (HotNews), Daniel Ionașcu (journalist Adevărul), stood out quantitatively. These news articles included various positions on the communication of representatives of commercial banks, the NBR and other relevant actors and concentrated 45% of the materials on public communication. Other published materials were analyses of the communication strategy of credit institutions with the general public.

Among the statements made by the representatives of the banking system regarding the communication activity, the most visible ones in the analyzed media emphasized the erosion of credibility and the need to restore trust. For example, Sergiu Oprescu, the president of the Romanian Association of Banks (RAB), declared that the credit institutions lost the "populist-media battle": "I don't think we managed to communicate very well on this subject. It's a guilt we must take on. I think we have fallen into a lack of credibility and that is why our message has not penetrated" (Olescu, 2016b, March 3). In his turn, Radu Grațian Ghețea, president of CEC Bank and honorary president of RAB at the time, stressed that "Another challenge is the relationship with customers and the recovery of trust in banks" (Olescu, 2016b, March 3). The NBR governor spoke publicly about the lack of reaction on behalf of commercial banks:

> Banks have always preferred to stand behind the NBR under some kind of protection and because of this the idea that we are their lawyer has been strengthened, said NBR governor Mugur Isărescu, continuing to criticize the passivity of the Romanian Association of Banks. (Medrega, 2016, March 7)

Marius Dunca, former president of Romania's National Consumer Protection Authority, also criticized the banks, accusing them of trying to manipulate public opinion by denigrating the law (Olescu, 2016c, March 18).

Returning to the evaluation of the central bank's communication by editorialists and commentators, bursa.ro stands out with 13 critical opinion materials out of the total of 23 evaluated in the present research. The main criticisms were focused on eroding the trust in the NBR, on the label of being the banks' lawyer, on errors made while using several contradictory voices in the NBR's communication. To these were added comments about engaging in numerous "people versus people" and "institutions versus people" conflicts. Based on all these aspects, the editorialists always emphasized the need for a change in the central bank's communication with stakeholders and for a greater openness to the general public.

For example, the absence of NBR representatives in the debate on the giving in payment law, organized by the Bursa newspaper and the Legal Commission of the Chamber of Deputies—"Giving in payment law—arguments for and against," on March 14, 2016, was the subject of a comment made by Make—"Why I was interested in the small communication problems of the banking system. The NBR is close to the verge on its abuse of independence" (Make, 2016c, March 15). According to the editorialist, the NBR was absent from the debates because it did not have sufficient arguments and solidarity with the commercial banks. In another editorial signed in March ("With or without the adoption of the giving in payment law") (Make, 2016d, March 21), Make emphasizes: "Banking communication has been the subject of my criticism and will continue to be." The editorialist of bursa.ro assesses the loss of credibility of the banking system in three segments: verbal communication, because credit institutions refused the dialogue with debtors and parliamentarians, "eroding the infallibility of the NBR" and the attitude of banks who showed solidarity in court against their clients and against the lawyer Gheorghe Piperea. Make believes that:

> Condemnation was widespread, and it reached even the NBR governor because he defended himself against the label of <<lawyer of banks>> when he should have presented himself as <<defender of the entire banking system>> against the clientele. (Make, 2016d, March 21)

The chairman of the Bursa press group considers that the publication he represents is at odds with other publications and that it has fallen into the category of bankers' "enemies" because he also published messages from supporters of the bill, "and not (as the media did in general) only of the opposing banking party." The results obtained in response to RQ3 confirm Make's observation regarding the more intense media coverage of the supporters' messages by bursa.ro, since, out of the four publications analyzed, the main promoters recorded the most prominent exposures in bursa.ro (Daniel Zamfir is mentioned in 43% of the articles and Gheorghe Piperea—in 29%). At the same time, the bankers' messages also recorded the most intense exposure in this publication (in more than half of the articles).

At the same time, Make draws attention to the escalation of the conflict around the giving in payment law and on simplification "when assessing the balance of power between for and against eliminating the rational assessment of arguments." Laurențiu Mitrache ("Justice and Responsibility," March 15, 2016) from bursa.ro, agrees that the conflict between supporters and opponents of the legislative initiative has captured public debate and is defined by more attacks on the other side and less arguing on one's side.

Through Make's voice, bursa.ro also drew attention to the communication on several voices, sometimes discordant (for example, the governor Mugur Isărescu, the director of the Financial Stability Directorate, Eugen Rădulescu and the Communication Department) of the number of notifications to the giving in payment law. After an estimate made by Eugen Rădulescu at the beginning of June 2016 and explained by the NBR Communication Directorate as Rădulescu's self-assessment and not an official statistic of the central bank, the NBR governor confirmed at the end of June that the number of notifications had reached a few thousand. According to Make, this statement confirmed Eugen Rădulescu's estimate and contradicted the position expressed by the Communication Department:

> Either Eugen Rădulescu and Mugur Isărescu are magicians, and their numbers appear when they utter a magic formula, or the NBR communicators simply lied. Or they quickly set to work and obtained, in just a month, data from the market. (Make, 2016e, July 1)

Make also criticized both the way in which the NBR responded to written requests during the analyzed period ("Is it really the National Bank of Romania who is inviting me to a contest of making fun of each other?" March 7, 2016a), as well as the governor's statements that "the NBR informs the public correctly and we are recognized internationally as an extremely serious institution" ("Filming eagles. The NBR does not correctly inform the public") (Make, 2016b, March 8).

The need to change the communication strategy of the central bank was underlined by the same editorialist (Make) and in editorial replies to the opinions expressed by Adrian Vasilescu and Lucian Croitoru, advisers of the NBR governor, in "Cordial controversies. Adrian Vasilescu writes well, but about what he wants to," (Make, 2016i, October 3) and "The NBR believes that it is under an electoral attack. Lucian Croitoru poisons the wells" (Make, 2016g, August 19). Again, the biased attitude in debates towards banks, poor communication with stakeholders—"Disastrous lack of quality of communication with both the general public and the limited public of the journalists' guild" and the erosion of the NBR's image as a result of its involvement in various conflicts, was discussed. Make also identifies "The remarkable change of speech among the members of the NBR leadership" (Make, 2016h, September 21). Daniel Dăianu, NBR board member in 2016, argued that—"If the banks win, they still lose," thus highlighting the mistakes done by banks towards their clients.

In August 2016, the central bank sent to the media an official position on the attacks by hostile stakeholders—"The National Bank of Romania strongly and unequivocally rejects attacks on the central bank's reputation," signed by spokesman Dan Suciu, stating that "The Central Bank will not respond to a campaign aimed at denigrating the institution with no aim of properly informing the public." The position was assessed by zf.ro as "quite unusual for a central bank" to enter a direct dispute—"Without mentioning the name, as the spokesman refers to Lucian Isar, who has an old dispute with the NBR" (Ziarul Financiar, 2016, August 9). The NBR statement generated a new editorial in bursa.ro ("The Romanian people invite you to dinner, Mr. Isărescu!" (Make, 2016f, August 10), in which Make highlights the conflicts "people versus people" and "institutions versus people" and reiterates the opinion that the central bank, as an institution of the Romanian state, must show a greater openness to the general public: "The NBR should revise its attitude towards the public."

Cristian Hoştiuc, the editorial director of Ziarul Financiar, also believed that the poor communication between the NBR and the commercial banks contributed to the wave of trust granted to the initiators and supporters of the giving in payment law ("It is not the customers' fault that they came to trust more in Piperea and Zamfir than in the bankers. Can the increase in the advance be mitigated by the decrease in the price of the apartments?") (Hoştiuc, 2016b, January 31). The main vulnerabilities reported were the lack of an impact assessment, the reactive attitude of credit institutions, and the erosion of confidence in the NBR:

> At the level of public opinion, the deputy Daniel Zamfir and the lawyer Gheorghe Piperea are heroes, because they manage to defeat the bankers and to improve the financial situation of several hundred thousand debtors. The heads of banks are hiding in this debate, considering that they should not get dirty by entering the parliamentary mire of talks or those on television. Bankers have been hiding behind the NBR, hoping that the confidence in the NBR will be enough to turn debates in their favor. In the crisis of francs and bank rates, confidence in the NBR has also eroded. (Hoştiuc, 2016b, January 31)

In another editorial, "The problem of the National Bank is not when the governor Mugur Isărescu will retire, but when Mr. Adrian Vasilescu will do so" (zf.ro, February 21, 2016), Cristian Hoştiuc appreciates that the main messages of NBR and of the bankers did not penetrate because the arguments of the central bank representatives were "dry and cold, legal and threatening" compared to the "logical-populist arguments of the lawmakers" and so the gap between experts and the general public is increasingly obvious: "In the same circle, of the NBR, economists and bankers end up no longer having a common language with the street, with the public, in the end with their customers" (Hoştiuc, 2016a, February 21). The editorialist considers that, among the NBR communicators, Adrian Vasilescu remains the closest to the public and expresses his concern about finding the next representative communicator for the institution: "A governor of the National Bank is sure to be found, but a good communicator who inspires confidence, peace and understanding in the NBR to the general public will be very difficult to find. And this was best seen in the discussions on the giving in payment law" (Hoştiuc, 2016a, February 21).

Referring to losing the media battle on the giving in payment law, Cristian Hoştiuc is of the opinion that this is caused by the defensive attitude of the bankers who "came down from the ivory tower and attack together," but also by the rise of social networks that have contributed to the much faster transmission of messages from the bottom up, from the general public to the media and elites, a "distribution channel that has a frighteningly fast and powerful spread" of customer dissatisfaction ("Facebook defeated even the bankers: how did a minority (those with loans in francs) manage to take the lead even in the courts and turn customers against the banks?") (Hoştiuc, 2016c, March 12).

In hotnews.ro and adevarul.ro, the comments regarding the communication were scattered and focused on the lack of any communication bridges between the supporters and opponents of the law and on the effects on the credibility of the central bank:

> Simple conclusion: Banks play their card extremely badly. Moreover, the credibility of the central broadcasting institution seems to be at stake. As it stands now, the law is perverse, with second-rate effects difficult to estimate. But in the parallel universes, very few people take into account what others say over a year. Especially if it is electoral . . . ("Two parallel worlds. Proponents and detractors of the giving in payment law break any bridges themselves, and in these conditions, it seems clear who will be the winner"). (Popa, 2016e, March 14)

In his turn, the adevarul.ro journalist Daniel Ionaşcu pointed out the absence of banks and the NBR from public debates considered important and analyzed the communication strategy on this subject:

> Mugur Isărescu, the governor of the NBR, criticized the law from a distance, while the bank employers published in the press acid warnings about the law, which they say will block lending, collapse the construction sector and lead to higher rents (. . .) At Monday's debate, however, organized by the Bursa newspaper and the Legal Committee of the Chamber of Deputies, they refused to participate. (Ionaşcu, 2016, March 14)

In conclusion, the main positions in the media (editorials, comments, opinions, etc.) regarding the NBR's communication strategy in the context of the giving in payment law have highlighted the need to change the central bank's communication, a greater openness to the general public, disengagement from conflicts, and better coordination of public statements. In the editorialists' perception, the central bank's poor communication contributed to the eroding public confidence in the NBR. These observations confirm those expressed both by the representatives of the institution, in the qualitative research, as well as the perception of the specialized and the general public, expressed in the applied questionnaires. In interviews, some NBR respondents tied the erosion of public confidence to strategic communication of the central bank. This was the third most frequently used argument after the communication strategy with opposing stakeholders and the low level of public financial education. At the same time, the statistically significant correlations established between the assessments of the level of trust and clarity of the NBR messages made by the two categories of public show that trust in the central bank can be restored by the institution's efforts toward greater clarity, simplification, and accessibility of messages.

## 7.5 Conclusions

The content analysis of the articles on the giving in payment law published, in 2016, by bursa.ro, zf.ro, hotnews.ro, and adevarul.ro shows that the online press in Romania reported this topic in a relatively similar way compared to the use of the five frames: conflict, economic repercussions, responsibility, human interest, and moral values. The economic framework was the most visible, an intuitive result as both the initiators and the opponents of the law used arguments regarding possible financial and economic effects. The responsibility frame comes in third place in the financial press and in the general media the most frequently used frames were human interest (hotnews.ro) and the moral frame (adevarul.ro).

The intensity of the framing reflects a clear difference between the two evaluated financial portals, zf.ro and bursa.ro, the framing of the conflict being even more intensely reported in bursa.ro than in the generalist portal adevarul.ro. Although the framing of human interest is frequently used in social news, the analysis highlighted another unexpected result: the highest intensity of framing, among all online publications, was recorded by bursa.ro. The moral frame was the least used and with the least intensity. At the same time, the use of the moral framework once again reflected the differences between the two newspapers with a financial profile, the averages registered by bursa.ro and zf.ro being at opposite poles. Based on these results, we appreciate that the differences in the way in which the frames were used in the financial press may suggest the existence of a split in this press segment.

The content analysis reconfirms the perception of the representatives of the central bank, namely that the NBR was, disproportionately compared to the other actors, the most visible actor in the media against the giving in payment law. The representatives of commercial banks come in a distant second, which helps understand the "bank lawyer" label attributed to the NBR. In the perception of the publishers of the evaluated publications, the faulty communication of the central bank contributed to the erosion of the public trust in the NBR. The main positions of the media on the NBR's communication strategy underlined the need to change the central bank's communication, greater openness to the general public, disengagement from conflicts, and better coordination of public statements.

A critical limitation of the deductive approach applied in this research, especially for RQ1 and RQ2, maybe that the five classifications were known in advance. Researchers point out that "this method is limited to existing frames and, therefore, the researcher is unable to observe how the classification of a subject varies over time" (Matthes & Kohring, 2008, p. 275). Secondly, the research focuses exclusively on media framing so that, from an overall perspective, an analysis of the framing used by the public for the interpretation of press texts could bring new information. Therefore, starting from the results of this study, the transition of media frames to the general public and the links between the framing of news and their effects on readers can be investigated. The third vulnerability of this research may be the construction of a manual content analysis, while a computer-assisted method could cover a much larger number of articles and eliminate the subjectivity of the researcher.

Future research could also focus on how publications with the same editorial profile influence each other on the giving in payment law, but also on how they can be differentiated. This research could be complemented by in-depth interviews with journalists who reported on the subject of the law, as social actors, an X-ray of their positions determined by their economic, social, and cultural capital.

We believe that data on how NBR messages were presented and framed by the media during turbulent times may be relevant given that the online media is the main source of information for the general public about the central bank and could influence its opinion. Along with the interview method applied to NBR representatives and the sociological survey based on questionnaires addressed to the general and specialized public, this analysis contributes to identifying the central points of central bank communication in relation to stakeholders and the main changes needed in public communication.

## References


Alicandro, G., Malvezzi, M., Gallus, S., La Vecchia, C., Negri, E., & Bertuccio, P. (2019). Worldwide trends in suicide mortality from 1990 to 2015 with a focus on the global recession time frame. *International Journal of Public Health, 64*(5), 785–795. https://doi.org/10.1007/s00038-019-01219-y

Bach, T., Weber, M., & Quiring, O. (2013). News frames, inter-media frame transfer and the financial crisis. *Zeszyty Prasoznawcze, 56*(1), 90–110. https://doi.org/10.4467/2299-6362PZ.13.008.1026

Badiu, A., & Niță, O. G. (2016). Impactul economico—financiar al dării în plată. Academia de Studii Economice. București. *Romanian Statistical Review Supplement, 7*(2016), 36–42. Retrieved from http://www.revistadestatistica.ro/supliment/wp-content/uploads/2016/08/RRSS_08_2016_A4ro.pdf

Cacciatore, M. A., Scheufele, D. A., & Iyengar, S. (2016). The end of framing as we know it. . . and the future of media effects. *Mass Communication and Society, 19*(1), 7–23. https://doi.org/10.1080/15205436.2015.1068811

Capella, J., & Jamieson, K. (1997). *Spiral of cynism. The press and the public good.* Oxford University Press.

Corbu, N., Ştefăniţă, O., Oprea, D., & Udrea, G. (2015). The European Union–From Agenda Setting and Media Frames to Citizens' Conversations. *Romanian Journal of Communication and Public Relations, 17*(1), 41–57. Retrieved from https://www.journalofcommunication.ro/index.php/journalofcommunication/article/download/114/167

Damstra, A., & Vliegenthart, R. (2018). (Un) covering the economic crisis? Over-time and inter-media differences in salience and framing. *Journalism Studies, 19*(7), 983–1003. https://doi.org/10.1080/1461670X.2016.1246377

Dimitrova, D. V., Kaid, L. L., Williams, A. P., & Trammell, K. D. (2005). War on the web: The immediate news framing of Gulf War II. *Harvard International Journal of Press/Politics, 10*(1), 22–44. https://doi.org/10.1177/1081180X05275595

Economou, M., Madianos, M., Peppou, L. E., Theleritis, C., Patelakis, A., & Stefanis, C. (2013). Suicidal ideation and reported suicide attempts in Greece during the economic crisis. *World Psychiatry, 12*(1), 53–59. https://doi.org/10.1002/wps.20296

Entman, R. M. (1993). Framing: Toward clarification of a fractured paradigm. *Journal of Communication, 43*(4), 51–58.

Entman, R. M. (2003). Cascading activation: Contesting the White House's frame after 9/11. *Political Communication, 20*(4), 415–432. https://doi.org/10.1080/10584600390244176

Falasca, K. (2014). Framing the financial crisis: An unexpected interaction between the government and the press. *Observatorio, 8*(1), 01–21. Retrieved from http://www.scielo.mec.pt/scielo.php?script=sci_arttext&pid=S1646-59542014000100001

Fountoulakis, K. N., Gonda, X., Dome, P., Theodorakis, P. N., & Rihmer, Z. (2014). Possible delayed effect of unemployment on suicidal rates: The case of Hungary. *Annals of General Psychiatry, 13*(1), 12. https://doi.org/10.1186/1744-859X-13-12

Gamson, W. A., Croteau, D., Hoynes, W., & Sasson, T. (1992). Media images and the social construction of reality. *Annual Review of Sociology, 18*(1), 373–393.

Gitlin, T. (1980). *The whole world is watching: Mass media in the making and unmaking of the new left.* University of California.

Goffman, E. (1986) [1974]. *Frame analysis. An essay on the organization of experience*. Northeastern University Press.

Harcup, T., & O'Neill, D. (2017). What is news? News values revisited (again). *Journalism Studies, 18*(12), 1470–1488. https://doi.org/10.1080/1461670X.2016.1150193

Iacob, R. (2020). Blind spots in the spotlight: Media reporting on the National Bank of Romania's answers to financial crisis aftershock. *Mediální studia/Media studies, 14*(1), 126–146.

Matthes, J., & Kohring, M. (2008). The content analysis of media frames: Toward improving reliability and validity. *Journal of Communication, 58*(2), 258–279. https://doi.org/10.1111/j.1460-2466.2008.00384.x

Morosan, G., & Scurtu, L. E. (2019). Regulation of the Romanian banking system. Effects on the market economy. *Ecoforum Journal, 8*(1) http://ecoforumjournal.ro/index.php/eco/article/view/939/561#

Mylonas, Y. (2012). Media and the economic crisis of the EU: The 'culturalization' of a systemic crisis and Bild-Zeitung's framing of Greece. *tripleC: Communication, Capitalism and Critique. Open Access Journal for a Global Sustainable Information Society, 10*(2), 646–671.

National Bank of Romania. (2016). *Annual report—2016.* Retrieved from https://www.bnr.ro/PublicationDocuments.aspx?icid=6874

Pan, Z., & Kosicki, G. M. (1993). Framing analysis: An approach to news discourse. *Political Communication, 10*(1), 55–75.

Petrescu, C. E. H., & Stan, A. E. (2017). Trends related to the post-crisis evolution of non-performing loans in European Union and Romania. In *Proceedings of the International*

*Management Conference (Vol. 11, no. 1)* (pp. 1054–1062). Faculty of Management, Academy of Economic Studies, Bucharest. Retrieved from http://conference.management.ase.ro/archives/2017/pdf/5_20.pdf

Radu, L., & Ştefăniţă, O. (2012). Framing the economic crisis in the Romanian online media. *Romanian Journal of Communication and Public Relations, 14*(2), 29–46. Retrieved from https://journalofcommunication.ro/oldsite/archive2/026/26/rjcpr_26_full.pdf#page=30

Reese, S. D. (2001). Framing public life. A bridging model for media research. In S. D. Reese, H. G. Oscar, & E. G. August (Eds.), *Framing public life: Perspectives on media and our understanding of the social world* (pp. 7–31). Lawrence Erlbaum Associates.

Reuters Institute. (2020). *Digital news report* (p. 80). Retrieved from https://reutersinstitute.politics.ox.ac.uk/sites/default/files/2020-06/DNR_2020_FINAL.pdf

Scheufele, D. A., & Iyengar, S. (2011). The state of framing research: A call for new directions. In*The Oxford handbook of political communication theories* (pp. 1–26). Oxford University Press. https://doi.org/10.1093/oxfordhb/9780199793471.013.47

Semetko, H. A., & Valkenburg, P. M. (2000). Framing European politics: A content analysis of press and television news. *Journal of Communication, 52*(2), 93–109.

Shoemaker, P. J., & Reese, S. D. (2014). *Mediating the message in the 21st century: A media sociology perspective*. Routledge.

Tankard, J. W., Jr. (2001). The empirical approach to the study of media framing. In S. D. Reese, O. H. Gandy Jr., & A. E. Grant (Eds.), *Framing public life: Perspectives on media and our understanding of the social world* (pp. 95–106). Routledge.

Van Gorp, B. (2007). The constructionist approach to framing: Bringing culture back in. *Journal of Communication, 57*(1), 60–78. https://doi.org/10.1111/j.1460-2466.2006.00329.x

## *Quoted Online Articles (From Coded Articles)*

Ghinea, R. (2016, 25 February). Isărescu, despre legea dării în plată:Există o confuzie mare în societate,nu o putem lăsa să persiste. *zf.ro*. Retrieved from https://www.zfcorporate.ro/banci-asigurari/isarescu-despre-legea-darii-in-plata-exista-o-confuzie-mare-in-societate-nu-o-putem-lasa-sa-persiste-15087240

Hoştiuc, C. (2016a, February 21). Problema Băncii Naţionale nu este când se va retrage guvernatorul Mugur Isărescu, ci când nu va mai fi domnul Adrian Vasilescu. *zf.ro*. Retrieved from https://www.zf.ro/eveniment/problema-bancii-nationale-nu-este-cand-se-va-retrage-guvernatorul-mugur-isarescu-ci-cand-nu-va-mai-fi-domnul-adrian-vasilescu-15082559

Hoştiuc, C. (2016b, January 31). Nu este vina clienţilor că au ajuns să aibă încredere mai mult în Piperea şi Zamfir decât în bancheri. Poate creşterea avansului să fie acoperită de scăderea preţului apartamentelor? *zf.ro*. Retrieved from https://www.zf.ro/opinii/nu-este-vina-clientilor-ca-au-ajuns-sa-aiba-incredere-mai-mult-in-piperea-si-zamfir-decat-in-bancheri-poate-cresterea-avansului-sa-fie-acoperita-de-scaderea-pretului-apartamentelor-15014517

Hoştiuc, C. (2016c, March 12). Facebook-ul i-a învins şi pe bancheri: cum a ajuns o minoritate (cei cu credite în franci) să preia conducerea chiar şi în sălile de judecată şi să întoarcă clienţii împotriva băncilor? *zf.ro*. Retrieved from https://www.zf.ro/opinii/facebook-ul-i-a-invins-si-pe-bancheri-cum-a-ajuns-o-minoritate-cei-cu-credite-in-franci-sa-preia-conducerea-chiar-si-in-salile-de-judecata-si-sa-intoarca-clientii-impotriva-bancilor-15105079

Ionaşcu, D. (2016, March 14). Cum s-au lăsat bancherii singuri în ofsaid pe legea dării în plată. Critică proiectul, dar ocolesc dezbaterea când sunt faţă în faţă cu consumatorii. *adevarul.ro*. Retrieved from https://adevarul.ro/economie/bani/cum-s-au-lasat-bancherii-singuri-ofsaid-legea-darii-plata-critica-proiectul-ocolesc-dezbaterea-fata-fata-consumatorii-1_56e6f2365ab6550cb8d76129/index.html

Make. (2016a, March 7). Oare este chiar Banca Națională a României cea care mă invită să ne luăm la mişto? *bursa.ro*. Retrieved from https://www.bursa.ro/oare-este-chiar-banca-nationala-a-romaniei-cea-care-ma-invita-sa-ne-luam-la-misto-49822922
Make. (2016b, March 8). Filmând vulturi. BNR nu informează publicul în mod corect. *bursa.ro*. Retrieved from https://www.bursa.ro/filmand-vulturi-bnr-nu-informeaza-publicul-in-mod-corect-82632924
Make. (2016c, March 15). De ce m-au interesat măruntele probleme de comunicare ale sistemului bancar. BNR frizează abuzul de independență. *bursa.ro*. Retrieved from http://www.bursa.ro/de-ce-m-au-interesat-maruntele-probleme-de-comunicare-ale-sistemului-bancar-bnr-frizeaza-abuzul-de-independenta-61092923.
Make. (2016d, March 21). Cu sau fără adoptarea legii dării în plată. *bursa.ro*. Retrieved from https://www.bursa.ro/cu-sau-fara-adoptarea-legii-darii-in-plata-43143922
Make. (2016e, July 1). După ce BNR a spus că nu are informații, magicianul Isărescu scoate cifrele dării în plată din joben. *bursa.ro*. Retrieved from http://www.bursa.ro/dupa-ce-bnr-a-spus-ca-nu-are-informatii-magicianul-isarescu-scoate-cifrele-darii-in-plata-din-joben-85051034
Make. (2016f, August 10). Poporul român vă invită la masă, domnule Isărescu! *bursa.ro*. Retrieved from https://www.bursa.ro/poporul-roman-va-invita-la-masa-domnule-isarescu-61464038
Make. (2016g, August 19). BNR creed că este atacată electoral. Lucian Croitoru otrăveşte fântânile. *bursa.ro*. Retrieved from https://www.bursa.ro/bnr-crede-ca-este-atacata-electoral-lucian-croitoru-otraveste-fantanile-81825039
Make. (2016h, September 21). Remarcabila schimbare de discurs printre membrii conducerii BNR. *bursa.ro*. Retrieved from http://www.bursa.ro/remarcabila-schimbare-de-discurs-printre-membrii-conducerii-bnr-07177035
Make. (2016i, October 3). Polemici cordiale. Adrian Vasilescu scrie bine, dar despre ceea ce vrea. *bursa.ro*. Retrieved from https://www.bursa.ro/polemici-cordiale-adrian-vasilescu-scrie-bine-dar-despre-ceea-ce-vrea-22858036.
Manu, F. (2016, January 7). Isărescu: Legea darii in plata trebuie să-i protejeze pe cei cu credite de locuințe. *adevarul.ro*. Retrieved from https://adevarul.ro/economie/stiri-economice/isarescu-legea-darii-plata-trebuie-sa-i-protejeze-cei-credite-locuinte-1_568e832037115986c63d4d8f/index.html
Medrega, C. (2016, March 7). Guvernatorul Băncii Naționale atacă dur băncile: Au preferat să stea în spatele BNR sub un fel de protecție. *zf.ro*. Retrieved from https://www.zf.ro/banci-si-asigurari/guvernatorul-bancii-nationale-ataca-dur-bancile-au-preferat-sa-stea-in-spatele-bnr-sub-un-fel-de-protectie-15098562
Mitrache, L. (2016, March 15). Dreptate şi răspundere. *bursa.ro*. Retrieved from http://www.bursa.ro/opinii-dreptate-si-raspundere-29092921
Olescu, E. (2016a, January 5). Daniel Cătălin Zamfir: "Se impune sesiune parlamentară extraordinară pentru adoptarea Legii dării în plată". *bursa.ro*. Retrieved from http://www.bursa.ro/daniel-catalin-zamfir-se-impune-sesiune-parlamentara-extraordinara-pentru-adoptarea-legii-darii-i...&s=politica&articol=286837.html
Olescu, E. (2016b, March 3). Sergiu Oprescu, ARB: "Băncile au pierdut bătălia populisto-mediatică pe Legea dării în plată". *bursa.ro*. Retrieved from https://www.bursa.ro/sergiu-oprescu-arb-bancile-au-pierdut-batalia-populisto-mediatica-pe-legea-darii-in-plata-66402923
Olescu, E. (2016c, March 18). MARIUS DUNCA, FOST PREŞEDINTE ANPC: "Sunt şocat de modul în care băncile dezinformează consumatorii". *bursa.ro*. Retrieved from https://www.bursa.ro/marius-dunca-fost-presedinte-anpc-sunt-socat-de-modul-in-care-bancile-dezinformeaza-consumatorii-01823925
Olescu, E. (2016d, March 31). Controverse în Comisia Juridică din Camera Deputaților, pe Legea dării în plată. *bursa.ro*. Retrieved from https://www.bursa.ro/controverse-in-comisia-juridica-din-camera-deputatilor-pe-legea-darii-in-plata-68324928
Olescu, E. (2016e, April 13). Legea Dării în plată a fost adoptată de Parliament. *bursa*.ro. Retrieved from http://www.bursa.ro/legea-darii-in-plata-a-fost-adoptata-de-parlament-03335925

Oncu, M. (2016, February 28). 250 de oameni, la un marş de susţinere a legii dării în plată. *zf.ro*. Retrieved from https://www.zf.ro/eveniment/250-de-oameni-la-un-mars-de-sustinere-a-legii-darii-in-plata-15090171

Popa, D. (2016a, January 15). Un an de la explozia francului elveţian. Ce s-a promis şi ce s-a realizat pentru a-i sprijini pe cei împrumutaţi în CHF. *hotnews.ro*. Retrieved from https://economie.hotnews.ro/stiri-finante_banci-20730453-explozia-francului-elvetian-promis-realizat-pentru-sprijini-cei-imprumutati-chf.htm

Popa, D. (2016b, February 17). Circ maxim la şedinta comisiilor Economică şi Juridică a Senatului pe tema legii dării în plată. Legea se va aplica şi programului Prima Casă. *hotnews.ro*. Retrieved from https://economie.hotnews.ro/stiri-finante_banci-20801485-live-text-comisiile-economica-juridica-senatului-discuta-miercuri-legea-darii-plata.htm

Popa, D. (2016c, March 7). Isarescu, BNR: Gestul total nefericit de a arunca cu bani pe treptele BNR echivaleaza cu terfelirea tricolorului sau cu fluieratul atunci cand se canta imnul national. *hotnews.ro*. Retrieved from https://economie.hotnews.ro/stiri-finante_banci-20848653-isarescu-bnr-gestul-total-nefericit-arunca-bani-treptele-bnr-echivaleaza-terfelirea-tricolorului-sau-fluieratul-atunci-cand-canta-imnul-national.htm

Popa, D. (2016d, March 8). Bogdan Glăvan, prof. de economie: Când FC Barcelona o încasează de la Juventus Colentina. Replică la Eugen Radulescu. *hotnews.ro*. Retrieved from https://economie.hotnews.ro/stiri-finante_banci-20852321-bogdan-glavan-prof-economie-cand-barcelona-incaseaza-juventus-colentina-replica-eugen-radulescu.htm

Popa, D. (2016e, March 14). Două lumi paralele. Susţinătorii dării în plată şi contestatarii legii îşi rup singuri orice punţi de legatură, iar în aceste condiţii pare clar cine va ieşi căştigător. *hotnews.ro*. Retrieved from https://economie.hotnews.ro/stiri-finante_banci-20865037-doua-lumi-paralele-sustinatorii-darii-plata-contestatarii-legii-isi-rup-singuri-orice-punti-legatura-iar-aceste-conditii-pare-clar-cine-iesi-castigator.htm

Popescu, L. (2016, March 3). Băsescu îl atacă direct pe guvernatorul BNR: Nu-şi asumă nicio responsabilitate pentru perioada când s-au dat credite. *zf.ro*. Retrieved from https://www.zf.ro/banci-si-asigurari/basescu-il-ataca-direct-pe-guvernatorul-bnr-nu-si-asuma-nicio-responsabilitate-pentru-perioada-cand-s-au-dat-credite-15094686

Vasiescu, A. (2016, March 15). Alin Iacob: "Legea darii in plata va încuraja creditarea responsabilă". *bursa.ro*. Retrieved from https://www.bursa.ro/alin-iacob-aursf-legea-darii-in-plata-va-incuraja-creditarea-responsabila-00392925

Vlad, A. (2016, September 25). Peste 200 de clienţi cu credite în franci elveţieni au protestat în Bucureşti, cerând Legea conversiei la cursul istoric. *adevarul.ro*. Retrieved from https://adevarul.ro/economie/bani/peste-200-clienti-credite-franci-elvetieni-protestat-bucuresti-cerand-legea-conversiei-cursul-istoric-1_57e7cfc85ab6550cb8f9b4ad/index.html

Ziarul Financiar. (2016, August 9). BNR iese la atac să se războiască cu bloggerii, într-o poziţie neobişnuită pentru o bancă centrală. *zf.ro*. Retrieved from https://www.zf.ro/banci-si-asigurari/bnr-banca-nationala-a-romaniei-respinge-ferm-si-fara-echivoc-atacurile-la-adresa-reputatiei-bancii-centrale-15555466

# Chapter 8
# Conclusions

What remains following this research on the changes in the public communication of the National Bank of Romania in the post-crisis period? Did the NBR capitalize on the 2008 crisis or did it waste it?

The results of all the studies conducted for this research show that the transparency of the NBR has been on an upward trend in the post-crisis period. However, public confidence and understanding remain low. The central bank communicated more often, diversified its topics, communication channels, showed an increased interest in adapting the specialized language and made progress, including in the transparency of monetary communication. Undoubtedly, the pressure of different categories of the public, against the background of crisis communication situations involving the central bank in the context of the Great Recession and technological advancement, has generated essential changes in the NBR's strategic communication, inscribed it in what specialists call the second communication revolution, focused on opening up to the general public and regaining their trust. The NBR has become more attentive to the reactions and perceptions of different audiences.

## 8.1 The Public Expects the Next Level of Transparency

The NBR was no exception to the intensified communication that characterized central banks in general after 2008. Certainly, compared to the pre-crisis period, the NBR communicated more with various categories of the public. This has been confirmed by both central bankers and the general and specialist public. However, we identified a difference in perception between the two categories of public and the NBR representatives: while only about a third of survey respondents considered that the NBR communicated more, 90% of BNR officials agreed. The difference shows that the NBR must continue to change and must intensify its communication efforts, especially toward the general public.

© The Author(s), under exclusive license to Springer Nature Switzerland AG 2022

R. Iacob, *Blind Spots in the Spotlight*, Financial and Monetary Policy Studies 53,
https://doi.org/10.1007/978-3-031-04067-2_8

If, regarding the frequency of communication, opinions were unanimous, on the quality of communication, the opinions were more nuanced.

According to the 20 NBR representatives interviewed, the central bank communicated in several voices, diversified its communication topics, made changes in the way messages were elaborated and structured. The interviewees were of the opinion that the NBR has assumed too much responsibility outside its mandate, entered into too much controversy on monetary and nonmonetary issues and accepted that it has answers to all questions. All this has increased the vulnerability of the central bank. However, the research did not identify a consensus on the central bank's best communication strategy in terms of multi-voice versus single-voice communication, and some respondents felt that strategic silence on certain topics with potential crisis communication can shorten the duration of their exposure to the media.

The results on the jargon adaptation show that this "double-edged sword" is a concern for NBR representatives. Respondents have seen visible progress in simplifying the language and continue to call for the use of non-elitist language for the general public. In addition to simplifying the language, for the correct and clear transmission of messages to the general public, the NBR also considers the involvement of other categories of stakeholders (journalists, specialists in academia, etc.).

The specialized public considered that the reasons for the decrease in the visibility of the central bank's messages regarding inflation, after 2008, were first and foremost the jargon, followed by the communication in several voices, through several representatives, in the same time frame, the parallel approach of many topics and the NBR's involvement in public debates on issues that, in the opinion of the specialized public, should not have been the subject of the central bank's communication. The public is also interested in the use of graphic and video media in disseminating information.

Regarding the three communication situations analyzed—the crisis of Greek-owned banks, the credit crisis in Swiss francs, and the legislative changes in the banking sector—central bankers believe that the NBR's messages were difficult to convey to the general public or did not reach the way in which the central bank constructed and transmitted the messages (without empathy, transmitted in several voices, late, reactive in some situations), due to the messages launched by other stakeholders that competed with those of the NBR, and due to how the media intervened in the framing process, giving the articles a negative tone and labeling the central bank as "bank lawyer." In addition, the commercial banks withdrew from the debates, were silent, did not strengthen the NBR's messages. And the way in which the media framed the official statements of the NBR representatives regarding the management of the crisis had a major impact on the transmission of information to the general public.

In turn, the two categories of public believe that the messages on monetary and nonmonetary issues closer to the object of activity of the central bank were also most clearly communicated in the post-crisis period, the perceived level of clarity decreased as topics moved away from the mandate of the NBR. About 30% of both the specialized public and the general public believe that the central bank's messages on nonmonetary issues in the post-crisis period were clear. Again, the results confirmed, but not to the same intensity, the observations of the NBR representatives.

Regarding the communication channels used during the period under review, the interviewees emphasized the role of the media as the primary source of information for the general public about central banks and stressed the need for the central bank to adapt to changing media. According to NBR representatives, the most effective communication channel in the post-crisis period for transmitting messages to the public was the TV, followed by the online and print media. In order to reach various audiences, the NBR used the media mainly as a neutral tool for the transmission of information and as a tool for amplifying messages.

The general public and the specialized public follow mostly online media and TV to be informed about the NBR's messages. Radio is also one of the most favorably evaluated sources, with a higher relevance compared to print media for both audiences. For the general public, Facebook ranks third as a source of information about decisions and other information provided by central bank representatives, while for the general public, this social network is ranked sixth in importance after radio and events. Therefore, for the efficient transmission of messages to the general and specialized public, the central bank should focus its online communication efforts, including on its website and its Facebook page. At the same time, we believe that the NBR could focus on capitalizing on radio as a communication channel.

The two online surveys also highlighted the importance of events organized by the NBR, both for the specialized public and for the general public. As for the other social networks (LinkedIn, YouTube, Twitter), the results reflect that they have an insignificant impact on the audiences and that they do not represent communication channels through which the NBR messages reach the public.

In terms of monetary communication, three-quarters of the interviewees consider that, after 2008, it was transparent, clear, and efficient, and the opinions of the NBR representatives agree with the studies on the transparency of central banks, which show that monetary policy has the best effects if it is predictable. Some respondents appreciate that progress has been made toward simplifying and making messages more transparent, especially for the specialized public. The role of the media in transmitting NBR messages is assessed differently: on the one hand, it distorts and simplifies the central bank's messages, seeking "sensationalism" or "more popularly formulated messages," on the other—the media, and especially television, are appreciated for their role in the efficiency of monetary communication. The publication of the minutes, a decision in the direction of transparency taken by the NBR in 2016, is not considered a reversible change after the end of the effects of the economic and financial crisis of 2008, according to three-quarters of respondents.

As pointed out earlier, communication on monetary issues and on issues that are close to the NBR's objectives was assessed by both categories of the public as clearer in the post-crisis period, compared to the messages on topics that exceeded the central bank's mandate. This confirms the comments made by the interviewees in the qualitative analysis. From the perspective of the specialized public, there is still room for simplification of the language and reduction of the number of pages in the specialized reports of the NBR. In addition, over 65% of the respondents in the specialized public believe that the NBR should move to the next level of communication after overcoming the economic crisis.

## 8.2 The Road to Trust Must Be Paved with Education and Clarity

The research also highlighted relevant aspects of how the NBR representatives perceived the erosion of public trust in the institution, and of the level of trust of the two categories of public in the NBR. Respondents' comments on the impact of the 2008 crisis on the NBR's reputation and credibility confirm that the erosion of trust has not bypassed Romania's central bank. Even if Romania did not face bank failures or the need to implement unconventional monetary policy measures during the Great Recession, public confidence has not yet been restored.

The extent of the decline in public confidence in the NBR was assessed differently by respondents: in the perception of more than half of respondents, the NBR was affected by a "big" and "very high" crisis of confidence after 2008, while the rest of the respondents consider that it was only an insignificant breach of trust or that it was a failed attempt at erosion by some stakeholders. Six complementary factors explain, according to central bankers, the decline in public confidence in the NBR during the financial crisis: (1) the communication strategy of hostile stakeholders (interest groups that launched public attacks on the institution and its management, commercial banks that did not communicate together with the NBR on topics that affected their activity, a part of the media that fixed certain negative frames in connection with the central bank); (2) the low level of public financial education on the Romanian market; (3) strategic communication of the central bank; (4) the very high level of credibility achieved by the NBR before 2008 and in the first part of the crisis; (5) assuming, on the basis of a high reputation, duties which have gone beyond the traditional mandate of the central bank; and (6) the widespread loss of public confidence in the major players in the global financial markets after 2008.

The analysis of the data collected through questionnaires confirms that the trust of both categories of public in the NBR was eroded in the post-crisis period. Based on the significant correlations identified between the level of confidence in the NBR and the assessment of the clarity of the central bank's messages after 2008, as well as between the level of confidence and the level of knowledge of the central bank's business objective, and also in line with the opinion of the central bankers interviewed, we believe that confidence in the NBR can be regained through the institution's efforts toward greater clarity in communication and through better informing the public on the role and responsibilities of the institution.

## 8.3 Blind Spots in the Media Light

The abundance of monetary and nonmonetary communication topics, as well as the involvement in numerous public debates and controversies, put the central bank in the spotlight after 2008. The NBR came to the attention of the media and was forced to participate in a series of debates on topics such as consumer protection, taxation, changes in the legal framework applicable to the banking system, the level of income of its own employees, immunity, and the management of international reserves.

The analysis of the articles published in 2016 on the giving in payment law, in bursa.ro, zf.ro, hotnews.ro, and adevarul.ro shows that the online press in Romania reported this topic in a relatively similar way compared to the use of the five frames: conflict, economic repercussions, responsibility, human interest, and moral values. The economic framework was the most visible, followed by the conflict frame, intuitive result by the nature of the subject, both the initiators and the opponents of the law bringing arguments regarding possible financial and economic effects. The responsibility frame comes in third only in the financial media, while in the general press, the framing of the human interest (hotnews.ro) and the moral one (adevarul.ro) were presented more frequently.

The intensity of the framing reflects a clear difference between the two evaluated financial portals, zf.ro and bursa.ro, the framing of the conflict being even more intensely reported in bursa.ro than in the generalist portal adevarul.ro. Although the framing of human interest is frequently used in social news, the analysis highlighted another unexpected result: the highest intensity of this frame, among all online publications, was recorded by bursa.ro, a financial portal. The moral framework was the least used and with the least intensity. At the same time, the use of the moral framework once again reflected the differences between the two newspapers with a financial profile, the averages registered by bursa.ro and zf.ro being at opposite poles. Based on these results, we believe that the differences in how the framing in the financial media was used reflect the existence of a split on this press segment.

The content analysis reconfirms the perception of the representatives of the central bank, namely that the NBR was, disproportionately compared to the other actors, the most visible actor in the media against the giving in payment law, the representatives of commercial banks following at a great distance, which had a contribution to the labelling of "bank lawyer."

The main positions in the media (editorials, comments, opinions, etc.) regarding the NBR's communication strategy in the context of the giving in payment highlighted the expectations of this stakeholder regarding the need to change the central bank's communication, a greater openness to the general public, a disengagement from conflicts and a better coordination of public statements. In the editorialists' perception, the central bank's poor communication contributed to the erosion of public confidence in the NBR.

* * *

We believe that all these changes would not have happened so fast and so visibly without the 2008 crisis, given the long road of central bank communication from hermeticism to transparency, the speed of reaction and the reactivity of these institutions, and the short history—of only 30 years—of communication as a monetary policy tool. From this point of view, the crisis has caused the central bank to communicate more, to gain experience in crisis communication, and to test new tactics. After the adoption of the inflation targeting as a monetary policy strategy, in 2005, when communication became an important tool of monetary policy, we can say that the Great Recession was a second turning point in changing the NBR's public communication, representing the framework for an exercise such as trial and error in strategic communication, with greater openness to the general public.

We consider that a careful assessment of the results of these changes and of the perception of different audiences can provide the central bank with a significant benchmark so that it can effectively respond to the public's expectations regarding its next level of communication. Currently, we appreciate that it is no longer possible to build a communication strategy for central banks without considering the perception and opinion of their different stakeholders. The retreat in the "ivory tower" has become history, and, as Clea Bourne (2016) plastically announced, "The mythical 'Age of the Central Banker' was over." The second revolution in the communication of the central bank of Romania will probably remain among the most important opportunities in the post-crisis period, whose degree of capitalization can be assessed by reporting the level of understanding and trust in the institution of the general public. Or, as we have shown, the NBR still has to recover the level of confidence eroded in the crisis, through efforts to inform and educate the general public about its main responsibilities, in a language as clear as possible.

As central bankers themselves admit that they need to simplify their discourse, we believe that all communication efforts must begin with a revolution in the language used. The main directions can be the use of non-elitist language, the adaptation of professional jargon, and a simplification of communication, in a format that allows, including through listening, the building of bridges to the public. Central banks are not only obliged to fulfil their mandate, but must provide society with compelling reasons for the measures they take (Issing, 2005). And the success or failure of monetary policy, as well as the preservation of historical authority, is based on the ability of central bankers to communicate clearly, openly, sincerely with all audiences about their actions.

Central bankers have gone public more than during the pre-crisis period have assumed responsibilities that have often exceeded their mandates, in an economy from which, however, the big projects were missing. But the slow recovery of economic growth after 2008 has discouraged the recovery of confidence in central banks more than all communication mistakes could have done (Bourne, 2016). However, we believe that the communication activity of central banks, including the NBR, no matter how professional, alone cannot overcome the crisis of confidence and cannot diminish the real gap between the perception of those inside the financial industry and those outside. Therefore, it is necessary that the main transformation, as reflected in central banks' communication, take place primarily at the level of their activity. Central banks should go beyond the "scapegoats" of the crisis.

After all, their main role in the financial crisis—to prevent the collapse of the banking sector—has been fulfilled, with central banks preventing the onset of a second Great Depression. Moreover, Romania has not faced a banking crisis since 2008.

* * *

This multi-angle analysis of the NBR's communication provides recent data on key changes in the post-crisis period, and we believe that this research can be followed by a longitudinal study to capture, using the proposed research design, changes in the key roles of actors at the origin of the changes in the new context of economic crisis, this time caused by the COVID-19 health crisis.

As Interviewee no. 1 observed, after 2008, the NBR broke with the textbook: "After the crisis, textbooks will be rewritten, including those on economics, (. . .) and definitely those on communication, as the public communication system has changed completely." The revolution in communication continues.

## References

Bourne, C. (2016). *Trust, power and public relations in financial markets*. London; New York: Taylor & Francis.

Issing, O. (2005). Communication, transparency, accountability: Monetary policy in the twenty-first century. *Federal Reserve Bank of St. Louis Review, 87 (March/April 2005)*. Retrieved from http://homepage.ntu.edu.tw/~nankuang/Money%20and%20Banking%20Supplement/12/Communication,%20Transparency,%20Accountability.pdf

# Correction to: Blind Spots in the Spotlight

**Correction to:**
**R. Iacob, *Blind Spots in the Spotlight*,**
**Financial and Monetary Policy Studies 53**
**https://doi.org/10.1007/978-3-031-04067-2**

This book was inadvertently published without the following corrections:
Chapter 1:

- On page 2, the missing footnotes 1 and 2 have been included now.

Chapter 6: In section "6.2.4 Who Informs the Public?"

- On page 142, second paragraph, the word "general" has been replaced with "specialized".
- On page 143, third paragraph, the phrase "with 84%, increasing" has been replaced with "with 76%, decreasing".
- On page 143, the first column in table 6.7 has been modified now.

The updated original versions of the chapters can be found at
https://doi.org/10.1007/978-3-031-04067-2_1
https://doi.org/10.1007/978-3-031-04067-2_6

© The Author(s), under exclusive license to Springer Nature Switzerland AG 2022

R. Iacob, *Blind Spots in the Spotlight*, Financial and Monetary Policy Studies 53,
https://doi.org/10.1007/978-3-031-04067-2_9

# Annexes

## Annex A: The Roles of the Main Stakeholders Involved in the Second Revolution in NBR's Communication, After 2008

© The Author(s), under exclusive license to Springer Nature Switzerland AG 2022

R. Iacob, *Blind Spots in the Spotlight*, Financial and Monetary Policy Studies 53,
https://doi.org/10.1007/978-3-031-04067-2

| Stakeholder | Contribution to the communication change | Role played in democracy | Powers | Conflicts | Motivation for conflicts | Trust crisis | Communications channels | Who mediates the messages? | Response to change |
|---|---|---|---|---|---|---|---|---|---|
| Parliament | Legislative power generates unintended changes in NBR's public communication | To adopt laws | Legislative power, elected by the citizens | Institutions versus institutions (Parliament versus NBR)<br><br>People versus people (personal attacks) | Popularity, winning votes<br><br>Personal financial interests | Parliament and government have the lowest levels of trust (INSCOP Research) | Social networks, mainstream mass media | Politicians<br>Lawyers<br>Analysts<br>Mass media | Proactive |
| Mass media | The framing of nonmonetary and monetary topics influences<br><br>Public opinion and perception of the central bank | To crystallize public opinion, the primary source of information of the public | Inform the electorate/consumers.<br><br>Influence public opinion about institutions, including Parliament and the central bank | Institutions versus institutions (mass media versus NBR)<br><br>People versus people (personal attacks) | Inform the public<br><br>Personal financial interests<br><br>Financing | Newsrooms—vulnerable to economic and political pressures<br><br>Generalized decline in trust in experts | Mainstream mass media<br><br>Social networks | Journalists<br>Columnists | Interactive<br><br>Proactive |
| NBR | Nonmonetary communication during crises led to reactive changes in NBR's overall public communication | Ensure and maintain price stability | Unelected power directly by citizens<br><br>The Administration Council consists of 9 members appointed by the Romanian Parliament for a 5-year term | Institutions versus institutions (NBR versus Parliament; NBR versus mass media; NBR versus banks)<br><br>Institutions versus people (NBR versus public at large; NBR versus | Financial stability<br><br>Property rights<br><br>Depositors' protection<br><br>Contributes to maintaining macroeconomic balances | Generalized decline in trust in experts<br><br>Nonmonetary crisis communications<br><br>Criticism of central banks in the 2008 crisis: blind spots, silo thinking, villains, the great | Mainstream mass media and social media (limited) | NBR representatives<br>Mass media<br>Analysts<br>Bankers<br>Academia | Reactive, partially interactive |

(continued)

(continued)

| Stakeholder | Contribution to the communication change | Role played in democracy | Powers | Conflicts | Motivation for conflicts | Trust crisis | Communications channels | Who mediates the messages? | Response to change |
|---|---|---|---|---|---|---|---|---|---|
| | | | | lawyers, journalists, financial analysts) | | divide, the only game in town | | | |
| Banks and specialized public | Participants in financial markets which—intentionally or not—generate changes in central bank's public communication | Contribute to the efficient distribution of financial resources in the economy, by attracting deposits from depositors and by providing loans to creditworthy borrowers<br><br>Represent other countries' interests in Romania | Electorate | Institutions versus institutions (banks versus Parliament; banks versus NBR)<br><br>Institutions versus people (banks versus borrowers, versus lawyers, analysts, etc.) | Financial interests, business interests, personal interests | Banks—the origin of the 2008 crisis | Social media and mainstream mass media | Analysts<br>Mass-media<br>Professional associations<br>Clients | Very reactive |
| Public at large | Free market participants which—intentionally or not—contribute to the second revolution in NBR's public communication | Elect representatives who deliberate and decide on the country's legislation, vote for leaders<br><br>Who represent their ideas<br><br>Participate in the free market (loans/savings) | Electorate | People versus institutions (against NBR, against banks, against government, etc.) | Personal financial interests | Cultural conflicts between the general public and experts | Social networks and mainstream mass media | Mass-media<br>Lawyers<br>Organizations/<br>Debtors' associations<br>Opinion leaders<br>Influencers | Reactive |

## Annex B: Interview Grid—Questions Regarding NBR's Communication, Addressed to NBR's Representatives

**The Experience of the Beginning**

1. How did your career as a communications officer/advisor/consultant/specialist at the National Bank of Romania start?
2. What was NBR's communication activity when you joined the bank? (frequency of public appearances, such as press conferences, statements, interviews, press releases, seminars, etc.)
3. What was the central bank's relationship with the media back then, what were the main topics on the public agenda for which you were asked to deliver official statements?

**Nonmonetary Communication**
**Pre-crisis period**

4. Can you give an example of a crisis communication situation that you managed or were involved in at the beginning of your career at the NBR?
5. What were the key changes you implemented in the central bank's communication strategy up to 2008 and what were the main determining factors?
6. How were these changes received by economic journalists and how were they presented to the public (positive/negative tonality)?

**Post-crisis period**

7. What impact do you appreciate the 2008 crisis had on NBR's communication? What was NBR's first public communication after the collapse of Lehman Brothers, what key messages did the central bank launch, and what were the main questions received from the public and from the media?
8. How has the frequency of public statements made by NBR's representatives changed since the beginning of the crisis?
9. In your view, what were the most effective communication channels and tools used after 2008? Why? What did not work as expected and why?
10. Please evaluate NBR's communication strategy on the following topics:

    10.1. The crisis of Greek-owned banks
    10.2. The Swiss franc crisis
    10.3. The giving in payment law

11. Has the NBR experienced a crisis of public confidence in the wake of the 2008 economic and financial crisis?
12. (If a crisis of confidence is confirmed): How have you been using communication in the NBR's efforts to mitigate the effects of this confidence crisis and to restore public's confidence?
13. (If the crisis of confidence has been mentioned): How long do you estimate it will take to restore public's confidence in the financial industry and what

communication rules do you think institutions in this industry should generally follow?

14. Regarding the impact that other monetary policy instruments had on public confidence, how would you describe the role of communication in relation to these other monetary policy instruments?
15. Central bankers themselves criticized the jargon used by central banks. Even NBR's representatives have announced, in the last year, the goal of abandoning jargon and getting closer to the public. More precisely, what do you need to change, in terms of discourse, and how will you do it?
16. What limits do you take into consideration when "translating" and adapting the central banks' discourse to the general public?
17. Where does the NBR currently stand in adapting its language to the level of public understanding?
18. Will the NBR have an active, precise presence in the next 2–3 years on social networks (focus on Facebook)?
19. Do you think that some of the changes in the discourse and communication strategy of the NBR following the 2008 crisis are reversible? Please motivate your answers.
20. What are, in terms of public communication, the main lessons learned, tested, validated by the NBR after 2008?

**Monetary Communication**

With a relatively short history of communication, how do you assess the monetary communication activity of the National Bank of Romania, mainly after 2008:

21. Was it effective, clear, what role did it play in steering the expectations of the general public and mitigating uncertainties during this period?
22. Were all the analysis and forecasting models used by the NBR prior to 2008 validated during the crisis?
23. (If they were invalidated) How did you communicate this to the public?
24. How were the monetary policy meetings conducted during the crisis, what keywords were used, what can you tell us about the topics discussed?
25. Do you consider that some changes in communication, such as the publication of minutes of monetary policy meetings, are reversible? Please motivate your answer.

**Closing Remarks**

26. Looking back, what would you change or improve in your communication activity after 2008, if you would have that chance?

As we are approaching the end of our interview, please let me know if you have any additional topics you would like to discuss?

Thank you!

# Annex C: Online Survey on NBR's Communication Targeting the Specialized Public (Conducted During May–July 2018 Period)

As part of an academic project, we are conducting a research on the communication of the National Bank of Romania (NBR) after the 2008 economic and financial crisis. You have been randomly selected to answer this questionnaire. There are no right or wrong answers; the validity of the survey depends on the honesty of your answers. Please be assured that your answers are confidential, and the data collected through this questionnaire will be used for academic purposes only. Completing the questions requires a maximum of 15 min.

Thank you in advance!

1. **Do you consider that things are going in a good direction in Romania from an economic point of view? Please tick the answer that corresponds to your opinion:**

   □ The direction is right
   □ The direction is neither right nor wrong
   □ The direction is wrong
   □ I don't know/I won't answer

2. **Overall, how satisfied are you with your living standard? Please tick the answer that corresponds to your opinion:**

   □ Very satisfied
   □ Quite satisfied
   □ Neither satisfied nor dissatisfied
   □ Not very satisfied
   □ Not at all satisfied
   □ I don't know/I won't answer

3. **Compared to a year ago, how is your economic situation? Please tick the answer that corresponds to your opinion:**

   □ Much better
   □ Better
   □ The same
   □ Worse
   □ Much worse
   □ I don't know/I won't answer

4. **A year from now, what do you expect your economic situation to be? Tick the answer that corresponds to your opinion:**

   □ Much better
   □ Better
   □ The same

☐ Worse
☐ Much worse
☐ I don't know/I won't answer

5. **How would you describe the current economic situation in Romanians compared to last year? Tick the answer that corresponds to your opinion:**

☐ Much better
☐ Better
☐ The same
☐ Worse
☐ Much worse
☐ I don't know/I won't answer

6. **A year from now, how do you expect the general, economic situation of Romanians to be? Tick the answer that corresponds to your opinion:**

☐ Much better
☐ Better
☐ The same
☐ Worse
☐ Much worse
☐ I don't know/I won't answer

7. **In your opinion, to what extent do the decisions of the National Bank of Romania influence the state of the Romanian economy? Pick a rank from 1 to 7 (where 1 is extremely low and 7 is extremely high):**

1 2 3 4 5 6 7

8. **In your opinion, what is the main objective of the National Bank of Romania? Please choose a single answer:**

☐ Sets the interest rates for loans and deposits
☐ Ensures and maintains price stability
☐ Sets exchange rates
☐ Protects customers in their contractual relationship with banks
☐ Sets income tax rates
☐ Lends money to the Romanian state
☐ I don't know/I won't answer
☐ Other (please mention)

9. **In your opinion, what are the main tasks of the National Bank of Romania? (multiple choice answer)**

| Answers | Yes | No | I don't know/I won't answer |
|---|---|---|---|
| 1. To design and implement the monetary policy and the exchange rate policy | 1 | 2 | 99 |
| 2. To set the exchange rate regime and to oversee its implementation | 1 | 2 | 99 |
| 3. To authorize credit institutions | 1 | 2 | 99 |
| 4. To regulate credit institutions | 1 | 2 | 99 |
| 5. To draft the fiscal policy of Romania | 1 | 2 | 99 |
| 6. To issue banknotes and coins as legal tender to be used in Romania | 1 | 2 | 99 |
| 7. To manage the gold reserve and the other international reserves of Romania | 1 | 2 | 99 |
| 8. To monitor and control the foreign exchange transactions in Romania | 1 | 2 | 99 |
| 9. To supervise credit institutions | 1 | 2 | 99 |
| 10. To apply Romania's fiscal policy | 1 | 2 | 99 |
| 11. To grant loans to Romanians | 1 | 2 | 99 |
| 12. To attract deposits from the Romanian population | 1 | 2 | 99 |

10. **To what extent are you satisfied with the decisions taken by the National Bank of Romania to maintain price stability during the financial crisis? Please tick the answer that corresponds to your opinion:**

    □ Very satisfied
    □ Satisfied
    □ Neither satisfied nor unsatisfied
    □ Unsatisfied
    □ Very unsatisfied
    □ I don't know/I won't answer

11. **How would you rate NBR's communication on price developments between 2008 and 2017:**

    □ Less visible compared to the pre-crisis period
    □ As visible as before 2008
    □ More visible compared to the pre-crisis period
    □ I don't know/I won't answer

12. **If you answered: "Less visible compared to the pre-crisis period," what do you think has reduced the visibility of messages on price developments? Please tick all answers that define your opinion (multiple choice answer):**

    □ Tackling several topics in parallel
    □ Communicating on several voices, through several representatives, in the same timeframe
    □ Jargon—specialized language—used by communicators

☐ Public involvement in topics that should not have been the subject of NBR communication
☐ I don't know/I won't answer
☐ Other reasons (please mention them)

13. **Based on the messages sent by the representatives of the National Bank of Romania, how do you expect consumer goods prices to evolve in 2018? Please choose one of the answers:**

☐ Prices will decrease significantly
☐ Prices will decrease
☐ Prices will stagnate
☐ Prices will increase
☐ Prices will increase significantly
☐ I don't know/I won't answer

14. **To what extent do you consider that the NBR maintained its independence from the Romanian Government (meaning that the NBR did not ask and/or accept instructions from the Government) during the financial crisis?**

☐ Very much
☐ A lot
☐ The financial crisis had no impact on the independence of the NBR
☐ A little
☐ Very little
☐ I don't know/I won't answer

15. **How would you rate general NBR's communication during the financial crisis (*we define effective communication as clear messaging to the target audience in the shortest possible time) (where 1 is extremely ineffective and 7 is extremely effective):**

1 2 3 4 5 6 7

16. **How would you rate general NBR's overall credibility during the financial crisis (where 1 is extremely unreliable and 7 is extremely credible):**

1 2 3 4 5 6 7

17. **How important are, for you, NBR's messages? Please tick the answer that applies to you:**

☐ Not important at all
☐ Slightly important
☐ Neither important nor unimportant
☐ Important
☐ Extremely important
☐ I don't know/I won't answer

18. **Please evaluate the frequency of the messages you receive from the NBR:**

☐ Very rare
☐ Rare
☐ Neither frequent, nor rare
☐ Frequent
☐ Very frequent
☐ I don't know/I won't answer

19. **What are the channels and networks through which the messages sent by the NBR reach you? Please tick all that apply (multiple choices):**

☐ TV
☐ Online media
☐ Print media
☐ Radio
☐ Facebook
☐ YouTube
☐ Twitter
☐ LinkedIn
☐ NBR website: www.bnro.ro
☐ NBR blog: www.opiniibnr.ro
☐ Events organized by the NBR
☐ Events organized by other organizations
☐ E-mail
☐ Informal meetings
☐ I don't know/I won't answer
☐ Other channels (please name them):

20. **In your opinion, how much has the NBR been communicating with the public compared to before 2008?**

☐ Much less
☐ Less
☐ No change
☐ More
☐ Much more
☐ Hard to tell

21. **What do you think the NBR should do in terms of communication following the economic crisis? Please choose one answer:**

☐ To revert completely
☐ To revert somewhat
☐ To remain the current level of communication
☐ To move to a next level of communication
☐ It is too early to judge

22. **What should the changes in NBR's communication now target? Please tick all the answers that define your opinion (multiple choice answer):**

☐ Adapt the specialized language (jargon) it uses
☐ Diversify its communication channels
☐ Increase the frequency of public appearances
☐ Decrease the frequency of public appearances
☐ Increase the number of its communicators
☐ Decrease the number of its communicators
☐ Increase the size of published reports
☐ Decrease the size of published reports
☐ Use infographics in the presentation of published reports
☐ Other

23. **Please indicate to what extent the language used by the NBR in the following publications and periodicals is easy for you to understand and interpret:**

| Publications | Very small extent | Small extent | Neither to a small extent nor to a large extent | Large extent | Very large extent | I don't know/I won't answer |
|---|---|---|---|---|---|---|
| Annual reports | 1 | 2 | 3 | 4 | 5 | 99 |
| Reports on inflation | 1 | 2 | 3 | 4 | 5 | 99 |
| Reports on financial stability | 1 | 2 | 3 | 4 | 5 | 99 |
| Monthly bulletins | 1 | 2 | 3 | 4 | 5 | 99 |
| Minutes of the monetary policy meetings | 1 | 2 | 3 | 4 | 5 | 99 |

24. **Please assess the size of the regular reports and information published by the NBR:**

| Publications | Very short | Short | Neither short nor long | Long | Very long | I don't know/I won't answer |
|---|---|---|---|---|---|---|
| Annual reports | 1 | 2 | 3 | 4 | 5 | 99 |
| Reports on inflation | 1 | 2 | 3 | 4 | 5 | 99 |
| Reports on financial stability | 1 | 2 | 3 | 4 | 5 | 99 |
| Monthly bulletins | 1 | 2 | 3 | 4 | 5 | 99 |
| Minutes of the monetary policy meetings | 1 | 2 | 3 | 4 | 5 | 99 |

25. **Below is a list of topics on which the NBR made public statements during the financial crisis. How would you rate the clarity of the discourse used by the central bank's representatives (we define clarity as using both messages that are easy to follow and to understand and language adapted to each topic)?**

| Topics | Very unclear | Unclear | Neither clear nor unclear | Clear | Very clear | I don't know/ I won't answer |
|---|---|---|---|---|---|---|
| 1. Monetary policy decisions | 1 | 2 | 3 | 4 | 5 | 99 |
| 2. Evolution of inflation | 1 | 2 | 3 | 4 | 5 | 99 |
| 3. Banking system | 1 | 2 | 3 | 4 | 5 | 99 |
| 4. Lending activity | 1 | 2 | 3 | 4 | 5 | 99 |
| 5. Economic crisis | 1 | 2 | 3 | 4 | 5 | 99 |
| 6. Crisis of Swiss-francs loans | 1 | 2 | 3 | 4 | 5 | 99 |
| 7. Giving in payment law | 1 | 2 | 3 | 4 | 5 | 99 |
| 8. Crisis of Greek capital banks | 1 | 2 | 3 | 4 | 5 | 99 |
| 9. Changes in the Fiscal Code | 1 | 2 | 3 | 4 | 5 | 99 |
| 10. Brexit | 1 | 2 | 3 | 4 | 5 | 99 |
| 11. Financing from the International Monetary Fund | 1 | 2 | 3 | 4 | 5 | 99 |
| 12. Romania's gold reserve | 1 | 2 | 3 | 4 | 5 | 99 |
| 13. Income of the NBR's employees | 1 | 2 | 3 | 4 | 5 | 99 |
| 14. National Committee for Macroprudential Oversight | 1 | 2 | 3 | 4 | 5 | 99 |
| 15. Fiscal policy | 1 | 2 | 3 | 4 | 5 | 99 |
| 16. Adoption of the Euro | 1 | 2 | 3 | 4 | 5 | 99 |

26. **To what extent do you consider that the NBR's public interventions were justified on the following issues during the financial crisis:**

| Topics | Very legitimate | Legitimate | Neither legitimate nor illegitimate | Illegitimate | Very illegitimate | I didn't follow/I can't assess |
|---|---|---|---|---|---|---|
| 1. Monetary policy decisions | 1 | 2 | 3 | 4 | 5 | 99 |
| 2. Evolution of inflation | 1 | 2 | 3 | 4 | 5 | 99 |

(continued)

(continued)

| Topics | Very legitimate | Legitimate | Neither legitimate nor illegitimate | Illegitimate | Very illegitimate | I didn't follow/I can't assess |
|---|---|---|---|---|---|---|
| 3. Banking system | 1 | 2 | 3 | 4 | 5 | 99 |
| 4. Lending activity | 1 | 2 | 3 | 4 | 5 | 99 |
| 5. Economic crisis | 1 | 2 | 3 | 4 | 5 | 99 |
| 6. Crisis of Swiss-francs loans | 1 | 2 | 3 | 4 | 5 | 99 |
| 7. Giving in payment law | 1 | 2 | 3 | 4 | 5 | 99 |
| 8. Crisis of Greek capital banks | 1 | 2 | 3 | 4 | 5 | 99 |
| 9. Changes in Fiscal Code | 1 | 2 | 3 | 4 | 5 | 99 |
| 10. Brexit | 1 | 2 | 3 | 4 | 5 | 99 |
| 11. Financing from the International Monetary Fund | 1 | 2 | 3 | 4 | 5 | 99 |
| 12. Romania's gold reserve | 1 | 2 | 3 | 4 | 5 | 99 |
| 13. Incomes of the NBR's employees | 1 | 2 | 3 | 4 | 5 | 99 |
| 14. National Committee for Macroprudential Oversight | 1 | 2 | 3 | 4 | 5 | 99 |
| 15. Fiscal policy | 1 | 2 | 3 | 4 | 5 | 99 |
| 16. Adoption of the Euro | 1 | 2 | 3 | 4 | 5 | 99 |

27. **In your view, how did the NBR communicate its main objective—to ensure and maintain price stability—between 2008 and 2017?**

    □ With less visibility compared to the pre-crisis period
    □ With same visibility as before 2008
    □ With greater visibility compared to the pre-crisis period
    □ I don't know/I won't answer

28. **If you answered: "With less visibility compared to the pre-crisis period," what do you think has reduced the visibility of NBR's messages on its main objective? Please tick all answers that define your opinion (multiple choice answer):**

☐ Tackling several topics in parallel
☐ Communicating on several voices, through several representatives, in the same timeframe
☐ Using jargon—specialized language
☐ Public involvement in topics that should not have been the subject of NBR communication
☐ I don't know/I won't answer
☐ Other reasons (please mention them)

29. **In your opinion, which NBR representatives were visible after 2008? Please tick all answers that define your opinion (multiple choice answer):**

☐ Mugur Isărescu (Governor)
☐ Adrian Vasilescu (Strategy Consultant)
☐ Dan Suciu (Communication Director)
☐ Valentin Lazea (Chief Economist)
☐ Liviu Voinea (Deputy Governor during the financial crisis)
☐ Florin Georgescu (Vice Chairman of the Board)
☐ Eugen Rădulescu (Director of the Stability Department)
☐ Daniel Dăianu (Member of the Board)
☐ Lucian Croitoru (Senior Advisor to Governor)
☐ Nicolae Cinteză (Director of Bank Supervision)
☐ Ruxandra Avram (Director of Financial Market Infrastructures and Payments Oversight)
☐ I don't know/I won't answer
☐ Other NBR's representatives (please mention their names):

30. **In your opinion, to what extent did the following NBR representatives communicate clearly to the target audience during the financial crisis (we define clarity as using both messages that are easy to follow and to understand and language adapted to each topic)?**

| Representatives | Very unclear | Unclear | Neither clear nor unclear | Clear | Very clear | I don't know/I won't answer |
|---|---|---|---|---|---|---|
| Mugur Isărescu | 1 | 2 | 3 | 4 | 5 | 99 |
| Adrian Vasilescu | 1 | 2 | 3 | 4 | 5 | 99 |
| Dan Suciu | 1 | 2 | 3 | 4 | 5 | 99 |
| Valentin Lazea | 1 | 2 | 3 | 4 | 5 | 99 |
| Liviu Voinea | 1 | 2 | 3 | 4 | 5 | 99 |
| Florin Georgescu | 1 | 2 | 3 | 4 | 5 | 99 |
| Eugen Rădulescu | 1 | 2 | 3 | 4 | 5 | 99 |
| Daniel Dăianu | 1 | 2 | 3 | 4 | 5 | 99 |
| Lucian Croitoru | 1 | 2 | 3 | 4 | 5 | 99 |

(continued)

(continued)

| Representatives | Very unclear | Unclear | Neither clear nor unclear | Clear | Very clear | I don't know/I won't answer |
|---|---|---|---|---|---|---|
| Nicolae Cinteză | 1 | 2 | 3 | 4 | 5 | 99 |
| Ruxandra Avram | 1 | 2 | 3 | 4 | 5 | 99 |

31. **Do you consider that the messages of the NBR's representatives published on the NBR's blog are useful to you in clarifying the officially released information?**

□ Yes
□ No
□ I don't know/I won't answer

32. **Do you follow the NBR on Twitter?**

□ Yes
□ No

33. **Do you follow the NBR on YouTube?**

□ Yes
□ No

34. **Do you follow the NBR on LinkedIn?**

□ Yes
□ No

35. **In your opinion, would an official NBR Facebook account be useful to you in more quickly finding out information?**

□ Yes
□ No
□ I don't know/I won't answer

36. **Have you ever marched against the NBR?**

□ Yes
□ No

37. **If you answered Yes to the previous question, please mention the reason of your protest (open question):**

________________________________________________

38. **If you have participated in a protest organized against the NBR, please evaluate the messages that the central bank sent on the issue that generated the protest:**

☐ Very useful
☐ Useful
☐ Neither useful nor useless
☐ Useless
☐ Very useless
☐ I don't know/I won't answer

39. **What are your contractual relationships with commercial banks? Tick all that apply (multiple choice answer):**

☐ I have a mortgage
☐ I have a credit for personal needs
☐ I have a leasing contract
☐ I have a credit card
☐ I have deposits
☐ I have a debit card
☐ I don't have any contractual relationships with banks
☐ I don't know/I won't answer
☐ Other

40. **What are your contractual relationships with non-financial institutions (NFIs)? Tick all that apply (multiple choice answer):**

☐ I have a loan without guarantees
☐ I have a guaranteed loan
☐ I don't have any contractual relationships with NFIs
☐ I don't know/I won't answer
☐ Other

41. **Have you ever taken legal action against a commercial bank?**

☐ Yes
☐ No
☐ I don't know/I won't answer

42. **Have you ever taken legal action against NFIs?**

☐ Yes
☐ No
☐ I don't know/I won't answer

43. **What is your most recent academic degree?**

☐ No degree
☐ Primary school
☐ Elementary school
☐ Unfinished vocational school/high school
☐ High school
☐ Post-secondary education
☐ University

☐ Master
☐ PhD
☐ Chartered Financial Analyst (CFA)
☐ Master of Business Administration (MBA)
☐ I don't know/I don't answer
☐ Other

44. **Which of the following descriptions corresponds with your current occupational status?**

☐ Employer/employee (including self-employed, small entrepreneurs, and employers)
☐ Student
☐ Unemployed, actively searching for a job
☐ Unemployed, not searching for a job
☐ Retired because of illness or disability
☐ Retired
☐ In the armed forces
☐ Volunteer, with a contract
☐ Volunteer, without a contract
☐ Domestic (housework, caregiver)
☐ I don't know/I don't answer
☐ Other (please specify):

45. **If you are employed, including self-employed, a small entrepreneur or an employer, in which field do you work? Please tick the option that applies to you:**

☐ Food industry
☐ Automotive industry
☐ Banking industry
☐ IT&C industry
☐ Education system
☐ Agriculture
☐ Trade
☐ Tourism
☐ Media (financial)
☐ Real estate
☐ Construction
☐ Transport
☐ Natural resources
☐ Creative industries
☐ Government sector
☐ Services
☐ Bar and restaurant industry
☐ Energy
☐ Public Relations

☐ Advocacy
☐ Healthcare
☐ Military
☐ Another field (please specify):

46. **What is your current net monthly income (in RON*):**

☐ Under 2.000 RON
☐ 2.001–3.000 RON
☐ 3.001–4.000 RON
☐ 4.001–5.000 RON
☐ 5.001–7.000 RON
☐ 7.001–9.000 RON
☐ 9.001–11.000 RON
☐ 11.001–15.000 RON
☐ Above 15.000 RON
☐ I don't know/I won't answer

*The average EUR value (expressed in RON/leu, Romanian currency) for the whole year 2018 is 4.6535 RON

47. **You live in a/an . . . environment:**

☐ Urban
☐ Rural

48. **Please tick your gender:**

☐ Male
☐ Female
☐ I won't answer

49. **Please mention your age:**

## Annex D: Online Survey on NBR's Communication Targeting the General Public (Conducted Between July 2019 and October 2019)

As part of an academic project, we are conducting a research on the communication of the National Bank of Romania (NBR) with the general public for the past years. There are no right or wrong answers; the validity of the survey depends on the honesty of your answers. Please be assured that your answers are confidential, and the data collected through this questionnaire will be used for academic purposes only. Completing the questions requires a maximum of 7 min.

Thank you in advance!

1. **How satisfied are you overall with your living standard? Please tick the answer that corresponds to your opinion:**

☐ Very satisfied
☐ Quite satisfied
☐ Neither satisfied nor dissatisfied
☐ Not very satisfied
☐ Not at all satisfied
☐ I don't know/I won't answer

2. **Compared to a year ago, how is your economic situation? Please tick the answer that corresponds to your opinion:**

☐ Much better
☐ Better
☐ The same
☐ Worse
☐ Much worse
☐ I don't know/I won't answer

3. **A year from now, what do you expect your economic situation to be? Tick the answer that corresponds to your opinion:**

☐ Much better
☐ Better
☐ The same
☐ Worse
☐ Much worse
☐ I don't know/I won't answer

4. **How often do you get information from the media (print, online, TV) on economic or business topics?**

☐ Very often
☐ Often
☐ Never
☐ Rarely
☐ Very rarely
☐ I don't know/I won't answer

5. **How important are, to you, the messages that the NBR sends?**

☐ Not important at all
☐ Minor importance
☐ Neither important nor unimportant
☐ Important
☐ Very important
☐ I don't know/I won't answer

6. **In your opinion, what influence have to the decisions of the NBR on the Romanian economy?**

   □ Extremely little influence
   □ Little influence
   □ No influence
   □ Some influence
   □ A lot of influence
   □ I don't know/I won't answer

7. **How much trust do you have in the NBR?**

   □ Very much
   □ Much
   □ Neither much nor little (I don't know the institution)
   □ Little
   □ Very little
   □ I don't know/I won't answer

8. **Based on the messages sent by the representatives of the NBR, how do you expect consumer goods prices to evolve in the short term? Please choose one of the answers:**

   □ Prices will decrease significantly
   □ Prices will decrease
   □ Prices will stagnate
   □ Prices will increase
   □ Prices will increase significantly
   □ I don't know/I won't answer

9. **In your opinion, what is the main objective pursued by the NBR? Please choose a single answer:**

   □ Sets the interest rates for loans and deposits
   □ Ensures and maintains price stability
   □ Sets exchange rates
   □ Protects customers in their contractual relationship with banks
   □ Sets income tax rates
   □ Lends money to the Romanian state
   □ Lends money to the banks
   □ I don't know/I won't answer
   □ Other (please mention):

10. **In your opinion, what are the main tasks of the NBR? (multiple choice answer)**

| Answers | Yes | No | I don't know/I won't answer |
|---|---|---|---|
| 1. To design and implement the monetary policy and the exchange rate policy | 1 | 2 | 99 |
| 2. To set the exchange rate regime and to oversee its implementation | 1 | 2 | 99 |
| 3. To authorize credit institutions | 1 | 2 | 99 |
| 4. To regulate credit institutions | 1 | 2 | 99 |
| 5. To draft the fiscal policy of Romania | 1 | 2 | 99 |
| 6. To issue banknotes and coins as legal tender to be used in Romania | 1 | 2 | 99 |
| 7. To manage the gold reserve and the other international reserves of Romania | 1 | 2 | 99 |
| 8. To monitor and control the foreign exchange transactions in Romania | 1 | 2 | 99 |
| 9. To supervise credit institutions | 1 | 2 | 99 |
| 10. To apply Romania's fiscal policy | 1 | 2 | 99 |
| 11. To grant loans to Romanians | 1 | 2 | 99 |
| 12. To attract deposits from the Romanian population | 1 | 2 | 99 |

11. **How would you rate NBR's communication frequency with the general public over the last 10 years compared to pre-2008:**

    □ Much less
    □ Less
    □ No change
    □ More
    □ Much more
    □ I don't know/I won't answer

12. **How would you rate NBR's general communication after 2008 (we define effective communication as clear messaging to the target audience in the shortest possible time):**

    □ Extremely inefficient
    □ Inefficient
    □ Neither inefficient nor efficient
    □ Efficient
    □ Extremely efficient
    □ I don't know/I won't answer

13. **How would you rate NBR's overall credibility during the financial crisis:**

    □ Extremely not trustworthy
    □ Not trustworthy
    □ Neither trustworthy nor not trustworthy
    □ Trustworthy

☐ Extremely trustworthy
☐ I don't know/I won't answer

14. **Please evaluate the frequency of the messages you receive from the NBR:**

☐ Very rare
☐ Rare
☐ Neither frequent nor rare
☐ Frequent
☐ Very frequent
☐ I don't know/I won't answer

15. **What are the channels and networks you receive NBR messages? Please tick all that apply (multiple choice answer):**

☐ TV
☐ Online media
☐ Print media
☐ Radio
☐ Facebook
☐ YouTube
☐ Twitter
☐ LinkedIn
☐ NBR website: www.bnro.ro
☐ NBR blog: www.opiniibnr.ro
☐ Events organized by the NBR
☐ Events organized by other organizations
☐ E-mail
☐ Informal meetings
☐ I don't know/I won't answer
☐ Other channels (please name them):

16. **How would you rate the language currently used by NBR's representatives?**

☐ Very unclear
☐ Unclear
☐ Neither unclear nor clear
☐ Clear
☐ Very clear
☐ I don't know/I won't answer

17. **What should the changes in NBR's communication now target? Please tick all the answers that define your opinion (multiple choice answer):**

☐ Adapt the specialized language (jargon) it uses
☐ Diversify its communication channels
☐ Increase the frequency of public appearances
☐ Decrease the frequency of public appearances

☐ Increase the number of its communicators
☐ Decrease the number of its communicators
☐ Increase the size of published reports
☐ Decrease the size of published reports
☐ Use infographics in the presentation of published reports
☐ Use video productions in the presentation of published reports
☐ Other:

18. **In your opinion, which NBR representatives were visible after 2008? Please tick all answers that define your opinion (multiple choice answer):**

☐ Mugur Isărescu (Governor)
☐ Adrian Vasilescu (Strategy Consultant)
☐ Dan Suciu (Communication Director)
☐ Valentin Lazea (Chief Economist)
☐ Liviu Voinea (Deputy Governor during the financial crisis)
☐ Florin Georgescu (Vice Chairman of the Board)
☐ Eugen Rădulescu (Director of the Stability Department)
☐ Daniel Dăianu (Member of the Board)
☐ Lucian Croitoru (Senior Advisor to Governor)
☐ Nicolae Cinteză (Director of Bank Supervision)
☐ Ruxandra Avram (Director of Financial Market Infrastructures and Payments Oversight)
☐ I don't know/I won't answer
☐ Other NBR's representatives (please mention their names):

19. **On what topics has the NBR been visible to you over the past year? Please choose all the answers you consider appropriate (multiple choice answer):**

☐ Consumer price developments
☐ Credit interest rates developments
☐ Deposit rates developments
☐ Romanian economy's development
☐ Romanian banks' situation
☐ ROBOR index evolution (*ROBOR—Romanian Interbank Offer Rate is the average interest rate for loans in national currency granted on the interbank market)
☐ New lending requirements for population
☐ New lending requirements for companies
☐ A new possible financial crisis
☐ New taxes on commercial banks
☐ Romania's gold reserve
☐ Evolution of the exchange rate
☐ Adoption of the Euro
☐ Other:

20. **In your opinion, would an official NBR Facebook account be useful to you in more quickly finding out information?**

☐ Yes
☐ No
☐ I don't know/I won't answer

21. **Do you consider that the NBR's presence on the social network Instagram, with an official account, would be useful for you to find out more quickly the information transmitted?**

☐ Yes
☐ No
☐ I don't know/I won't answer

22. **Have you ever marched against the NBR?**

☐ Yes
☐ No

23. **If you have participated in a protest organized against the NBR, please evaluate the messages that the central bank sent on the issue that generated the protest:**

☐ Very useful
☐ Useful
☐ Neither useful nor useless
☐ Useless
☐ Very useless
☐ I don't know/I won't answer

24. **What are your contractual relationships with commercial banks? Tick all that apply (multiple choice answer):**

☐ I have a mortgage
☐ I have a credit for personal needs
☐ I have a leasing contract
☐ I have a credit card
☐ I have deposits
☐ I have a debit card
☐ I don't have any contractual relationships with banks
☐ I don't know/I won't answer
☐ Other:

25. **Do you have studies in economics, finance, or other related fields?**

☐ Yes
☐ No
☐ I don't know/I won't answer

26. **What is your most recent academic degree?**

☐ No degree
☐ Primary school
☐ Elementary school
☐ Unfinished vocational school/high school
☐ High school
☐ Post-secondary education
☐ University
☐ Master
☐ PhD
☐ Chartered Financial Analyst (CFA)
☐ Master of Business Administration (MBA)
☐ I don't know/I don't answer
☐ Other:

27. **Which of the following descriptions corresponds with your current occupational status?**

☐ Employer/employee (including self-employed, small entrepreneurs, and employers)
☐ Student
☐ Unemployed, actively searching for a job
☐ Unemployed, not searching for a job
☐ Retired because of illness or disability
☐ Retired
☐ In the armed forces
☐ Volunteer, with a contract
☐ Volunteer, without a contract
☐ Domestic (housework, caregiver)
☐ I don't know/I don't answer
☐ Other (please specify):

28. **If you are employed, including self-employed, small entrepreneur, and employer, in which field do you work? Please tick the option that applies to you:**

☐ Food industry
☐ Automotive industry
☐ Banking industry
☐ IT&C industry
☐ Education system
☐ Agriculture
☐ Trade
☐ Tourism
☐ Media (general)
☐ Real estate

☐ Construction
☐ Transport
☐ Natural resources
☐ Creative industries
☐ Government sector
☐ Services
☐ Bar and restaurant industry
☐ Energy
☐ Public relations
☐ Advocacy
☐ Healthcare
☐ Military
☐ Another field (please specify):

29. **What is your current net monthly income (in RON*):**

☐ Under 2.000 RON
☐ 2.001–3.000 RON
☐ 3.001–4.000 RON
☐ 4.001–5.000 RON
☐ 5.001–7.000 RON
☐ 7.001–9.000 RON
☐ 9.001–11.000 RON
☐ 11.001–15.000 RON
☐ Above 15.000 RON
☐ I don't know/I won't answer

*The average EUR value (expressed in RON/leu, Romanian currency) for the whole year 2019 is 4.7452 RON

30. **You live in a/an ... environment:**

☐ Urban
☐ Rural

31. **Please tick your gender:**

☐ Male
☐ Female
☐ I won't answer

32. **Please mention your age:**

## Annex E: Grid Analysis of Online News on the Giving in Payment Law (2016)

**A. General Information**

A1. Online publication

1. Bursa
2. Ziarul Financiar
3. HotNews
4. Adevărul

A2. Day's code (six digits: year/month/day) 20160101

A3. Word count

A4. Views count (traffic)

A5. Placement

1. Opening page/main article
2. Right article on page/secondary article
3. Base article/secondary
4. Column news

A6. Comments count

**B. Thematic (Agenda)**

B1. Material type

1. Article/news
2. Analysis
3. Column/View/Editorial

B2. Tone of the news

1. Positive
2. Neutral
3. Negative

B3. Actors featured in the news

B31. NBR's Governor (Mugur Isărescu) is present in the news

1. Yes
2. No

B311. If YES, space allocated to the Governor (word count)

B312. If YES, space allocated to the Governor's statements (word count)

B313. If YES, space allocated to the Governor-related presentations (word count)

[NOTE: B312 + B313= B311]

B314. If YES, is the article referring to his competence (e.g.: skilled, strategic, expert in the laws governing the functioning of the institution, and appreciated)?

1. Yes, in a positive way
2. Yes, in a negative way
3. No

B315. If YES, is the article referring to his integrity (e.g.: correct, honest, corrupted, and power-hungry)?

1. Yes, in a positive way
2. Yes, in a negative way
3. No

B41. NBR's Strategy Consultant Adrian Vasilescu is present in the news

1. Yes
2. No

B411. If YES, space allocated to the Strategy Consultant (word count)
B412. If YES, space allocated to the Strategy Consultant's statements (word count)
B413. If YES, space allocated to the Strategy Consultant-related presentations (word count)

[NOTE: B412 + B413 = B411]
B414. If YES, is the article referring to his competence (e.g.: skilled, strategic, expert in the laws governing the functioning of the institution, and appreciated)?

1. Yes, in a positive way
2. Yes, in a negative way
3. No

B415. If YES, is the article referring to his integrity (e.g.: correct, honest, corrupted, and power-hungry)?

1. Yes, in a positive way
2. Yes, in a negative way
3. No

B51. NBR's Vice-Governor Bogdan Olteanu is present in the news

1. Yes
2. No

B511. If YES, space allocated to the Vice-Governor (word count)
B512. If YES, space allocated to the Vice-Governor's statements (word count)
B513. If YES, space allocated to the Vice-Governor-related presentations (word count)

[NOTE: B512 + B513 = B511]
B514. If YES, is the article referring to his competence (e.g.: skilled, strategic, expert in the laws governing the functioning of the institution, and appreciated)?

1. Yes, in a positive way
2. Yes, in a negative way
3. No

B515. If YES, is the article referring to his integrity (e.g.: correct, honest, corrupted, and power-hungry)?

1. Yes, in a positive way
2. Yes, in a negative way
3. No

B61. NBR's Director of the Stability Department Eugen Rădulescu is present in the news

1. Yes
2. No

B611. If YES, space allocated to the Director of the Stability Department (word count)
B612. If YES, space allocated to the Director of the Stability Department's statements (word count)
B613. If YES, space allocated to the Director of the Stability Department-related presentations (word count)

[NOTE: B612 + B613 = B611]

B614. If YES, is the article referring to his competence (e.g.: skilled, strategic, expert in the laws governing the functioning of the institution, and appreciated)?

1. Yes, in a positive way
2. Yes, in a negative way
3. No

B615. If YES, is the article referring to his integrity (e.g.: correct, honest, corrupted, and power-hungry)?

1. Yes, in a positive way
2. Yes, in a negative way
3. No

B71. NBR's Director of Bank Supervision Nicolae Cinteză is present in the news

1. Yes
2. No

B711. If YES, space allocated to the Director of Bank Supervision (word count)
B712. If YES, space allocated to the Director of Bank Supervision's statements (word count)
B713. If YES, space allocated to the Director of Bank Supervision-related presentations (word count)

[NOTE: B712 + B713 = B711]

B714. If YES, is the article referring to his competence (e.g.: skilled, strategic, expert in the laws governing the functioning of the institution, and appreciated)?

1. Yes, in a positive way
2. Yes, in a negative way
3. No

B715. If YES, is the article referring to his integrity (e.g.: correct, honest, corrupted, and power-hungry)?

1. Yes, in a positive way
2. Yes, in a negative way
3. No

B81. Deputy Governor Liviu Voinea is present in the news

1. Yes
2. No

B811. If YES, space allocated to the Deputy Governor (word count)
B812. If YES, space allocated to the Deputy Governor's statements (word count)
B813. If YES, space allocated to the Deputy Governor-related presentations (word count)

[NOTE: B812 + B813 = B811]
B814. If YES, is the article referring to his competence (e.g.: skilled, strategic, expert in the laws governing the functioning of the institution, and appreciated)?

1. Yes, in a positive way
2. Yes, in a negative way
3. No

B815. If YES, is the article referring to his integrity (e.g.: correct, honest, corrupted, and power-hungry)?

1. Yes, in a positive way
2. Yes, in a negative way
3. No

B91. NBR's Member of the Board Daniel Dăianu is present in the news

1. Yes
2. No

B911. If YES, space allocated to the Member of the Board (word count)
B912. If YES, space allocated to the Member of the Board's statements (word count)
B913. If YES, space allocated to the Member of the Board-related presentations (word count)

[NOTE: B912 + B913 = B911]
B914. If YES, is the article referring to his competence (e.g.: skilled, strategic, expert in the laws governing the functioning of the institution, and appreciated)?

1. Yes, in a positive way
2. Yes, in a negative way
3. No

B915. If YES, is the article referring to his integrity (e.g.: correct, honest, corrupted, and power-hungry)?

1. Yes, in a positive way
2. Yes, in a negative way
3. No

B101. NBR's Vice Chairman of the Board Florin Georgescu is present in the news

1. Yes
2. No

B1011. If YES, space allocated to the Vice Chairman of the Board (word count)
B1012. If YES, space allocated to the Vice Chairman of the Board's statements (word count)
B1013. If YES, space allocated to the Vice Chairman of the Board-related presentations (word count)

[NOTE: B1012 + B1013 = B1011]
B1014. If YES, is the article referring to his competence (e.g.: skilled, strategic, expert in the laws governing the functioning of the institution, and appreciated)?

1. Yes, in a positive way
2. Yes, in a negative way
3. No

B1015. If YES, is the article referring to his integrity (e.g.: correct, honest, corrupted, and power-hungry)?

1. Yes, in a positive way
2. Yes, in a negative way
3. No

**C. Frames**
C1. The responsibility frame—NBR is responsible for different consequences during the 2008 crisis

C11. Does the article attribute the responsibility for this issue/situation/problem to NBR?

1. Yes
2. No

C12. Does the article suggest that the NBR can alleviate the situation/problem of consumers/institutions/companies?

1. Yes
2. No

C13. Does the article suggest solutions to solve the situation/problem?

1. Yes
2. No

C14. Does the article suggest that the problem requires urgent action from the NBR?

1. Yes
2. No

C2. The conflict frame—NBR in conflict with certain institutions, companies, consumers

C21. Does the article reflect disagreement/conflicts between the NBR and other institutions, companies, consumer groups, lawyers, etc. related to the giving in payment law debates?

1. Yes
2. No

C22. Does the article present specific reproaches directly targeted at the NBR from other involved parties in the debate (such as other institutions, companies, consumer groups, and lawyers)?

1. Yes
2. No

C23. Does the article include both perspectives or all the aspects of the situation/problem?

1. Yes
2. No

C24. Does the article refer to winners and losers?

1. Yes
2. No

C3. Economic consequences frame—due to NBR's decisions

C31. Does the article mention financial consequences (losses or gains) for other institutions/companies/consumer groups generated by the NBR previous actions/decisions?

1. Yes
2. No

C32. Does the article mention expenses/costs for consumers/institutions/companies?

1. Yes
2. No

C33. Does the article refer to economic consequences due to NBR action/decision/inaction?

1. Yes
2. No

C4. Morality frame—assessing the NBR's decisions and actions from this perspective

C41. Does the article contain any moral message?

1. Yes
2. No

C42. Does the article refer to morality, God, and other religious tenets?

1. Yes
2. No

C43. Does the article offer specific social prescriptions about how the NBR representatives should behave?

1. Yes
2. No

C5. Human interest frame—NBR and debtor's interests

C51. Does the article emphasize if consumers/institutions/companies are affected by this situation?

1. Yes
2. No

C52. Does the article provide case studies or a "human face" of the issue?

1. Yes
2. No

C53. Does the article make use of adjectives, metaphors, etc. that can generate feelings of outrage, empathy, sympathy, or compassion for those affected by the situation?

1. Yes
2. No

C54. Does the article go into the private lives of the people affected by the situation?

1. Yes
2. No

C55. Does the article contain visual information that might generate feelings of outrage, empathy, sympathy, or compassion for those affected by the situation?

1. Yes
2. No

**D. Subject, Title (for All the Materials)**

D1. News topic (one sentence)

______________________________________________

D2. News title

______________________________________________

**E1: Sources Supporting the Giving in Payment Law (Direct Quotations)**

E11. Daniel Cătălin Zamfir (politician)

1. Yes
2. No

E12. Gheorghe Piperea (lawyer)

1. Yes
2. No

E13. Association of Romanian Users of Financial Services

1. Yes
2. No

E14. Group of Clients with CHF Loans/Other organized groups of clients

1. Yes
2. No

E15. Individual clients (case studies)

1. Yes
2. No

E16. Political parties

1. Yes
2. No

E17. Fiscal consultants, experts

1. Yes
2. No

E18. Romania's National Consumer Protection Authority

1. Yes
2. No

**E2: Sources Against the Giving in Payment Law (Direct Quotations)**
E21. NBR

1. Yes
2. No

E22. Council of Banking Employers in Romania

1. Yes
2. No

E23. Romanian Association of Banks

1. Yes
2. No

E24. Banks/bankers

1. Yes
2. No

E25. European Central Bank and other European institutions

1. Yes
2. No

E26. Presidency

1. Yes
2. No

E27. Political parties

1. Yes
2. No

E28. Fiscal consultants, specialists, including THE Association of Financial and Banking Analysts of Romania

1. Yes
2. No

E29. Superior Council of Magistracy (advisory role)

1. Yes
2. No

E30. Ministry of Justice (advisory role)

1. Yes
2. No

The manufacturer's authorised representative in the EU is Springer Nature Customer Service Centre GmbH, Europaplatz 3, 69115 Heidelberg, Germany. If you have any concerns regarding our products, please contact ProductSafety@springernature.com

Printed and bound by CPI Group (UK) Ltd, Croydon, CR0 4YY
22/09/2026
02221055-0005